유학영어
길라잡이

Study abroad

유학영어 길라잡이

Jennifer M. Yi · 김미연 · 김영하 · 박혜원 · 이원희 지음

HU:iNE

머리말

북미권으로 여행은 물론 학업이나 취업을 목적으로 유학을 떠나는 사람들이 늘어나고 있다. 이 책은 어학연수나 유학을 계획하고 있는 사람들을 위한 지침서이다. 무엇보다 학생들에게 유학 생활에 좋은 가이드가 될 수 있도록 대화문을 실제 상황을 바탕으로 만드는 데 중점을 두었다.

공항, 집, 대중교통, 학교, 은행, 병원을 주제로 구성하였으며, 중심이 되는 대화문은 각 상황에 꼭 필요한 단어와 문장으로 이루어져 있다. 대화문은 길이가 길고 삽화와 함께 소개되어 있어 영어를 좀 더 생동감 있고 즐겁게 배울 수 있을 것이다. 단어와 문장을 다양하게 활용하는 방법과 함께 유학 생활 정보를 실어 매일 아침 눈 뜨면 낯선 학교로 가야 하는 즐겁고도 고단한 유학 생활에 도움이 되도록 하였다.

마지막으로 책의 밑그림을 그려주시고 오랜 기간 동안 이끌어주신 제니퍼 교수님께 가장 먼저 감사하다는 말씀을 드리고 싶고, 같이 고생한 저자들과 결실의 기쁨을 나누고 싶다. 옆에서 사랑 가득한 도움을 준 가족과 기대하는 마음으로 응원해 준 친구들에게도 감사의 마음을 전한다. 마지막까지 애써주신 한국외국어대학교 지식출판원 관계자 여러분께도 감사드린다.

저자 일동

책의 구성

이 책은 북미권 국가로 어학 연수나 유학을 가려는 학생은 물론 영어를 자연스럽게 말하고자 하는 학생들에게도 매우 유용한 책입니다. 처음부터 끝까지 영어로만 구성된 이 책은 말하기와 쓰기, 듣기와 읽기의 모든 영역을 골고루 연습할 수 있는 기회를 제공합니다. 길이가 긴 메인 다이알로그를 시작으로 천천히 책의 구성을 따라가 보십시오.

Main Dialogue

Situation: The dialogue is between the reservation receptionist and the customer, and is taking place from the time of calling the receptionist in confirming a ticket. [S=Susan Morris (reservation receptionist), P=Jiyeon Park (customer)]

S: Good morning, this is Mavis Airlines, Susan speaking.

P: I booked an online ticket to Seattle a few days ago, and called just to confirm the reservation.

S: Let me check your reservation first, and then I may be able to help you. What's your reservation number?

P: It's T96PR21.

S: Please give me a minute to upload the file to check it… Only to confirm, what is your name?

P: Park, Jiyeon. Park is my last name; that's P-A-R-K, and Jiyeon is spelled J-I-Y-E-O-N.

S: All right. You booked a ticket for May 14th from Shanghai to Seattle for one person. Your plane leaves at 20:30 with flight number MA404. Your reservation went through okay.

P: Thank you.

[a few days later, calling the airline again]

S: Good afternoon, Mavis Airlines. May I help you?

P: Yes, please. I booked an online flight ticket for the 14th of May to Seattle. However, I am in an urgent situation where I need to find ways to get there in this week. Would you be able to help me?

S: Let me check our website. How many people will you be traveling with?

P: Just by myself. The tickets were all booked when I checked the website.

S: If you don't mind having a layover, then I can squeeze you in. I found one cancellation a few minutes ago with one layover in Los Angeles.

P: That's great! What day is the ticket for?

S: That's for April 27th, the flight leaving at 19:15.

길이가 긴 메인 다이알로그

이 책은 메인 다이알로그의 길이가 길기 때문에 영어로 대화할 때 대화를 길고 자연스럽게 이어가는 연습을 할 수 있습니다.

Useful Expressions

Read the definition of useful expressions and the example sentences.

1. **book**: to reserve or to arrange in advance with a hotel, restaurant, theater, etc. to have a room, seat, or ticket on a particular date
   A: Did you book a flight to New York for next week?
   B: Not yet. I'm on the waiting list. They say there isn't any nonstop flight left.

2. **discounted ticket**: a ticket that is offered with less than the usual price
   A: Do you offer special price for kids?
   B: How old is your kid?
   A: Five.
   B: Sorry, we don't offer a discounted ticket for kids older than 48 months.

3. **penalty**: a punishment in the form of a financial payment
   A: Could I cancel my flight now?
   B: Let's see. Yes, you can, but there will be a penalty.
   A: Oh, sugar. Well, I still need to cancel it.

4. **put on**: to pay for something especially with the card
   A: How will you pay for this item?
   B: Could I put it on my Visa? Or should I pay in cash?
   A: Sure, we accept Visa.

5. **itinerary**: a schedule or plan for a journey
   A: What time are we leaving tomorrow?
   B: I'm not so sure. Don't you have a flight itinerary with you?
   A: Oh, yes! I will check that out.

중요한 단어 학습

메인 다이알로그에서 나왔던 표현 중 중요한 단어를 정해서 그 뜻과 예문을 담았습니다. 중요한 표현은 외워두면 큰 도움이 됩니다.

Additional Expressions

booking reference code, one-way ticket, ISP (Internet Service Provider), registered member, stop off, holding a ticket, airfare, payout, travel insurance, meal request

관련 단어 학습

메인 다이얼로그의 내용과 관련된 단어 및 표현 10개를 담았습니다. 사전을 찾아서 스스로 공부하면서 단어 지식을 확장시킵니다.

Exercise for Useful Expressions

Fill in the blanks with appropriate words from the list provided below. Use the words only once.

Johnny decided to go to Bahamas for one week with a couple of his friends during his spring vacation. He __________ a round-trip ticket. Even with a student __________ rate, the flight ticket was $980. However, being a student and not having much cash, he had to __________ it __________ his American Visa card. He planned the __________, had a fabulous time during the vacation, and paid all his expenses with his credit card. When he came back home, his bill was waiting for him. He was shocked to see his credit card debt of $2,350, which included __________ for one day overdue. Who can rescue Johnny from his debt?

itinerary	penalty	discounted	check out
booked	put on	punishment	confirming

문제 풀이를 통한 중요한 단어 학습

메인 다이얼로그에서 사용되었던 중요한 단어를 학습한 다음, 연습 문제를 풀어보면서 실력을 다집니다.

Conversation Starters

A reservation receptionist of the travel agency and a customer are having a conversation to book a flight ticket. In your own words, complete the following conversation. (R: receptionist, C: customer)

중요한 문장 연습

이제 단어나 표현을 공부했으면 실제로 대화를 하는 방법을 배울 차례입니다. 메인 다이얼로그에서 나왔던 질문과 답변을 생각하면서 스스로 문장을 만들어 봅니다.

Dialogue Practice

Roleplay booking a flight ticket. Part 1 and 2 provide example questions for each role that may be used in the role play.

Part 1: RECEPTIONIST

1) What's your reservation number?	It's K95QS31.
2) Only to confirm, what is your name?	Aram, Kim. Kim is my last name.
3) How many people will you be traveling with?	Two, my sister and I.
4) Do you mind having a layover to squeeze you in?	No, not at all, as long as I can get there earlier.

유용한 질문과 대답 연습

학생은 대답하는 문장만 연습하는 경향이 있습니다. 그래서 입장을 바꿔 질문과 대답하는 문장을 모두 연습해 봅니다. Part 3는 질문과 대답을 연결하는 문제입니다.

Useful Tips

E-ticket

This is an electronic ticket that one can book at home through online. In the past, tickets are mailed by the travel agency to the customer's home. These days, online has become a popular means for booking a flight ticket. After the customer pays for the ticket with a credit card, the e-ticket will be emailed to the customer with an itinerary confirmation. The customer can print out the e-ticket and take it to the check-in counter.

알아두면 도움이 되는 생활 팁

북미권 국가에서 살면서 공부한다는 것은 큰 모험입니다. 막상 부딪히면 당황할 수 있는 문화의 차이점을 미리 익히고 주어진 환경을 적극적으로 활용하는 방법을 알려드립니다.

Self-made Dialogues

Role-play: Given the role of A and B, create your own dialogue.

Role A (customer)

You are Emma and planning a family trip to Miami on the 23rd of July and booked the e-ticket about 3 days ago. However, you didn't get any email from the airlines. Call the airline to confirm the booking. A week later, your grandfather passed away from a heart attack. You want to delay the trip by 2 weeks. You decide to pay the penalty.

Role B (receptionist)

You are Julian, a receptionist of a travel agent for Best Travel company. Tell Emma that you are sorry and find out her name and the date of trip to confirm the ticket. Check the booking information on your screen, and tell her that if she delays the ticket, she has to pay 10% penalty of the ticket price.

대화문 직접 만들기

이 책은 학생들이 대화를 길게 이어갈 수 있도록 충분한 연습 기회를 제공합니다. 그 마지막 단계로 질문과 답변을 직접 해보는 순서입니다.

Word in Use

Study how *put on* can be used various ways in a sentence.

1. Put your jacket on, it's freezing out there.
   [PUT + noun phrase + ON: to dress oneself in a clothing]
2. She puts on 10 pounds last year.
   [PUT ON + noun phrase: to become heavier, especially by the amount]
3. The advertisement on that magazine puts pressure on losing weight.
   [PUT + noun + ON: to force or try to persuade someone to do something]
4. I don't believe you because you're putting me on all the time.
   [Be-verb + PUTting + pronoun + ON: to tease somebody]

한 단어의 확장

유용하게 쓰일 수 있는 단어 하나를 선정하여 다양한 쓰임새를 공부합니다. 앞서 공부했던 한 단어가 얼마나 다양하게 쓰이는지 확인해 봅니다.

Grammar Table

Review of grammar on *how*

1. to ask a question about means, manner, or instrument
   How do you spell your name?
2. to ask to describe one's feeling or to state opinions about something
   How was the party last night?
3. *How* can also come before an adjective, an adverb, or a quantity word, in asking questions about degree, distance, frequency, and length of time.
   How far can you swim from here? [How + adverb]
   How many people will you be travelling with? [How + quantity word]
4. *How + about* frequently introduces suggestions in conversation.
   How about on the 14th?

간단한 문법

기본적인 문법을 공부할 수 있습니다. 간단하지만 헷갈리거나 잊었던 기본 문법을 학습합니다.

Unit	Unit Title	Section	Section Title	Function
1	At the Airport	1	Book a ticket	a) call to confirm the reservation b) call to change the itinerary c) ask for any discount ticket
		2	Check in at the airport	a) decide a seat and have bags checked b) go through the security check
		3	Get servicies in the plane	a) find the seat b) ask changing a seat is possible c) decide a meal d) ask questions regarding the embarkment form
		4	Go through the customs	a) answer the questions at the customs office b) go through the customs c) have bags checked and talk about the regulations
		5	"Report for the baggage lost/ problems"	a) ask where the baggage claim is b) ask about the lost baggages and take care of problems
2	At Home	1	Make dinner	a) talk about the American traditional dish b) learn how to cook the dish from the host lady c) talk about the ingredients and understand the cooking procedure
		2	Watch TV	a) ask about favorite or preferred TV programs b) introduce the story of the drama c) decide to watch the movie together
		3	Have a family reunion	a) invite a friend to the family reunion party b) meet all the family members and know their names c) talk about meals, drinks, and traditions
		4	Find a place to move	a) call the agent to confirm the information from the ad b) check the apartment's conditions, dicuss price and facilities c) pay the rent and security deposit and decide the moving date
		5	Install TV, Internet, and cell phone	a) ask a friend how to install a phone, TV, and Internet b) discuss the kinds of cell phone services c) search the websites and disscuss options d) talk about a converter
		6	Prepare for a garage sale	a) decide to have a garage sale b) dicuss how to prepare the goods c) talk about prices and refreshment

Unit	Unit Title	Section	Section Title	Function
3	Transpor-tation	1	Understand public transportation schedule	a) ask the destination and schedule to the bus driver b) find ways to transfer buses c) get a bus schedule
		2	Take a taxi	a) call the cab and ask questions b) tell the driver where to drop off c) handle the overcharge problem
		3	Buy a car	a) ask where the second-hand auto shop is and tell what is needed b) get information about the cars from the dealer c) negotiate the price
		4	Maintain a car	a) take a car to the garage and get an inspection b) call to talk about what's been done and the cost c) understand the basic check up
		5	Get or renew a driver's license	a) talk about how to take a permit test b) get a permit and a doctor's signature
		6	Drive a car	a) ask how to put gas b) get stopped by a piolice and talk about regulations
4	Campus Life	1	Go to the library	a) ask about the library tour b) decide to buy a photocopying card c) get to know the interlibrary loan and request it
		2	Get to know about the course	a) meet a classmate and get information about the class b) talk about reading packets and secondhand books c) discuss credits, professors, and plagiarism
		3	Get a student credit card	a) ask whether to get a credit card at a concession b) get information about the card at a bank c) understand the limits and penalty
		4	Look for a part time job	a) call the office to get the information b) have an interview
		5	Register classes and pay tuition	a) visit the advisor to get help on major courses b) ask whether to audit a class c) visit the financial office and apply the financial aid
		6	Get involved in extracurricular activities	a) get to know an RA and what to do b) ask about a sorority club c) understand the qualifications and what the club does for voluntary work

Unit	Unit Title	Section	Section Title	Function
5	At the Bank	1	Open or close a bank account	a) open savings and checking accounts b) ask questions about writing a check c) ask about an automatic transfer
		2	Deposit or withdraw money	a) try to cash in checks b) withdraw some money c) understand how to read the bank account
		3	Solve problems related to banks	a) request for a copy of bank statement b) learn how to check the balance c) report a lost credit card
		4	Transfer or wire money	a) call to ask about transwiring money internationally b) wire money overseas
6	At the Hospital	1	Find a good doctor and make an appointment	a) describe symtoms b) check insurance and get the doctor's number c) make an appointment with the doctor's office
		2	Have a health interview	a) fill out the form and ask about it to the nurse b) describe physical state to the doctor c) get the result from the doctor
		3	Perform CPR and give a simple first aid	a) ask how to CPR b) understand the procedure of it c) learn how to use a first basic aid
		4	Identify an appropriate department	a) ask about hospital departments and describe physical state b) visit a friend at a hospital c) discuss diet and MRI
		5	Go to the drugstore	a) ask the reason to take MRI and blood test b) get the result and prescription from a doctor c) fill the prescription and ask how to refill it
		6	Discuss how to work out	a) talk about working out, weight, and skin b) decide to sign up for the free yoga class

Unit	Unit Title	Section	Useful Expressions	Useful/Cultural Tips	Word in Use	Grammar Table
1	At the Airport	1	book, discounted ticket, penalty, put on, itinerary	E-ticket	put on	how
		2	check in, access, carry-on, direct flight, proceed	Baggage allowance	cehck in	must/have to (obligation) vs. should (suggestion)
		3	compartment, stow, motion sickness, embarkment, declare	In-flight special and medical meals	declare	would you mind verb-ing?
		4	go through, customs, produce, contagious, regultion	Types of visa	produce	sentence inversion
		5	baggage claim, carousel, pick up, put down, make a delivery	Tips for lost luggage	claim	present perfect progressive
2	At Home	1	gravy, poultry seasoning, thyme, trim, sprinkle	How to make Bibimbap	place	adjective ending -ing and -ed
		2	episode, part with, catch up, rerun, rate	Rating information	catch	will and be going to
		3	reunion, dorm, eggnog misltetoe, tease	Eggnog & Mistletoe	major	let's + verb
		4	furnished, utility room, lease, upfront, put down	Abbreviations related to a house	address	borrow vs. lend
		5	bundle, prepaid, promotional, waive, converter	Installing internet + TV + phone	bill	need as an auxiliary
		6	categorize, retail, bargain, be short of, refreshment	A garage sale vs. a flea market	change	present tense and present continuous tense
3	Transpor-tation	1	transfer, run, slot, kiosk, route	Passes	run	asking frequency: how often
		2	dispatcher, flat rate, depart, drop off, settle	Giving a tip to a tixi driver	settle	on time vs. in time
		3	passenger car, fit in, launch, warranty, take for a spin	Kelly Book Price	launch	subjunctive verbs
		4	inspection, sqeeze in, registration, garage, anti-freezer	Car inspection	inspection	relative pronouns as prepositional complement
		5	examinee, expire, permit, vision test, terminal	DMV	permit	help
		6	prepay, PIN, nozzle, accumulate, suspend	AAA (American Automobile Association)	suspend	auxiliary verbs to express obligation

Unit	Unit Title	Section	Useful Expressions	Useful/Cultural Tips	Word in Use	Grammar Table
4	Campus Life	1	take through,periodical, refundable card fee, value, interlibrary loan	University ID card	value	adverb clause of conditions: if / unless
		2	reading packets, grab a bite, credits, punctual, plagiarize	Used or secondhand books	punctual	noun clause: what
		3	concession, cosign, gaurdian, come in handy, by all means	Student credit cards	cosign	adjective clause pronouns
		4	position, statistics, cover letter, qualification, indicate	Part time jobs	position	future progressive vs. simple future
		5	liberal arts, obligatory, elective course, audit, tuition	Three types of students loans	audit	adjective clause pronouns as the object
		6	RA, sorority, finalize, initiation, consecutive	Fraternities and sororities	finalize	verb infinitive vs. verb gerund
5	At the Bank	1	account, deposit, bounce, balance, set up	Bank accounts	order	present perfect with since and for
		2	clear, endorse, slip, transaction, subtract	Bank statement	check	passive and past forms of infinitives
		3	bank statement, loan agency, overdraw, issue, registered mail	SSN	cause	passive
		4	wire, beneficiary, assign, jot down, exchange rate	Different types of money	start	each and every
6	At the Hospital	1	porridge, upcoming, PMS, symptom, OBGYN	White page & Yellow page	cover	used to
		2	allergic, run, urine, soothe, negative	Medical insurance in USA	lie	whether and if
		3	CPR, chest compression, antiseptic, sterilize, dressing	Cardiopulmonary resuscitation (CPR)	practice	determiners: the, a, an
		4	chiropractics, crouch, consult, posture, gastroscope	Tips for visiting hospitalized patients	consult	let, make, have, get
		5	thyroid gland, tumor, biopsy, nausea, generic drug	How to fill prescription	fill	adverbs with comparative
		6	work out, dedicated, fair, clogged pore, enhancing	University gym	work out	during, while, for

목차

A Map to Being an Excellent English Speaker

Unit 1

AT THE AIRPORT

Section 1 **Book a ticket**
Section 2 **Check in at the airport**
Section 3 **Get services in the plane**
Section 4 **Go through the customs**
Section 5 **Report for the baggage lost**

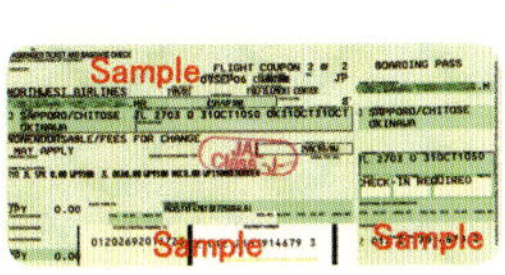

A Map to Being an Excellent English Speaker

Section 1 Book a ticket

Main Dialogue

Situation: The dialogue is between the reservation receptionist and the customer, and is taking place from the time of calling the receptionist in confirming a ticket. [S=Susan Morris (reservation receptionist), P=Jiyeon Park (customer)]

S: Good morning, this is Mavis Airlines, Susan speaking.

P: I booked an online ticket to Seattle a few days ago, and called just to confirm the reservation.

S: Let me check your reservation first, and then I may be able to help you. What's your reservation number?

P: It's T96PR21.

S: Please give me a minute to upload the file to check it… Only to confirm, what is your name?

P: Park, Jiyeon. Park is my last name; that's P-A-R-K, and Jiyeon is spelled J-I-Y-E-O-N.

S: All right. You booked a ticket for May 14th from Shanghai to Seattle for one person. Your plane leaves at 20:30 with flight number MA404. Your reservation went through okay.

P: Thank you.

[a few days later, calling the airline again]

S: Good afternoon, Mavis Airlines. May I help you?

P: Yes, please. I booked an online flight ticket for the 14th of May to Seattle. However, I am in an urgent situation where I need to find ways to get there in this week. Would you be able to help me?

S: Let me check our website. How many people will you be traveling with?

P: Just by myself. The tickets were all booked when I checked the website.

S: If you don't mind having a layover, then I can squeeze you in. I found one cancellation a few minutes ago with one layover in Los Angeles.

P: That's great! What day is the ticket for?

S: That's for April 27th, the flight leaving at 19:15.

P: How much would the round-trip ticket cost?

S: It would be $1,643.

P: Do you have any discounted tickets for students?

S: If you provide a copy of student ID card, you will get 20% off.

P: Then, could I reserve the ticket for that day?

S: Sure. Could I have your name?

P: My name is Park, Jiyeon. Park is my last name.

S: Hold on for a minute...You know you bought a non-refundable ticket, and will be charged for changing the date.

P: How much is the penalty?

S: It is 10% of the ticket price; that'll be $164.

P: I guess I have no choice. I will pay the extra fee.

S: How would you like to pay for the ticket?

P: I'd like to put it on my Visa card, including the penalty fee. The number is 5555-7878-4444-1000 and the expiration date is July 10th 2021.

S: Okay. What's your card security code? It's a 3-digit number that you will find on the back of the card, followed by a 4-digit number on the signature section.

P: Oh, I see. That's 4-2-5.

S: Okay, your reservation is completed. Is there anything else I can help you with?

P: No, that's all.

S: Your departure time is 19:15 hours on April 27th leaving with flight number MA404 from Pudong Airport and arriving at 15:20 hours on the same day at Los Angeles Airport. You will then transfer to another flight to Seattle. Your departing time is 17:42 hours, and the arrival time at Washington Airport is 20:25 hours. Your ticket number is MX235701.

P: Okay. Thanks.

S: When you receive the e-ticket through email, you should check the itinerary. Thank you and have a nice day.

Useful Expressions

Read the definition of useful expressions and the example sentences.

1. **book**: to reserve or to arrange in advance with a hotel, restaurant, theater, etc. to have a room, seat, or ticket on a particular date

A: Did you book a flight to New York for next week?

B: Not yet. I'm on the waiting list. They say there isn't any nonstop flight left.

2. **discounted ticket**: a ticket that is offered with less than the usual price

A: Do you offer special price for kids?

B: How old is your kid?

A: Five.

B: Sorry, we don't offer a discounted ticket for kids older than 48 months.

3. **penalty**: a punishment in the form of a financial payment

A: Could I cancel my flight now?

B: Let's see. Yes, you can, but there will be a penalty.

A: Oh, sugar. Well, I still need to cancel it.

4. **put on**: to pay for something especially with the card

A: How will you pay for this item?

B: Could I put it on my Visa? Or should I pay in cash?

A: Sure, we accept Visa.

5. **itinerary**: a schedule or plan for a journey

A: What time are we leaving tomorrow?

B: I'm not so sure. Don't you have a flight itinerary with you?

A: Oh, yes! I will check that out.

Additional Expressions

booking reference code, one-way ticket, ISP (Internet Service Provider), registered member, stop off, holding a ticket, airfare, payout, travel insurance, meal request

Exercise for Useful Expressions

Fill in the blanks with appropriate words from the list provided below. Use the words only once.

Johnny decided to go to Bahamas for one week with a couple of his friends during his spring vacation. He __________ a round-trip ticket. Even with a student __________ rate, the flight ticket was $980. However, being a student and not having much cash, he had to __________ it__________ his American Visa card. He planned the __________, had a fabulous time during the vacation, and paid all his expenses with his credit card. When he came back home, his bill was waiting for him. He was shocked to see his credit card debt of $2,350, which included __________ for one day overdue. Who can rescue Johnny from his debt?

itinerary	penalty	discounted	check out
booked	put on	punishment	confirming

Conversation Starters

A reservation receptionist of the travel agency and a customer are having a conversation to book a flight ticket. In your own words, complete the following conversation. (R: receptionist, C: customer)

Dialogue Practice

Roleplay booking a flight ticket. Part 1 and 2 provide example questions for each role that may be used in the role play.

Part 1: RECEPTIONIST

1) What's your reservation number?	It's K95QS31.
2) Only to confirm, what is your name?	Aram, Kim. Kim is my last name.
3) How many people will you be traveling with?	Two, my sister and I.
4) Do you mind having a layover to squeeze you in?	No, not at all, as long as I can get there earlier.

Part 2: CUSTOMER

1) What can I do for you?	I booked an online flight ticket, however I am in an urgent situation.
2) Have you checked the website?	The tickets were all booked when I checked the website.
3) Would it be okay to change your departure time?	I guess I have no choice.
4) How are you going to pay the fee?	I'd like to put them on my Visa card.

Part 3: Read the questions in the left column and match the best answer from the right column.

1) How much would the one-way ticket cost?	a) Since your ticket is non-refundable, it will be 15% of the ticket price.
2) How much is the cancellation fee?	b) Sure. Do you want to get it by registered mail or by email?
3) Can you reissue me a ticket?	c) What's your total mileage?
4) Will you purchase an open ticket?	d) It'd be $350.
5) Is there a direct flight?	e) Yes, for one year.
6) Can I get the ticket with my frequent mileage?	f) Yes, but it's more expensive.

Useful Tips

E-ticket

This is an electronic ticket that one can book at home through online. In the past, tickets are mailed by the travel agency to the customer's home. These days, online has become a popular means for booking a flight ticket. After the customer pays for the ticket with a credit card, the e-ticket will be emailed to the customer with an itinerary confirmation. The customer can print out the e-ticket and take it to the check-in counter.

WikiAirlines

YOUR TICKET-ITINERARY YOUR BOOKING NUMBER : WXIKXI

Flight	From		To		Aircraft	Class/Status
WK 2200	Montreal-Trudeau (YUL) Thu May-04-2006	17:15	Frankfurt (FRA) Fri May-05-2006	06:30+1	333	Y Confirmed
WK 2495	Frankfurt (FRA) T1 Fri May-05-2006	07:50	Amsterdam (AMS) Fri May-05-2006	09:00	321	Y Confirmed
WK 2293	Munich (MUC) T2 Mon May-22-2006	15:30	Montreal-Trudeau (YUL) Mon May-22-2006	17:50	340	Y Confirmed

Passenger Name	Ticket Number	Frequent Flyer Number	Special Needs
(1) JONES, JOHN/MR.	012-3456-789012	000-123-456	Meal: VGML

Purchase Description	Price	
Fare (LLXSOAR, LLXGSOAR)	CAD	558.00
Canada - Airport Improvement Fee		15.00
Canada - Security Duty		17.00
Canada - GST #1234-5678		1.05
Canada - QST #12345-678-901		1.20
Germany - Airport Security Tax		18.38
Germany - Airport Service Fees		37.76
Fuel Surcharge		161.00
Total Base Fare (per passenger)		809.39
Number of Passengers		1
TOTAL FARE	CAD	809.39

Ticket is non-endorsable, non-refundable
Changes allowed, subject to availability,
no later than 2 hours before departure.
Please read carefully all fare restrictions.

Have a pleasant flight!

Paid by Credit Card XXXX-XXXX-XXXX-1234

Self-made Dialogues

Role-play: Given the role of A and B, create your own dialogue.

Role A (customer)

You are Emma and planning a family trip to Miami on the 23rd of July and booked the e-ticket about 3 days ago. However, you didn't get any email from the airlines. Call the airline to confirm the booking. A week later, your grandfather passed away from a heart attack. You want to delay the trip by 2 weeks. You decide to pay the penalty.

Role B (receptionist)

You are Julian, a receptionist of a travel agent for Best Travel company. Tell Emma that you are sorry and find out her name and the date of trip to confirm the ticket. Check the booking information on your screen, and tell her that if she delays the ticket, she has to pay 10% penalty of the ticket price.

Word in Use

Study how *put on* can be used various ways in a sentence.

1. Put your jacket on, it's freezing out there.
   [PUT + noun phrase + ON: to dress oneself in a clothing]

2. She puts on 10 pounds last year.
   [PUT ON + noun phrase: to become heavier, especially by the amount]

3. The advertisement on that magazine puts pressure on losing weight.
   [PUT + noun + ON: to force or try to persuade someone to do something]

4. I don't believe you because you're putting me on all the time.
   [Be-verb + PUTting + pronoun + ON: to tease somebody]

Grammar Table

Review of grammar on *how*

1. to ask a question about means, manner, or instrument
   How do you spell your name?

2. to ask to describe one's feeling or to state opinions about something
   How was the party last night?

3. *How* can also come before an adjective, an adverb, or a quantity word, in asking questions about degree, distance, frequency, and length of time.
   How far can you swim from here? [How + adverb]
   How many people will you be travelling with? [How + quantity word]

4. *How* + *about* frequently introduces suggestions in conversation.
   How about on the 14th?

Section 2 Check in at the airport

Main Dialogue

Situation: The dialogue is between the receptionist and the customer and is taking place at the check-in counter of the airport. [R=receptionist, C=Cathy, S1=security guard 1, S2=security guard 2, S3=security guard 3]

[at the check-in counter]

R: Next in line please...Hello, can I have your ticket and passport, please?

C: Here you are.

R: Would you like a window or an aisle seat?

C: Aisle seat, please.

R: Okay, how many bags are you checking in?

C: Just two.

R: Did anyone else pack your bags or have access to them?

C: No, I packed them by myself.

R: Please put each bag on the scale. This bag weighs 30 kilograms and it overweighs by 3 kilograms. You will need to take something out or pay for the extra weights.

C: How much do I have to pay for the overweight?

R: It's 2% of your flight fare per each extra kilogram, so you will need to pay $53.

C: Okay, I'll just pay the overweight charge. Can I pay it by card?

R: No problem.

C: Here you are.

R: Do you have any carry-on luggage? It must also follow the regulation.

C: What's the policy on that?

R: Well, it must be no more than 10kg and the maximum size of 45" in the form of a *22" x 14" x 9" bag. I think your bag looks okay. Here is your boarding pass.

Your departure time is 16:45 to San Francisco, so you should go to the boarding gate number 7 by 15:45.

C: Excuse me. With a direct flight ticket, where should I check in my bags for customs inspection?

* You read 22 by 14 by 9 inches.

R: You'll need to get all your bags and go through the customs at the San Francisco Airport, which is the port of entry to the country.

C: Thanks.

R: You're welcome. You are all set and enjoy your flight.

[going through the security check]

S1: Please place your shoes, belts, electronic gadgets and metal objects into the tray, and walk through the security line. You also need to take your laptops and cellphone out and put them in the tray.

C: Okay.

S2: (scanning each person) Next.

S3: Please put your arms up in parallel position. (checking the customer with a metal detector.) Okay, please pick up all your belongings and follow me, ma'am.

C: Sure.

S3: I need you to open this bag for me. What's this?

C: My makeup.

S3: Anything over 50 milliliters of liquid is not permitted to carry on board. You'll have to leave it here and pick it up when you come back or have someone who isn't boarding pick it up for you.

C: Well, all right. I'll have to leave it here.

S3: Okay, you can proceed to the immigration booth.

Useful Expressions

Read the definition of useful expressions and the example sentences.

1. **check in**: to have bags, suitcases, and luggage shipped on a plane

   A: You should check in your luggage at least 3 hours before prior to the flight schedule.

   B: I know that, mom. Don't worry!

2. **access**: an opportunity or right to see, meet, or use something

   A: I lost my bag.

   B: Did anyone have access to your locker?

   A: No, after putting the bag in the locker, I locked and took the key out. When I came back and opened the locker, it was gone.

3. **carry-on**: a suitcase or other baggage that is small enough for a passenger to take in on board when travelling by, for example, airplane, train, or bus

   A: You should put name tags on all your carry-on luggage.

   B: That's a good idea, just in case I lose it.

4. **direct flight**: any flight between two points by an airline with no change in flight numbers or a stopover at an intermediate point

   A: Do I have to transfer the flight or is it a direct flight?

   B: You're transferring at Chicago, with a 40-minute layover.

5. **proceed**: to move forward without interruption or continue

   A: Your bags have been through the security check. You may proceed to the airport security checkpoint line.

   B: Is it going to take a long time? I need to catch my next flight within 20 minutes.

   A: In that case, follow me. I'll help you speed up the process.

Additional Expressions

stop-over, over-sized baggage, security checkpoint, pass through, name tag, non-stop flight, skycap, baggage claim tag, prohibited items, baggage registration

Exercise for Useful Expressions

Write the letter that matches the word with its definition.

1. carry-on	_______	a) a journey made by flying with a single flight without involving intermediate stops
2. direct flight	_______	b) a small size of luggage that can be carried by the passenger aboard and stowed on an airplane, train, or bus
3. access	_______	c) to ship one's baggage on the plane before getting the boarding pass from the counter
4. proceed	_______	d) a right to take advantage of or attain privilege to use something
5. check in	_______	e) to move on or keep going uninterrupted

Conversation Starters

A receptionist at the check-in counter and a customer are having a conversation at the airport. In your own words, complete the conversation. (R: receptionist, C: customer)

Dialogue Practice

Roleplay checking in at the counter. Part 1 and 2 provide example questions for each role that may be used in the roleplay.

Part 1: RECEPTIONIST

1) Would you like a window or an aisle seat?	I will take an aisle seat.
2) How many bags are you checking in?	I have three.
3) Do you have any carry-on luggage?	Yes. I have two small luggage.
4) Did anyone else pack your bags or have access to them?	No one had accessed to them.

Part 2: CUSTOMER

1) Which seat would you prefer, a window or an aisle?	Aisle seat please.
2) Has anyone packed or carried your bag for you?	No, I packed them by myself.
3) Will you pay overweight charge or take something out from the bag?	I'll just pay the overweight charge.
4) Did you follow the regulation?	I didn't know that. What's the policy on that?

Part 3: Read the questions in the left column and match the best answer from the right column.

1) How can I get to Departure Gate 5, please?	a) Take the escalator up to the next level and turn left. All the gates are upstairs.
2) How can I get a shuttle train to Terminal C?	b) The trains are free.
3) Where can I buy a ticket for the shuttle train?	c) Go out the main entrance and turn left. It runs every 5 minutes.
4) Excuse me, where are duty-free shops?	d) You'll find shops right in front of you after you go through the departure gate.

Useful Tips

Baggage allowance

The following is the baggage allowance for check-ins and carry-ons based on the economy class. If anything is over the allowance, the passenger must pay an extra fee.

airline	weight		size		number	
	check-in baggage	carry-on baggage	check-in baggage	carry-on baggage	check-in baggage	carry-on baggage
Korean Air	↓20-23kg (44-50lbs)	↓12kg (26lbs)	↓158cm* (62in)	↓115cm (45in)	1-2	1 (1bag+1personal item)
Asiana	↓20-23kg (44-50lbs)	↓10kg (22lbs)	↓158cm (62in)	↓115cm (45in)	2	1 (1bag+1personal item)
Cathay Pacific	↓20kg (44lbs)	↓7kg (15lbs)	↓157cm (62in)	↓115cm (45in)	2	1 (1bag+1personal item)
Air Canada	23kg (51lbs)	↓10kg (22lbs)	↓158cm (62in)	↓118cm (46.5in)	2	1

* The size of luggage which is sum of "width, length, and height".

Self-made Dialogues

Role-play: Given the role of A and B, create your own dialogue.

Role A (student)
You are Min, a college student, travelling to England and France by yourself. You want to have a window seat. You have 2 bags to check in and one of the bags is overweighed by 3 kilograms. You also have 2 more carry-on luggage. Now you are at the check-in counter.

Role B (receptionist)
You are Anna, a receptionist and need to ask which seat the customer wants to sit on, the number of carry-on luggage, and the bags the customer has. You need to explain about regulations on luggage: overweight luggage charges $15 per each extra kilo and the size of carry-on luggage is within 20x15x10. Also you need to repeat the final flight schedule to confirm the information that the departure time is 17:30 at boarding gate 8.

Word in Use

Study how *check in* can be used various ways in a sentence.

CHECK IN: to go to the desk at a hotel to state your arrival

1. Ma'am, don't forget to check in when you return from the meeting tonight.
   [CHECK IN + conjuction]

2. Peter checked in at a hotel 2 hours before.
   [CHECK IN + preposition]

CHECK IN: to leave the bags to be shipped on plane

3-1. I have no bags to check in but have one carry-on.
[to + CHECK IN]

3-2. It might take a while when you check in your bags at this time of day.
[CHECK IN + noun phrase]

Grammar Table

Review of grammar on *must/have to (obligation)* vs. *should (suggestion)*

To express obligation, you can usually use *must or have to + verb.*

Should can also be used to have the meaning of obligation, but *should + verb* is less stronger than *must + verb*. This is the way of giving advice or suggestion which means that what someone is talking about is a good thing to do: something that is right or desirable (but it is probably not done at the moment).

must / have to + verb	should + verb
It's essential. If this isn't done, there will be certain consequences of not following obligations. You *must* follow the regulations. You *must* clean your teeth after meals. In this country, you *have to* be over 17 before you're allowed to drive.	It's important, but not essential. If this isn't done, it is likely to be in trouble, but it is not certain. You *should* lose weight. The government *should* lower taxes.

Section 3 Get services in the plane

Main Dialogue

Situation: The dialogue is between the flight attendant and the customer. The dialogue is taking place from the moment of getting on to getting off the plane. [F= flight attendant, C=Cathy, P=passenger]

[in the plane]

F: May I see your boarding pass?

C: Here it is.

F: Your seat number is 23-C. It's on the right aisle. Would you please put your carry-on luggage either in the overhead compartment or stow it under the seat?

C: Would you help me to put the luggage in the compartment?

F: Sure.

C: Thanks, and can I have a glass of water? I have to take my medicine now.

F: Wait a minute… Here it is.

C: Thanks.

[a few minutes later]

C: Excuse me. Could I change the seat? This seat is really uncomfortable and I have motion sickness. Also it's located right by the restroom.

F: Let me check if there is any empty seat left.
(a few minutes later) I'm sorry but there's no vacancy left. Perhaps you can change the seat with this gentleman sitting in front of you.

C: Oh, no… (asking to the man) Excuse me, would you mind switching the seat?

P: Sorry, I have the same problem.

[during the meal time]

F: Would you please put the seat upright and put the armrests down? What would you like to drink? We have juice, soft drinks, beer and wine.

C: I'll have OJ.

F: Okay. We have chicken veal and meatloaf. Which would you like?

C: Meatloaf sounds good.

F: Here is your meal. Enjoy it.

C: Could you get me some coffee with sugar?

F: Sure. Give me a few minutes to serve the customers in this aisle. ... Here you are.

C: Thanks. By the way, how long is the remaining flight time?

F: You can check it on the screen in front of you. Here. We have about 9 hours and 45 minutes remaining.

[filling in the embarkment form]

C: Would you help me fill out the embarkment form?

F: Sure. You will need to fill out the personal section first.

C: What does question 9 mean?

F: "The city where you board" means the city you left from. That will be Seoul.

C: What about this question?

F: Oh, it's asking whether you are bringing any vegetables, meat or cash. Do you have anything to declare?

C: No, I don't.

F: In that case, just check 'no' to all these blocks and then sign here.

[about to land]

F: Please go back to your seat and get ready for the landing position. You need to put your seat upright and all electronic gadgets must be turned off.

C: Can I use the restroom?

F: Okay, but you need to hurry up.

Useful Expressions

Read the definition of useful expressions and the example sentences.

1. **compartment**: a separate or partitioned section within a larger enclosed area

   A: Ma'am, it's too big. This luggage won't fit in the overhead compartment.

   B: Do you think so? I guess I should take something out.

2. **stow**: to place or store something in a place

   A: You should also stow the luggage carrier under the seat.

   B: But it looks too big.

   A: Let me find some space to place it in the front. Just ask any flight attendant for it when you get off the plane and she will get it for you.

3. **motion sickness**: a feeling of nausea that some people have when traveling by car, boat, plane, etc.

   A: Are you okay? You look pale.

   B: I think I have motion sickness.

   A: Do you want me to ask the flight attendant to bring some kind of medicine?

4. **embarkment**: passengers or other vehicles going on board

   A: Do you have an extra embarkment form? I need one more for my mother.

   B: You don't need to fill out the separate form. You only need one for each family.

5. **declare**: to reveal or announce formally or publically

   A: Do I have to declare for carrying more than $10,000?

   B: Of course. If you don't, you will have to pay penalty in addition to tax.

Additional Expressions

cabin, declaration form, turbulence, life vest, reclined, taxing, safety instruction(regulation), oxygen mask, pressure on the ears, air sick

Exercise for Useful Expressions

Choose the most appropriate word for the blank.

1. My wife is often on her business trips and she constantly suffers from __________.
   a) amnesia b) motion sickness c) vomit d) morning sickness

2. The flight attendant requested to _______ the luggage into the compartment before the takeoff.
   a) replace b) carry to c) stow d) bestow

3. All passengers of the international flights must fill out the __________ form.
   a) compartment b) embarkment c) registration d) flight

4. The president finally _______ the third Monday of January a national holiday to celebrate the birthday of Dr. Martin Luther King.
   a) made a speech b) alarmed c) declared d) commented

5. I guess I need to put this carry-on bag in the overhead __________.
   a) embarkment b) shoulder c) spot d) compartment

Conversation Starters

A flight attendant and a customer are having a conversation in the plane. In your own words, complete the following conversation. (F: flight attendant, C: customer)

Dialogue Practice

Roleplay having a conversation in the plane. Part 1 and 2 provide example questions for each role that may be used in the role play.

Part 1: FLIGHT ATTENDANT

1) Would you please put your carry-on luggage either in the overhead compartment or stow it under the seat?	Oh, let me check if my bag fits under the seat first.
2) Would you please put the seat upright and put the armrests down?	Sure, I'll do that.
3) Which would you like, chicken veal or meat loaf?	Um… I'll have chicken veal, please.
4) Do you have anything to declare?	My watch I bought in Florida.

Part 2: CUSTOMER

1) Would you like to have some water?	Yes, please. I have to take my medicine.
2) What troubles you?	This seat is really uncomfortable
3) What do you want to drink, sir?	I'll have OJ.
4) Did you call for assistance?	I'd like to get help in filling out the embarkment form.

Part 3: Read the questions in the left column and match the best answer from the right column.

1) Could you fasten your seat belt, ma'am?	a) This monitor doesn't work well. Can I change the seat?
2) Would you mind passing the headphone, please?	b) I will after using the ladies room.
3) Is there something wrong, ma'am?	c) Oh, I'll bring it to you right away.
4) Excuse me. Can I have one more coffee?	d) Sure. Can I have one, too?

Useful Tips

In-flight special and medical meals

Airlines provide in-flight special and medical meals to those who have special dietary requirements. To request the special meals, a minimum of one day notice is needed by calling the airline or booking them on the website of the airline. The meals are categorized typically as follows.

Types of meal	Detail information
Vegan vegetarian	Does not contain meat, fish, fowl, eggs and dairy products.
Hindu	Does not contain beef, beef derivatives, veal or pork.
Muslim	Does not contain pork, by-products of pork or foodstuffs containing alcohol. For them, all meats are ritually slaughtered animals.
Diabetic	This meal is for those who need to manage blood sugar levels. Foods excluded are jams, sugars, syrups, cakes and chocolate.
Low salt	Excludes use of salt, MSG and baking powder, instead spices are used to flavor the meal.

Self-made Dialogues

Given the role of A and B, make a short conversation.

Role A (flight attendant)

Sarah Johnson is a flight attendant for Pacific Ocean Airlines stationed in Los Angeles.

Role B (student)

You are Joon Kim and going on a trip to California with your friends and this is your second time on the international flight.

Role A	Role B
Ask Joon to put his carry-on luggage on the overhead compartment	
	Say that you will stow it under the seat.
Say it will be fine.	
	Ask how you can ask for help during the flight.
Tell him to press the button located on the armrest.	
	Thank her for help.
During the meal time, ask what he would like to drink.	
	Answer whether you can have wine or not.
Say yes and ask him to choose between chicken and beef for the meal.	
	Say you want chicken and ask for an extra embarkment form.
Say you will get it for him later after serving the meal.	

Word in Use

Study how *declare* can be used various ways in a sentence.

DECLARE: to announce or decide officially

1. The doctor declared that his grandfather was dead.
   [DECLARE + conjunction]

2. The accused was declared guilty.
   [Be-verb + DECLAREd + adjective]

3-1. The US declared war on terrorism.
   [DECLARE + noun: to say officially or publicly that something is happening]

3-2. The state senator must declare his full income.
   [DECLARE + noun phrase: to tell the tax authorities how much money someone has earned]

4. The school suddenly declared off the upcoming prom and the seniors are against the decision.
   [DECLARE + preposition: to state that something is cancelled]

Grammar Table

Review of grammar on *would you mind verb-ing?*

Would you mind verb-ing form is used to suggest or to request something or to ask permission.

A: *Would* you *mind calling* me back?

B: Of course not. I'll call you back.

There are different ways of using this phrase with the same meaning.

Would you mind if I + verb?

A: Would you *mind if I smoke*?

B: Yes, this is a smoke-free area.

Would you mind my verb-ing?

A: Would you *mind my smoking*?

B: No, go ahead.

Section 4 Go through the customs

Main Dialogue

Situation: The dialogue is between customs officers and a customer, Tony, and is taking place from the time of getting the documents or a visa to be stamped at the customs desk. [O=customs officer, T=Tony]

[at the customs desk]

O: Your passport and entry card, please. Where are you traveling to?

T: I'm going to Seattle.

O: What's the purpose of your visit?

T: I'm here to study at the University of Washington.

O: What will you major in?

T: Industrial engineering.

O: How long will you stay in the United States?

T: I think it will take about 2 years to complete my study.

O: Where will you be staying?

T: I'll be staying with my host family living in Madison Park in northeast of Seattle.

O: Is this your first visit to the U.S.?

T: No, this is my second visit.

O: Okay, where is your I-90 form?

T: One second… here it is.

O: Your visa is expired.

T: What? That's a previous one. I have renewed my visa about a week ago. You will see it on the next page.

O: I see. All right, everything seems to be fine. You may proceed. Have a safe trip.

[going through the customs office]

O: Do you have anything to declare?

T: No, sir.

O: Can I see your passport and the customs declaration card?

T: Sure, here they are.

O: Would you stand in this line? Your bags need to be checked.

[turning for bags to be checked]

O: Could you put all your bags on the table and open them? Are you carrying any produce, meats or liquid?

T: No, I'm not.

O: What are these? You are carrying too many bottles of liquid.

T: They are soy bean sauce and sesame oil that my mother packed for me.

O: What is this?

T: That's dried fern. Is there any problem with carrying these items?

O: Yes, you are not allowed to carry these kinds of items overseas, especially these dried ferns which may carry some insects that are contagious. Sorry, but I have to take these away from you.

T: But they are completely dried under the sun. I need them.

O: It's still dangerous. Next time, you should read the regulations carefully.

O: I will. Can I go now?

T: Sure.

Useful Expressions

Read the definition of useful expressions and the example sentences.

1. **go through**: to examine or search carefully; to be approved

   A: Finally I'm next in line.

   B: Yeah, finally. I'm not sure why I get nervous whenever I go through the customs.

   A: Their questions are always the same. Relax!

2. **customs**: a government agency where the goods from other countries are checked whether to collect taxes or to prevent if they are illegal

   A: Why should I go through customs inspection?

   B: Do you have anything to declare?

   A: Nothing. I'm here only for a few days.

3. **produce**: things that are made or grown especially in farm

   A: Is cheese one of the ingredients of this dish?

   B: Yes, it is. Is there any problem, sir?

   A: Sorry, but my doctor recommended me not to eat any dairy produce.

4. **contagious**: spreading viruses and diseases from one person or animal to another

   A: Oh god. This lecture is really boring.

   B: Yeah, I see we are all yawning. I think yawning is more contagious than the common cold.

   A: Haha. Right. See over there. They are all yawning again.

5. **regulation**: a condition, law, or rule designed to govern or control procedure or behavior

   A: What regulation is applied here?

   B: I guess we need to be under the new regulations from yesterday.

Additional Expressions

immigration, border protection, pre-approved passengers, departure lounge, impose, crew, itinerant flights, official letter, I-94, delayed

Exercise for Useful Expressions

Choose the most appropriate word for the blank.

1. There are __________ applied to the boarders, so please read them carefully at the website.
   a) regulated b) related c) repetitions d) regulations

2. The farmer carried several __________ to the local store.
   a) production b) process c) produce d) professional

3. People suffered from the __________ disease.
   a) contain b) contest c) contact d) contagious

4. The customers __________ the security line one by one in order.
   a) went by b) went through c) run though d) drop by

5. The __________ is a place to declare and pay taxes if needed.
   a) customs b) customer c) costumes d) consumers

Conversation Starters

A customs officer and a customer are having a conversation at the customs office. In your own words, complete the following conversation. (O: customs officer, C: customer)

Dialogue Practice

Roleplay going through the customs office. Part 1 and 2 provide example questions for each role that may be used in the role play.

Part 1: CUSTOMS OFFICER

1) Where are you traveling to?	I'm traveling to Vancouver.
2) What's the purpose of your visit?	I'm here for just sightseeing.
3) Where will you be staying?	I'll be at a hotel in Manhattan.
4) Where are your l-90 form and the return ticket?	They are in this pocket. Let me grab them.

Part 2: CUSTOMER

1) How long do you intend to study?	I think it will take about 2 years to complete my study.
2) Do you have your passport and the customs declaration card?	Sure. Here they are.
3) How many times have you visited the United States?	This is my second visit.
4) What's in this bottle?	They are soy bean sauce and sesame oil that my mother packed for me.

Part 3: Read the questions in the left column and match the best answer from the right column.

1) How long will you be in the United States?	a) You can find it at the airport website or TSA (Transportation Security Administration) website.
2) When was your first time visiting to the States?	b) Yes, we are classmates.
3) Are you traveling in group?	c) Well, it was about 6 to 7 years ago.
4) Where are you going to stay in Virginia?	d) Just for two weeks.
5) Where can I find the regulations about produce or liquid?	e) I'm going to stay at the university dorm.

Useful Tips - Types of visa

Before traveling to the U.S., a citizen of a foreign country must obtain a nonimmigrant visa for temporary stay or an immigrant visa for permanent residence. The type of visa differs by the purpose of the travel.

1. F-1

This is a visa of non-immigrant students which allows foreigners to study (academic studies and/or language training programs) in the United States for a short term period. There are some restrictions applied to students in F-1 status. International students, who leave the United States and want to return to continue their studies, or want to transfer from a private school or program into a public school or program, need to obtain an I-20 to study in the United States.

2. I-90

This is a visa of application to renew or replace permanent resident card.

3. ESTA

This visa is for travelers and it stands for Electronic System for Travel Authorization.

Self-made Dialogues

Role-play: Given the role of A and B, create your own dialogue.

Role A (traveler)

Your name is Junichi. You've just arrived in Vancouver, Canada. You are at the customs desk at the airport, waiting to get your passport to be stamped. You are going to study at Hubble Institute of Art for 2 years, and you will stay in dorms. After you go through the customs, the customs officer will check your luggage to see if you have anything to declare. You are carrying several bottles of liquid in your bag and didn't know if you had to declare them or not. However, the customs officer indicates that they are against the regulation and decides to take them away from you. You decide to pay the tax.

Role B (officer)

You are an officer at the customs desk at the airport. Ask Junichi where he is travelling to, what the purpose of his visit is, and where he is going to stay. Junichi has some bottles of alcohol in his luggage. Tell him that he is not allowed and he has to pay tax on them. If not, you are going to take them away from him. If he decides to pay tax, it will be $24.90 plus $10.50 for penalty for not declaring the items.

Word in Use

Study how *produce* can be used various ways in a sentence.

PRODUCE: things that have been made or grown, especially things connected with farming

1. If you want to eat more foods containing dairy produce, read this list.
   [noun + PRODUCE]

2. This company provides the customers with a home delivery service of organic produce. It's really convenient.
   [adjective + PRODUCE]

3. You can grow all kinds of produce at your house! You should try it.
   [preposition + PRODUCE]

4. Bomi sold produce raised on her allotment in Jeju Island and it was a huge success.
   [verb + PRODUCE]

Grammar Table

Review of grammar on *sentence inversion*

Sentence inversion changes the word order of subject and verb in a sentence to give emphasis.

Never *should you* forget who your teacher is.
Only then *can you* lie to me.
Little *was a woman* more conscientious than she.
Not until I finished the work *did my mother allow* me to go out.

Not inverted sentences:

An inversion doesn't occur, when emphasizing objectives in general.

That day we will remember forever.

An inversion also doesn't occur, when adverbs or complements are emphasized and the subject is a pronoun. In this case, adverbs or complements are moved to the front of the sentence.

Adverb
He stood on the hill. = *On the hill* he stood.

Complement
He was very happy. = *Very happy* he was.

Section 5 Report for the baggage lost

Main Dialogue

Situation: The first dialogue is between a customer and an airport security guard, and the second is between the customer and the receptionist at the airline desk. The situation occurs from the point of finding the baggage claim section to filing out a baggage lost report. [C=customer, S1=security guard 1, S2=security guard 2, R=receptionist]

C: Excuse me, where is the "baggage claim"?

S1: It's on the second floor. If you go straight until you see the book store, you'll see the elevator across from the store. Take the elevator to the second floor. You will see the baggage carousels according to your flight number for the "baggage claim".

C: Sorry, but I did not get the direction clearly.

S1: Follow me. I will take you there.

C: Thanks.

[at the customer baggage claim section]

C: Excuse me, I can't find my bags. Where can I go and find out about them?

S2: You should go to the baggage lost claim section. There is an office in front of section D where they can help you locate your bags. Do you see the office?

C: Yes, thank you.

[at the baggage lost claim office]

R: Hello. Can I help you?

C: Yes, I can't find my bags. I've been waiting at the carousel for about 30 minutes. Can you help me finding them?

R: What airline did you fly with?

C: It was Katthy Airlines.

R: I can help you proceed the claim. Don't worry, this can happen, especially when there is not enough time between stopovers. What was the flight number?

C: It was KA402.

R: Let me check. Can I see your flight ticket and passport?

C: Here you are.

R: How many bags did you check in?

C: 2 bags.

R: According to the computer, your bags are still in Los Angeles. They'll be on the next flight and arrive in Seattle tomorrow.

C: Oh, no. What happened?

R: Looks like they were put on the wrong flight in L.A. Can you pick them up or do you want them to be delivered to your home?

C: Is it possible to have my baggage delivered to my home?

R: Sure, if you just fill out this form. Make sure to put down your correct address and any other contact information in Seattle.

C: (giving the completed form) Here is the form.

R: The driver will make the delivery between 9:00 and 12:00 tomorrow. Make sure that someone answers the phone when the driver calls before making the delivery.

C: Okay. Am I finished?

R: Yes, you are all set.

C: Thanks for helping me.

Useful Expressions

Read the definition of useful expressions and the example sentences.

1. **baggage claim**: a place where baggage is to be picked up

   A: Excuse me, sir. Can you tell me which way I should go for the baggage claim?

   B: I'm on that way. You can follow me.

   A: Thanks a million.

2. **carousel**: a moving belt that moves checked luggage from an opening and circulates it at the baggage claim area

   A: I don't really know which carrousel the baggage will be coming in on.

   B: I think you should check the screen.

   A: That's a good idea.

3. **pick up**: to collect something from a place

   A: Would you please go to the airport in this afternoon and pick up the baggage for me?

   B: Sure. What time should I leave?

4. **put down**: to write or to fill in something

   A: Please give me a form to report lost articles.

   B: Here you are, put down your information in the asterisked area, please.

5. **make a delivery**: to take goods to customers

   A: How long does it take to get the product?

   B: You will get your product tomorrow. We make a delivery within 24 hours.

Additional Expressions

regional offices, compensation claim, missing luggage, lost articles, offending item, luggage receipt, inventory, legislation, insurance policy, law suit

Exercise for Useful Expressions

Write the letter that matches its best answer.

1. Is it possible to make a delivery today?	_____	a) Follow this escalator to go two floors down; it's right by the escalator.
2. Please don't let your children walk on the carousel.	_____	b) I'm sorry. I will settle them down.
3. Can you put down the correct ID number?	_____	c) In that case, he will need to bring a proper photo ID card.
4. Sir, where is the baggage claim?	_____	d) It certainly is. Please put down the current address.
5. My husband will pick up the ticket for me in this afternoon.	_____	e) Did I make a mistake?

Conversation Starters

A customer and an airport security are having a conversation at the airline desk. In your own words, complete the following conversation. (C: customer, S: airport security, R: receptionist)

Dialogue Practice

Roleplay reporting the baggage problem. Part 1 and 2 provide example questions for each role that may be used in the role play.

Part 1: AIRPORT SECURITY / RECEPTIONIST AT THE AIRLINE DESK

1) What airline did you fly with?	It was Canada Airlines.
2) What was the flight number?	It was CA603.
3) How many bags did you check in?	I checked in only one bag.
4) Can you pick the bags up or do you want them to be delivered to your home?	I want to pick up my luggage.

Part 2: CUSTOMER

1) Do you see the sign over there on your right next to the restroom?	Sorry, but I did not get the direction clearly.
2) Where can I report the lost baggage?	You should go to the baggage lost claim section.
3) What can I help you?	Yes, I can't find my bags.
4) Do you have your boarding pass and passport with you?	Here you are.

Part 3: Read the questions in the left column and match the best answer from the right column.

1) Where can I pick up my baggage?	a) Sure. Let me check on it.
2) Could you help me find my luggage?	b) It's at the baggage carousels.
3) My baggage hasn't arrived. Who should I see about that?	c) Section D, you'll see it on the screen.
4) Do you know which carousel the luggage comes out?	d) Follow me. Most lost baggage will turn up soon.

Useful Tips - Tips for lost luggage

Losing the luggage in a plane travel is the one of the dreadful experiences that a person can go through. Following lost luggage tips will make the procedure a little easier.

1. Label all of the checked bags

Don't forget to tag the bags with the name, phone number and address on. Furthermore, it is important to define exactly what the baggage look like before checking them in; the brand, color and size. The best is to take a photo of your luggage.

2. Buy the luggage with bright colors / Tag the luggage with bright-colored ribbon

Try to choose a bright colored bag when buying it as most luggage looks alike in shapes, especially when it's dark color. For dark color bags, tie or tag it with yellow or red ribbons to recognize them easily.

Self-made Dialogues

Role-play: Given the role of A and B, create your own dialogue.

Role A (receptionist)

Your name is Andy and you are a receptionist of a claim office at the airport. A customer claims that she lost her bags. You ask the customer a flight number. You found out that her bags are put on the wrong flight, and need to coax her. Tell her that the bags will be arriving on the next flight. You also ask if she wants to pick up her bags at the airport or wants them to be delivered to her place. Lastly, tell her to come to the airport by 1:30 on the next day to the baggage claim section if she wants to pick up the bags.

Role B (traveler)

Your name is Sally and you are a traveler. When you got to the baggage claim area, you found out that your luggage was lost. You go to the claim office and ask for help. Tell the receptionist your flight number and ask him when the bags will be arriving. Also, tell him that you want to pick up your bags at the airport.

Word in Use

Study how *claim* can be used various ways in a sentence.

Noun

1. Even though he has denied the article's claim, he decided not to make any allegation.
   [possessive noun + CLAIM: a statement that something is true although it has not been proved and other people may not agree with it]

2. You can make a claim on your insurance policy.
   [verb + CLAIM: a request for a sum of money that someone believes he/she has a right to the government, etc.]

Verb

3. She claimed damages from breaking the contract.
   [CLAIM + noun: to ask for money from the government or a company because someone has a right to it]

4. You can claim back the tax on your purchases.
   [CLAIM + adverb: to ask or demand to have something returned because you have a right to it]

Grammar Table

Review of grammar on *present perfect progressive*

Form: have/has + been + verb-ing

Present perfect progressive is used to talk about an action or activity which began in the past and has continued up to the present. It is usually followed by a preposition 'for' or 'since.'

They *have been building* this bridge for 5 years.
I've been waiting here for about 30 minutes.

It's also used to talk about a job or activity which is not finished.

He *has been writing* the story of her life.

Unit 2

AT HOME

A Map to Being an Excellent English Speaker

Section 1 Make dinner

Main Dialogue

Situation: Cathy is a student who is staying with an American host family. One weekend, the lady of the house decided to prepare traditional American dishes for Thanksgiving. The dialogue takes place in the host family house from the time of talking about what to cook to serving them. [C=Cathy, L=the lady of the host family]

C: Good afternoon, ma'am.

L: Oh, hello. You are early from school today.

C: Ya, I want to watch you cook. When I go back to my country, I can talk about this experience to my family.

L: That's great! Have you had turkey before?

C: No, not yet.

L: On holidays, it's our family tradition to cook turkey.

C: I'm so excited.

L: Good. Today's menu is turkey with gravy, stuffing, and string bean casserole. The dessert is a blueberry pie.

C: Sounds good. I can already smell them.

L: Well, I have already prepared most dishes except turkey.

C: All right. What are the ingredients?

L: First, we need a turkey, 1/4 cup of olive oil, poultry seasoning, onions, carrots, potatoes, garlic, and a few leaves of rosemary and thyme.

C: Okay. What shall I do with this turkey?

L: First, we need to trim it. We should remove the neck, organs and any loose fat hanging from the body. Then, rinse inside and outside the turkey and pat dry it with paper towel. Could you pass the olive oil, please?

C: Here it is.

L: Thanks. Take about 1/4 cup of the oil, and mix it with poultry seasoning. Rub it thoroughly on the turkey with the seasoning. We also need to sprinkle the herbs inside and outside of it afterwards.

C: Let me help you with that.

L: Why don't you cut vegetables first? Chop up the onions, carrots, potatoes and garlic.

C: Okay. What are they for?

L: They will be stuffed into the turkey and some will be around the bird after mixing them with the seasoning. Don't forget to preheat the oven to about 350°F before you start cleaning the turkey.

C: Yes. I did as you have asked.

L: I think it's ready to put the turkey in the oven.

C: Right. I think so.

L: Place the bird breast side up and brush it with olive oil. You can also use butter. Okay, we are ready.

C: Why do you butter it?

L: So the skin doesn't get dried.

C: I see. Don't worry. I'll keep an eye on it. How long does it take to be cooked?

L: It depends on the size of the turkey. This is not a really big one, so it would take about 2 hours. And don't forget to brush it with oil or butter every 30 minutes until it's done.

C: I can't wait till it's done!

Useful Expressions

Read the definition of useful expressions and the example sentences.

1. **gravy**: brownish sauce made from the juice of cooked meat

   A: What can I get you, sir?

   B: I'll have mashed potato with gravy.

   A: Do you want the gravy on it or on the side?

2. **poultry seasoning**: a mixture of dried herbs and spices to flavor chicken or turkey

   A: Do you think we need to add more poultry seasoning for this size of chicken?

   B: Of course! Add 2 more tablespoons.

3. **thyme**: a type of mint herb used in cooking

   A: Add onions and cook it until it turns brown.

   B: And then?

   A: Sprinkle fresh minced thyme over the cooked onion.

4. **trim**: to make something neat by cutting or clipping

   A: What can I do with these celeries?

   B: Just trim some leaves on the top and wash them.

   A: I got it.

5. **sprinkle**: to scatter tiny pieces loosely onto something

   A: Sprinkle a pinch of powdered sugar over the strawberries.

   B: Can I put some more?

   A: No, that's too much.

Additional Expressions

broth, spatchcock, pour, frozen, dripping, smear, drain, slice, stick to, turn over

Exercise for Useful Expressions

Write the letter that matches the word with its definition.

1. poultry seasoning	______	a) to make something neater, smaller by cutting parts from it
2. trim	______	b) to throw tiny pieces of something
3. sprinkle	______	c) brown sauce made by mixing flour and juices that come out of meat while cooking
4. gravy	______	d) a blend of flavors (such as sage, marjoram, rosemary, black pepper, nutmeg, etc.) for cooking meat to remove its smell
5. thyme	______	e) various kinds of mints and garden herbs used in cooking meat or stew

Conversation Starters

The lady of the host family and a student are cooking Turkey. In your own words, complete the following conversation. (L: the lady of the host family, S: student)

Dialogue Practice

Roleplay cooking turkey. Part 1 and 2 provide example questions for each role that may be used in the role play.

Part 1: LADY OF THE HOST FAMILY

1) Have you had turkey before?	I haven't had so far.
2) Do you remember where I put the olive oil?	It's on the second shelf.
3) Could you pass the olive oil, please?	Sorry, you mean this one?
4) Why don't you cut vegetables first?	Sure, I can do that.

Part 2: STUDENT

1) Are you ready to enjoy our traditional turkey?	I'm so excited.
2) Would you pass the butter?	Here it is.
3) Did you preheat the oven?	Yes. I did as you have asked.
4) Will you check the oven?	Don't worry. I'll keep an eye on it.

Part 3: Read the questions in the left column and match the best answer from the right column.

1) What kind of dishes do you want to try?	a) At about 380°F.
2) Should I drain the pasta when it's done?	b) Poultry seasoning mostly
3) What seasoning do you use to cook lamb?	c) 7, including us.
4) To what degree should I preheat the oven?	d) A vegetable dish, like string beans casserole.
5) How many people are we going to serve?	e) Yes, please. I think it's done.

Useful Tips

How to make Bibimbap (mixed rice with vegetables)

Ingredients

rice, bean sprouts, spinach, zucchini, shiitake mushrooms, ground beef, carrots, eggs, salt, sugar, black pepper, soy sauce, hot pepper paste, sesame oil, vegetable oil, minced garlic, sesame seeds

Recipe

1. Cook rice and prepare a large plate to put all your ingredients on it.
2. Cut zucchini and carrots into thin strips, sauté them with a pinch of salt in a pan over high heat for 30 seconds. Place them on a plate.
3. Put bean sprouts into a pot of boiling water with a pinch of salt, boil them for 3 minutes, and drain and squeeze them lightly. Mix them with 1 clove of minced garlic and sesame oil. (Follow the same procedure for cooking spinach.)
4. On a heated stone bowl, put 1/2 teaspoon vegetable oil and preheat it for a few minutes. Afterwards, mix soy sauce, minced garlic, sesame oil, a pinch of sugar, and black pepper with ground beef, and stir fry it. Place the cooked meat on the plate along with cooked vegetables. (same procedure with Shiitake mushrooms after slicing them thin.)
5. Fry a sunny-side up egg.
6. Put cooked rice in the stone bowl, and place all the vegetables and meat neatly on top of the rice. Lastly, put the sunny-side up egg on it with sesame oil, sesame seeds, and hot pepper paste.
7. Lastly, mix all up and enjoy it!

Self-made Dialogues

Given the role of A and B, make a short conversation.

Role A (the lady of the host family)

You are Cheryl, and you are helping Sujin cook the traditional Korean dish (Bibimbap).

Role B (student)

You are Sujin from Korea, staying at an American host family, and you are preparing Bibimbap for them. (*check how to cook it from Useful Tips)

Role A	Role B
Ask what Sujin is going to cook.	
	Ask if Cheryl has ever had Korean traditional food before.
Say no.	
	Say that you're going to cook Bibimbap and explain what it is with ingredients.
Ask what you should do first.	
	Suggest that you should cook rice, wash and cut vegetables, and cook each of them separately.
Ask her how to cook zucchini.	
	Tell her to cut it into thin strips, sauté them in a pan over high heat for 30 seconds with a pinch of salt. (*Make use of the information from the Useful Tips)
Ask how many people you are going to serve.	
	Say four. Ask her to prepare eggs with sunny side up on a heated pan.
Ask her to pass oil and salt.	
	Say here they are. Ask her what to have for dessert.
Suggest a chocolate cake and say you've got some left in the fridge.	

Word in Use

Study how *place* can be used various ways in a sentence.

Verb: to put something in a specific place

1-1. He placed his hands on her face.

[PLACE + noun phrase]

1-2. That boy was placed in the care of his mother.

[Be-verb + PLACEd + preposition]

Noun: a position of a specific place

2-1. This will be a good place for study.

[adjective + PLACE]

2-2. Look, your room is so messy. Put everything in place, right now!

[preposition + PLACE]

Grammar Table

Review of grammar on *adjective ending -ing and –ed*

The past participles are used to describe people's feelings about the person or the subject.

I was very *interested* in the movies.

I was very *interesting* in the movies. (x)

Whereas, the present participles illustrate the things or people that cause the feelings.

It was an *interesting* movie.

I'm very *interested* in getting to know that actress.

I got *bored* because he was so *boring*.

I got *excited* because the game was very *exciting*.

→ Compare the following adjectives:

boring/bored, interesting/interested, tiring/tired, satisfying/satisfied, depressing/depressed, surprising/surprised, disappointing/disappointed, shocking/shocked, exciting/excited, exhausting/exhausted, confusing/confused

Section 2 Watch TV

Main Dialogue

Situation: The dialogue is between Terry and his friend Peter, and is taking place in the living room at the host family house. They are talking about TV programs. [T=Terry, P=Peter]

T: Hey, I missed the 5th episode of "Lost Forever" last night because of my assignment!

P: Do you watch that program, too? Most people around me seem to watch it.

T: Don't you like that program? It is one of the most popular programs these days.

P: Well, not for me. It's too mysterious to keep watching. I'm not that patient to keep watching the next episodes to find out what happens to the characters. Nothing gets solved.

T: That's why it attracts people.

P: I don't like that kind of drama. I think it will never come to an end.

T: Then, what's your favorite drama?

P: Do you know "Blue Books" on Channel 21?

T: I've heard of it but haven't watched it. What is it about?

P: It's about a bookstore owner and his two friends. The owner enjoys drinking, dislikes customers, and has trouble in parting with his beloved books.

T: Ha ha. How is it possible?

P: His friends are even funnier. His assistant is really sweet, but he's punished by the owner relentlessly just for the crime of existing.

T: Sounds really hilarious!

P: It's on Channel 21 at 10 o'clock every Friday night. You should watch it.

T: I will. Can I catch the previous episodes on the Internet?

P: I guess so, but you may have to pay for it. I have the first series in DVD. You can borrow mine.

T: Thanks! By the way, did you get to watch "Young and the Sleepless" yesterday?

P: No. I don't watch soap operas.

T: Then, I have to catch up from the reruns. Do you know that "Shinning of the Dead" is on the movie channel tonight?

P: Really? I've heard it's really funny. It's about survival from zombies, right?

T: Yeah. Do you want to watch it together?

P: Cool! Is it rated R?

T: I think it's rated for PG-13.

P: In that case, I am going to invite my friend and his sister. We can all watch it together.

T: All right. What time should I come down?

T: The movie starts from 9:30 p.m., so just come down to the living room about 10 minutes before the movie starts.

P: Okay. I'll make popcorns.

T: That's great! I'll get some soft drinks.

Useful Expressions

Read the definition of useful expressions and the example sentences.

1. **episode**: a part of dramatic work such as a serial television or radio program

A: What was the last episode of the show about?

B: John Aguel appeared and made fun of his sister.

A: I can't believe I missed that.

2. **part with**: to give something to someone else even in a condition of unwanted

A: I'm flat broke. What should I do?

B: How about parting with your expensive hobby of collecting shoes?

A: Yes. Maybe I should open a flea market.

3. **catch up**: to spend extra time doing something because it has not been done earlier

A: God, I missed the final episode of "The Big Splash Theory" season 2 last night!

B: Don't worry. You can catch it up on a cable channel tomorrow.

4. **rerun**: the same episode of a movie or television program that is shown on television again

A: Hey, there'll be a rerun of the documentary you've mentioned.

B: Great! I really want you to watch it this time!

5. **rate**: to officially judge and decide a film to be suitable for a particular age group of viewers

A: Can my son go to the movies with you tonight?

B: Not sure if it is rated PG-13.

A: Let me check its rating.

Additional Expressions

censorship, supporting actors, theater chains, film screening, home cinema, surround sound, spoiler, show time, movie trailers, tabloid TV show

Exercise for Useful Expressions

Fill in the blanks with appropriate words from the list provided below. Use the words only once.

Movie maniacs are eager to buy a new 3D TV to enjoy experiencing the 3D motion pictures. They want to upgrade their home theater system to __________ the newest technology which is equipped with an eyewear to provide the illusion of depth perception. Families especially with kids can enjoy the 3D movies at home by downloading new __________ of dramas or __________ of blockbuster action movies, while sitting on their sofa, having their favorite snacks, and going to the restroom whenever they want. However, the 3D contents so far are limited mostly to __________ R movies. The 3D TV is becoming another entertainment gadget of the home theater market.

episodes	ranked	reruns	catch up
rated	cast up	epidemic	part with

Conversation Starters

Two students are having a conversation about watching TV in the living room. In your own words, complete the following conversation. (S1: student 1, S2: student 2)

Dialogue Practice

Roleplay wathching TV with friends. Part 1 and Part 2 provide example questions for each role that may be used in the role play.

Part 1: STUDENT 1

1) Don't you like that program?	It's not surreal like many other TV dramas.
2) What's your favorite drama?	It is called "Dutch Brothers" and has been on the air since last week. It's hilarious!
3) What's the drama about?	It's about a man fell in love with a woman from the past.
4) What time should I come down?	Not today. I need to prepare for the English exam this Friday.

Part 2: STUDENT 2

1) Did you know that "Seven Wolves" on channel 2 was aired?	No. Most people around me seem to watch it.
2) Which channel is it on?	It's on Channel 21 at 10 o'clock every Friday night.
3) Why don't we watch "American Funny Story" together over the weekend?	I don't watch soap operas.
4) This DVD is too good to watch alone. Do you want to join me?	In that case, I'm going to invite my friend and his sister.

Part 3: Read the questions in the left column and match the best answer from the right column.

1) Why were you so into that movie?	a) It never lets me down! I liked it a lot.
2) When are you going to see the new animation that's showing in the theater now?	b) I don't know. Maybe this weekend?
3) How was the episode you watched last night?	c) I was captivated by the performances of the supporting actors of that movie.
4) Where are you going to watch the Super Ball game this Saturday?	d) I haven't decided yet. Do you have any place in mind?

Useful Tips

Rating information

Since 1990, the MPAA has reviewed and rated any type of motion pictures for its theme, language, violence, sex and drug use. The current motion films or movies are rated according to the age of the viewers into 5 types. Family can use the rating information to guide their under aged children in watching films or movies.

Rating symbol	Meaning
G	**G – General Audiences** All ages admitted. Nothing that would offend parents for viewing by children.
PG	**PG – Parental Guidance Suggested** Some material may not be suitable for children. Parents urged to give "parental guidance". May contain some material parents might not like for their young children.
PG-13	**PG-13 _ Parents Strongly Cautioned** Some material may be inappropriate for children under 13. Parents are urged to be cautious. Some material may be inappropriate for pre-teenagers.
R	**R – Restricted** Under 17 requires accompanying parent or adult guardian. Contains some adult material. Parents are urged to learn more about the film before taking their young children with them.
NC-17	**NC-17 _ Adults Only** No One 17 and Under Admitted. Clearly adult. Children are not admitted.

Self-made Dialogues

Role-play: Given the role of A and B, create your own dialogue.

Role A (student)
You are Tomoko and watching your favorite TV drama with your friend. Ask if your friend has watched this program before. This is your favorite program because of the characters of the drama. Introduce the story and the main characters of the drama. Tell him that it's aired at 8:50 p.m. on every Thursday. Invite your friend over to your apartment to watch it together next time.

Role B (student)
You are Taejin and watching a TV program with your friend, Tomoko, which you've never watched it before. Ask your friend why she likes that drama, and find out more about it, its story and the aired time. Based on the information, decide to accept or reject your friend's invitation.

Word in Use

Study how *catch* can be used various ways in a sentence.

Verb: to stop and arrest someone or capture something

1-1. Luckily, the policeman caught the pickpocket.
[CAUGHT + noun]

1-2. The wolf was finally caught alive.
[CAUGHT + adjective]

Noun: an act of stop and hold an object

2. Debbie threw the ball to me at a speed of 120 km/h and Jennifer was impressed by the catch.
[preposition + CATCH]

Grammar Table

Review of grammar on the difference between *will and be going to*

Will is used when the speaker has not decided to do something yet but decides to do it now; the decision is made at the time of speaking.

A: Let's have a party.

B: That's a good idea. We *will* invite a lot of friends.

Be going to is used when the speakers has already decided to do something.

A: Let's talk about the party. Will you invite your friends?

B: Yes, we *are going to* invite twelve friends.

Section 3 Have a family reunion

Main Dialogue

Situation: The first dialogue is between Tom and his friend Olivia on the phone, and Tom is inviting Olivia to his family reunion. The second dialogue occurs at Tom's place. [O=Olivia, T=Tom]

T: Hello, Olivia. It's me, Tom.

O: Hi, Tom. What're you up to?

T: Are you free on this Saturday? Do you want to come to my family reunion party?

O: But that's for your family members.

T: It'll be no problem. It's my family tradition to have a reunion party on every Christmas, and I want to invite you to the party.

O: Oh, really? That sounds great! I was never invited to such kind of a party while staying in America. I'd be delighted to go to your party.

T: It'll be so much fun. You'll have a chance to see my relatives from all over the country, and everyone puts the Christmas presents under the tree.

O: That sounds exciting!

T: We'll also watch some films and play games, stuff like that all day. So can you come in the afternoon, at about 2 o'clock?

O: Sure. What should I bring or is there anything you need help with?

T: Just come and enjoy. See you then, bye.

O: See you.

[at Tom's place]

O: Hello. Merry Christmas!

T: Merry Christmas! Come in. I'll introduce you to my family. Olivia, this is mom, dad, and my little brother. We are taking a biology class together.

O: Happy to meet you. I'm Olivia from Korea. .

T's mom: Nice to meet you, Olivia. I've heard so much about you. Call me Cheryl and make yourself at home.

O: Thank you, ma'am.

T's dad: Welcome. I'm Michael and very nice to meet you.

T: He is a math teacher at a junior high school.

T's brother: Hi, call me Liam. I've heard so much about you from Tom as well.

T: He is majoring in psychology at Portmayer University. He stays in the dorm and comes down only on holidays.

O: Nice to meet you, Liam .

T's mom: Would you care for something to drink? Do you want some eggnogs?

O: Sorry. I'm allergic to dairy products. Could I have some coffee?

T's mom: Sure.

T's brother: So are you here by yourself?

O: Ya, I've been in Portland for about six months. I like here and everyone is so kind.

T: Olivia is really smart. She gets As from all her classes so she helps me a lot.

T's brother: Hey, you guys are standing under the mistletoes. Do you know what you have to do if you stand under the mistletoes with another person? You have to kiss each other.

O: What? (blushing)

T: My brother is teasing you. Don't worry about it.

O: Wow, something smells good. What is it?

T: My mom's preparing turkey for dinner.

O: I have never had turkey before; it'll be my first time. I read so much about this kind of tradition, and books always talk about turkey in relation to the American tradition. However, I haven't experienced any. I can't wait till I taste it.

T: It's too early for dinner. Let's play Monopoly while waiting for dinner.

O: Sounds great!

Useful Expressions

Read the definition of useful expressions and the example sentences.

1. **reunion**: a social event where a group of people with a commonality gather especially those who have not met each other for a certain period of time

A: This is family picture taken on last Thanksgiving Day.

B: You have such a big family.

A: We had an annual family reunion on that day.

2. **dorm(abb. dormitory)**: a university building for students to reside during their study of a program

A: Where do you live?

B: I stay in dorm but I prefer having an apartment nearby the campus.

3. **eggnog**: a drink made from beaten eggs with sugar, milk and some alcohol mixed with them

A: This drink tastes like eggnog.

B: What is eggnog?

A: Ah, it's like an egg and milk combined with alcohol.

4. **mistletoe**: a plant with small red berries with pointy edges on the leaves and is often used as a Christmas decoration

A: Are you finished decorating your house for Christmas?

B: I'm almost finished except an ornament made with mistletoes.
I can't remember where I put it last Christmas.

5. **tease**: to laugh at someone and make jokes about them either in a friendly way or in order to annoy or embarrass them

A: Why are you crying?

B: My classmates tease me about my dimple.

A: Don't get upset. It makes you look cute.

Additional Expressions

extended family, offspring, genealogy, class reunion, military reunion, Christmas ornaments, commemoration, office Xmas party, venue, illumination

Exercise for Useful Expressions

Write the letter that matches its best answer.

1. Is it possible for guys to visit your dorm?	______	a) It traditionally consists of eggs, sugar, milk and rum or brandy.
2. What is eggnog made of?	______	b) Yes, it is. You'd better buy an artificial one at a store.
3. Is it true that the real mistletoe is poisonous to animals and kids?	______	c) No. This is only for female students.
4. Have you ever been to your high school reunion?	______	d) Definitely. That's where I met my husband.
5. What was your brother like when he was younger?	______	e) Well, he always teased me, so we fought all the time.

Conversation Starters

Two students are having a conversation about inviting a friend to the family reunion. In your own words, complete the following conversation. (S1: student 1, S2: student 2, M: s1's mom)

Dialogue Practice

Roleplay inviting a friend to the family reunion. Part 1 and 2 provide example questions for each role that may be used in the role play.

Part 1: STUDENT 1

1) Are you free on this Saturday?	Sure, what's on your mind?
2) Do you want to come to my family reunion party?	I'm not sure. I'd feel strange.
3) Can you come in this afternoon, at about 2 o'clock?	How about 3 instead, if it's okay with you?
4) Are you here by yourself?	Yes. I've been here studying at a graduate program for 1 year.

Part 2: STUDENT 2

1) Would you come to my family reunion party?	But that's for your family members.
2) Can I invite you to the party? It will be really fun.	Oh, really? That sounds great!
3) Would you have some eggnogs?	Sorry. I'm allergic to dairy products.
4) Have you been here long?	Ya, I've been here for about six months.

Part 3: Read the questions in the left column and match the best answer from the right column.

1) Do you have any plans for this Sunday?	a) I'm afraid not. I won't be in town on that day.
2) Would you like to come to my family reunion party in this Friday night?	b) Yes. Meggie and I are going hiking.
3) Oh, I like this smell. Is someone cooking?	c) No, it will be my first try.
4) Have you ever had eggnog before?	d) Yes, my dad is making a beef stew.

Useful Tips

Eggnog & Mistletoe

Eggnog is a well-known drink throughout Canada and the United States and is usually associated with winter celebrations such as Christmas and the New Year. It is a dairy-based beverage, traditionally made with milk, sugar, and eggs. A combination of alcoholic liquors is often added.

Mistletoe is a plant with red berries growing on the branches of some trees. It is often used as a Christmas decoration. It was used in festivals and marital ceremonies in Greece and became a tradition to exchange kisses under the mistletoes by couples as a promise to marry.

Self-made Dialogues

Role-play: Given the role of A and B, create your own dialogue.

Role A (student)
You are Emily and call your friend, Paulo, to invite him to your family reunion. You tell him that he doesn't need anything to bring or help with and should just come and enjoy the party. Tell him that he will have a chance to meet your family and relatives. Let him know that you will pick him up at his place at 5 p.m.

Role B (student)
You are Paulo from Brazil and has been in the States for one year to study at a undergraduate program. Emily calls you to invite you to her family reunion. Decide to either accept or reject the invitation. If you accept it, then ask if there is anything you can help with. Ask the time and place to meet for the party. If you reject it, then do it politely by giving your reason for it.

Word in Use

Study how *major* can be used various ways in a sentence.

Noun

1-1. Her major is engineering.

[adjective + MAJOR: the main subject that university students are studying]

1-2. Thanks to Major Jimmy Stuart we won in the end.

[preposition + MAJOR: the rank of an officer in the United States Army]

Verb: to study the main subject

2. I majored in science.

[MAJORed + preposition]

Adjective: important or serious

3-1. In the meantime there has been a major change in the political landscape of Seoul.

[MAJOR + noun]

3-2. Never mind. That was not major.

[verb + MAJOR]

Grammar Table

Review of grammar on *let's + verb*

Let's + verb is used as a way of making a suggestion for the speaker and hearer to do something.

Let's go dancing.

Let's eat out at the new restaurant near Sarang Street.

Answer: Yes, let's. / I'm afraid I can't.

Similar expressions

How about going dancing?

What about going dancing?

Why don't we go dancing?

Shall we go dancing?

Don't be confused with let us (=let's) from the imperative form of let (=allow).

Let me help you. (= Allow me to help you.)

Section 4 Find a place to move

Main Dialogue

Situation: The first dialogue is between an apartment management agent and the customer on the phone. The next dialogue takes place at the apartment to check the conditions of the place. The third dialogue occurs at the apartment management office to sign the lease. [A=apartment management agent, S=student]

A: Good afternoon, this is Forrent Management. Cindy speaking. How can I help you?

S: Hello, I'm interested in a two-bedroom apartment which I saw from a newspaper ad. Is it still available?

A: Which one did you see? We manage apartments located in several places. Could you give me the address?

S: The ad says it's on 89 Hills Lane, in East Lexington.

A: Oh, yes. It's a fully furnished one-bedroom apartment. Would you like to see it today?

S: Sure. What time can I see it?

A: How about around 3 in the afternoon?

S: Great. Should I meet you in front of the apartment building?

A: That will be fine.

S: Then I'll get there at around 3. My name is Emma Lee.

A: Okay, Emma. See you around 3:00.

[at the renting apartment]

A: As you see, this apartment is fully furnished.

S: It looks nice, but where is the washing machine?

A: There is one on each floor in utility rooms. There is also a laundromat located nearby this building.

S: Oh, that's convenient. How about nearby facilities around here?

A: There is Seven-Twelve convenient store located right in front of this building. Also, it takes only about 5 minutes to get to the nearest bus stop and a subway station.

S: That's great! How long do you think it takes to get to the Lexington University?

A: It takes about 7 minutes by bus and 20 minutes on foot.

S: I see. (looking around the apartment again) I think this carpet needs to be changed. It's stained and looks really worn out.

A: No problem. You cannot beat the price of $850 for rent including all utilities.

S: Um… I know the price is reasonable and I like this apartment. I think I'll take this. .

A: Great. We'll need to go to the office to do the paperwork.

[at the apartment management office]

A: Please fill out this form. I will need to photocopy your photo ID.

S: Here it is.

A: Thanks. As you know, it's a one-year lease. On the day you move in, you'll need to pay the security deposit and one-month rent upfront, a total of $1,700. Well, how much do you want to put down today?

S: $200. Then, when can I move in?

A: Since it's vacant, any day is okay.

S: That's good. I'd like to move in on this Saturday. Can you put a new carpet by then?

A: Sure. On Saturday, come to the office to get the keys after you pay the rest. You'll need to bring $1500 with you on that day. Sign here.

S: All right.

Useful Expressions

Read the definition of useful expressions and the example sentences.

1. **furnished**: supplied with the necessary furniture or appliances

   A: How's your new work place?

   B: It's an eco-friendly office. All rooms are furnished with recycled materials.

   A: That sounds awesome.

2. **utility room**: a room that contains machines such as washing machine, freezer, furnace, and utility lines running across

   A: Did you install a washing machine in each apartment?

   B: No. There are 3 machines on each floor in the utility room.

3. **lease**: a legal agreement that allows to use a building, a piece of equipment or some land for a period of time, usually in return for rent

   A: I think I'm going to sign the lease today.

   B: Make sure to read it carefully before you sign it.

4. **upfront**: paid in advance, before other payments are made

   A: You should pay one-month rent and the security deposit upfront before moving in.

   B: Is the security deposit refundable?

   A: Yes, of course.

5. **put down**: to pay part before paying up the total cost later, especially for a large amount of money

   A: How much do you want me to pay today?

   B: If you put down 10% today, we'll start working on your bookshelf tomorrow.

   A: I'll wire the money right away.

Additional Expressions

security gate, tenant, intercom, buzzer, dead-bolt lock, smoke detector, fire exit, janitor, honor the lease, sublease

Exercise for Useful Expressions

Choose the most appropriate word for the blank.

1. You can go to the ___________ to check out how many washers and dryers there are.
   a) restroom b) living room c) utility room d) family room

2. The best thing about this newly built apartment is that its fully ___________ with high quality solid oak wood furniture using eco-friendly materials only.
   a) flourished b) flown c) fulfilled d) furnished

3. Mr. Cruz had to pay one month rent ___________ and will pay the rest later.
   a) upfront b) down front c) front d) upside down

4. When you rent an apartment, you need to ___________ the security deposit, which is refundable.
   a) put out b) put down c) push down d) put up

5. I completely forgot that my ___________ expires next month.
   a) lease b) least c) sign d) constrict

Conversation Starters

An apartment agent and a student are having a conversation. In your own words, complete the following conversation. (A: apartment agent, S: student)

[at the renting apartment]

[at the apartment management office]

Dialogue Practice

Roleplay finding a place to move in. Part 1 and 2 provide example questions for each role that may be used in the role play.

Part 1: APARTMENT MANAGEMENT AGENT

1) Which apartment did you see?	The one from the university bulletin board.
2) Would you like to see it today?	I can't make it in this afternoon because of work.
3) How much do you want to put down today?	I'm not sure. What's the usual amount?
4) Is there anything else you need?	I might need a new microwave.

Part 2: STUDENT

1) Which apartment are you talking about?	The ad says it's on 89 Hills Lane, in East Lexington.
2) Do you have any requests before signing the lease?	I think this carpet needs to be changed.
3) Do you want to rent this apartment?	Yes. I think I'll take this.
4) When do you want to move in?	I'd like to move in on this Saturday.

Part 3: Read the questions in the left column and match the best answer from the right column.

1) What kind of apartment are you looking for?	a) I don't have anything particular in mind, but I prefer quiet neighborhood.
2) What's available for rent?	b) Living a few blocks away from campus might be a good idea.
3) Would you give me any suggestions on a good place to live?	c) Sorry. All apartments are occupied in this month.
4) Can I get a month to month lease?	d) Yes, but you can't break it.

Useful Tips

Abbreviations related to a house

In buying or renting a house, people search on the newspaper or on the Internet, or call the real estate agency directly. To search Internet, it can link to information on various types of housing. And people can select a desirable price range. The followings are some abbreviations which can be seen on ads on the newspaper or Internet.

apt	apartment
a/c	air conditioning
cent h/a	central heat and air
bd, br	bedroom
mbr	master bedroom
ba	bath
balc	balcony
blt	built-ins
mwv	microwave oven
sr	security deposit
W/D	washer (wsh) / dryer (d)
Agt/Bkr	agent / broker
3/2/2	3 bedrooms / 2 bathrooms / 2 car garage
2 1/2 bath	2 full bad and half bath
1 C	1 car garage (Gar : garage)

Self-made Dialogues

Develop the conversation by using prompt words in a bracket with a partner.

You are at the apartment with the real estate agent to check the condition of an apartment before you sign the lease. [A: agent, S: student]

S.____________________________________? (furniture/appliance: be furnished)

A. It is fully furnished with a TV, refrigerator, oven, microwave, closet, and a bed.

S.________________________________? (laundromat)

A. There are on the 2nd, 5th, and 7th floors in this building.

S.________________________________? (nearby facility such as a supermarket)

A. There is Seven-Twelve 24 hours open right in front of the building. And the bus stop and the subway station are within a 3-minute-walk from here.

S.________________________________? (change an old and stained carpet)

A. Before you move in? No problem.

S.________________________________? (ask to show another apartment)

A. Sure. Shall we go, then?

Word in Use

Study how *address* can be used various ways in a sentence.

Noun

1. I heard that there will be a presidential address on Channel 14 tonight, don't miss it.
   [ADDRESS + preposition: the act of delivering a formal speech to an audience]

Verb

2. The CEO didn't begin to address the central issue and everyone fretted about it.
   [ADDRESS + noun phrase: to give a speech to]

3. If you have any questions, they can be addressed to your professor.
   [Be-verb + ADDRESSed: to direct a question to someone]

Grammar Table

Review of grammar on the verb *borrow vs. lend*

The verbs *lend* and *borrow* are confusing because they have the same meaning, but at the same time they are used differently.

If a person *lends* something *to* somebody, he *gives something to someone* for a certain period of time.

If a person *borrows* something *from* somebody, he *takes something from someone* for a certain period of time.

lend something *to* somebody
lend somebody something
borrow something *from* somebody
borrow somebody something (X)

Tom: Can I *borrow* your pen, please?
Amy: Sorry. I don't have any pen right now. You can *borrow it from John*. He must have it. (NOT You can borrow John the pen.)
Tom: Oh, I see. John, can you *lend me your pen*, please?
John: Sure. I'll *lend it to you*. Here it is

Section 5

Install TV, Internet, and cell phone

Main Dialogue

Situation: The dialogue is between Brian and Jamie. Brian is a junior at a university. His family friend, Jamie, has just arrived in the States from Taiwan as an exchange student for 2 years. Jamie wants to get Internet, TV, and cell phone connections. Brian helps Jamie to settle things down at his place. [B=Brian, J=Jamie]

J: Hey, so this is your place. A nice view you got and it's pretty close to the school.

B: Yeah, not bad. I think an off campus apartment is much better for having privacy.

J: I can see that. It's cool.

B: So, did you get the Internet connection?

J: Not yet. I was hoping that you could help me because I don't have a Social Security Number(SSN).

B: No problem. I'm using a triple play service from X-Speed Company, which provides Internet, cable TV, and phone services as a bundle.

J: Hmm... How about cell phones?

B: Cell phone services have two kinds of contracts based on the term of commitment. Are you going to stay here for more than one year?

J: Yes. I've learned that I have to make a commitment to the contract for at least one year. Also, because I don't have an SSN, a phone company may charge me a high deposit fee for getting a smart phone. If I don't care for it and already have a credit card, I don't have to pay the deposit fee; instead, I can just use the prepaid service.

B: That's right. You know the deposit is refundable though. What about Internet and TV connections?

J: Yeah, I need them. Do you have any other suggestions?

B: No, but we can check the websites together. This company is the most widely used one among university students in this area. It says if you use Internet and TV with this offer, you pay 69 dollars a month.

J: Hmm, does it mean the service charges depend on the area you live in?

B: Right. This one seemed pretty cool at first. It says if you use double play, you only pay 49 dollars. This is a **promotional** pricing and is only for the first 6 months. Afterwards, the price may go way up to like 119 dollars or who knows. This is written in small letters on the bottom of the site. Make sure to read fine prints before signing anything.

J: By the way, did you know that XEN Network will come to the campus tomorrow to give out coupons?

B: No, I didn't know that. You should go and compare their pricing with this offer. Sometimes they may **waive** part of the high deposit fees if you sign up at a designated store.

J: I think I should.

B: Don't forget that there will be an extra charge for a box.

J: What do you mean?

B: This is called a **converter** which connects your computer to the LAN line. You can reuse the box without paying for it again.

J: I see. Thanks! I'll go to the promotional booth tomorrow and then decide what to get. Thanks a bunch again for helping me today.

Useful Expressions

Read the definition of useful expressions and the example sentences.

1. **bundle**: a group of things bound together for convenience

   A: They sell this program with chatting software as a bundle!

   B: Well, I don't need the chatting software. Can I buy this program only?

2. **prepaid**: paid before receiving or using it

   A: Oops... I don't have coins again, sorry.

   B: You can use a prepaid traffic card.

3. **promotional**: ideas, organizations, or events made to increase the sales

   A: Look at this promotional video.

   B: That's amazing. I think we should use it in doing homework for Marketing 101 class.

4. **waive**: to refrain from pressing or enforcing compliance with a rule or fee

   A: It seems that if I purchase one more book, the delivery charge can be waived.

   B: That's nice. Let's ask Karen if she needs to buy a book. I'm texting her.

5. **converter**: a device or a program that changes something from one to another

   A: I tried so many times to watch this video using my laptop but I failed. I don't know why.

   B: This video needs a converter program which converts it into the codes compatible with it.

Additional Expressions

bundle builder, rebate, activation, receiver, service level agreements, acceptable use policies, terms and conditions, applicable subsidiaries, anti-spyware, firewall software

Exercise for Useful Expressions

Choose the most appropriate word for the blank.

1. If you want to buy ___________ of socks, this weekend is the time.
   a) billing b) bush c) bundles d) drain

2. There are two kinds of ___________ cell phones you can choose.
   a) preferred b) receipt c) credit d) prepaid

3. We are going to begin a (an) ___________ tour for this book in Canada.
   a) prevail b) promotional c) inaugurate d) advanced

4. To sell more products B-mart decided to ___________ the sales tax.
   a) wait b) waive c) conduct d) give away

5. Please check if the ___________ is unplugged when you have bad Internet connections.
   a) converter b) inventor c) introduction d) conversion

Conversation Starters

Two friends are having a conversation about getting Internet, TV, and cell phone connections at home. In your own words, complete the following conversation. (S1: student 1, S2: student 2)

Dialogue Practice

Roleplay having a conversation about installing TV, phone, and Internet. Part 1 and 2 provide example questions for each role that may be used in the role play.

Part 1: STUDENT 1

1) Did you get the Internet connection?	No. I'm still looking for it.
2) Are you going to stay here for more than a year?	I'm not sure
3) Do you have an SSN?	No. I don't. Is that a problem?
4) What about Internet and TV connections?	I need your advice on them.

Part 2: STUDENT 2

1) Have you installed the Internet connection?	Not yet.
2) Are you planning to stay here over 2 years?	Yes. I'll stay here for almost 3 years.
3) Do you need TV and a home phone connection, too?	Yeah, I need them. Do you have any suggestions?
4) Don't you think you should go to the promotion booth?	I think I should.

Part 3: Read the questions in the left column and match the best answer from the right column.

1) What if I don't have a SSN yet?	a) Yes. I have installed mine.
2) Have you ever installed a converter by yourself?	b) You should be fine if you have a savings bank account.
3) How much can you pay for your Internet and TV every month?	c) That's what I want to do.
4) Do you want to compare their pricing with this option?	d) Well, I thought 60 dollars was reasonable.

Useful Tips

Installing Internet + TV + Phone

Installing Internet is crucial for many students who just arrived in the USA. These days many Internet companies provide a triple play which means that they provide Internet + TV + Phone services together as a bundle or a double play which means that they provide TV + Internet service as a bundle. Regarding a home phone, many international students tend to install a phone by VOIP which stands for voice over ip instead of installing a home phone through a phone company.

Each Internet company provides different bundles and services thus students should read the terms & conditions carefully. Some companies said their offer does not include any additional equipment fees, installation fees, taxes, or other assessments which subject to increase after the promotional period. After promotional period, the price will revert back to the current retail price. Some companies advertise that if their customers sign a 2-year agreement, they charge them only $69 per month for the first 6 months but afterwards, the price may not stay the same.

Self-made Dialogues

Role-play: Given the role of A and B, create your own dialogue.

Role A (student)
You are Aiden from Singapore. You've just arrived in the States as an exchange student for 2 years. You need to get TV, Internet and cell phone connected. You went to Jenny's, your family friend, and ask her for help. You ask her which company she is using and its price. You check some websites and ask her advice.

Role B (student)
You are Jenny, helping your friend Aiden. You give information regarding your Internet company you are using. You already checked some websites. You explain prices and policies of several companies you forwarded from the websites. You tell him that he should read the terms very carefully also tell him that the prices can be different from where he lives.

Word in Use

Study how *bill* can be used various ways in a sentence.

Noun: a piece of paper that shows how much you owe somebody for goods or services

1-1. Look at those bills piled up on your desk! You should pay them on time.
[BILL + adjective]

1-2. I couldn't pay off credit-card bills through a wire transfer. Do you know why?
[BILL + preposition]

Verb: to ask or demand for payment

2. You can bill the company for the business trip expenses.
[BILL + noun]

Grammar Table

Review of grammar on *need* as an auxiliary

Need is used as an auxiliary verb in the below sentences. Use the simple form of verb after *need* instead of an infinitive form *need to*. *Need* does not change its form according to the subject. For negative sentences, use *need not* meaning *don't have to*. *Need* as an auxiliary verb can also be an interrogative sentence by moving *need* to the front position of the sentence.

If he wants anything, he *need* ask.
She *need* hardly add that he is always welcome.

Need he have paid so much?
Need we reserve seats?

He *need not* have hurried.
You *needn't* work today.
They *need not* come.

Section 6 Prepare for a garage sale

Main Dialogue

Situation: The dialogue is between Sumin and her friends at Sumin's place, and they are planning to have a garage sale on weekends. [S=Sumin, T=Tim, Sumin's friend, Z=Zoe, Tim's sister]

S: I'm moving to a new apartment next Saturday and I have a few things that I want to get rid of before I move.

T: There is a garage sale in our neighborhood in this weekend. You can try to get rid of the things you don't use anymore by selling them at a cheap price.

S: That's an idea! I have books, old DVDs, and plastic model cars that have never been opened. I also have some old baseball cards to get rid of.

T: You can try to sell them.

S: I suppose.., extra cash can come in hand. Moving can cost me an arm and a leg. By the way, I don't know anything about having a garage sale. Will you help me?

T: Sure, I'm thinking about selling my MP3 which I used only twice. It's practically new, but I don't use it anymore.

Z: I want to help, too.

S: Thanks, Zoe. What do I need to do first?

T: After collecting all the items, you can categorize according to its use or whichever way helps to catch customers' eyes. Then, you can put them into separate boxes.

Z: You need to clean and wrap all of the items carefully as well.

S: How should I price the items?

T: I heard that they are usually 30% or 40% of the retail price for the best-conditioned items.

S: Really!

Z: You should put prices on everything.

T: Our neighbor, Mr. Hampton, already put the signs on the main street. He takes care of and manages such kind of events. He enjoys volunteering this kind of work.

Z: We should still have a sign for our own to attract people. How about including two or three items with special bargains or at a really cheap price to get customers' attention?

S: All right, I will sell model cars for $2. I paid $15 for each.

T: Then, I will sell my MP3 player for $15 which I paid $99. I want to get a new MP3 player which costs $109, but I'm short of money by $15.

Z: I'll make the signs.

S: What time does the garage sale start?

Z: The advertisement sign says 9, so we should be ready around that time. How about providing refreshments?

T: Let's prepare some lemonade.

S: I will buy a bag of lemonade mix. Zoe can help me make the drinks. Tim, why don't you get some paper cups?

T: Don't worry. That should be easy. By the way, I almost forgot to mention that we need to get ready for changes.

Z: Good thinking. We should go to the bank on Friday to get some bills and coins changed.

Useful Expressions

Read the definition of useful expressions and the example sentences.

1. **categorize**: to label people or things by giving them names or divide them to sets

   A: Could you categorize those books and put them in the novel or autobiography sections?

   B: Okay. But some books seem difficult to be categorized as either of them.

2. **retail**: selling goods in small quantities

   A: The retail price is usually 20% higher than the outlet stores.

   B: Wow, that's a huge difference.

3. **bargain**: purchase of buying goods cheaper than the usual cost

   A: When you go to an outdoor market, it's important to bargain with the merchant.

   B: Why is that so?

   A: If you don't, you might get overcharged.

4. **be short of**: not to have enough

   A: Do you have any coins? I'm short of a dime to get a drink from this vending machine.

   B: No, I put all my coins in a piggy bank before I left home.

5. **refreshment**: beverages or snacks provided during a meeting

   A: This seminar is lasting too long. I'm really hungry.

   B: Wait for 5 more minutes. They'll serve light refreshments during the next break.

Additional Expressions

rummage sale, yard sale, moving sale, white elephant sale, home appliance, driveway, carport, flea market venue, negotiable, thrift store

Exercise for Useful Expressions

Choose the one that has the most appropriate match between Q and A.

1. Q: How do we organize the stuffs we're going to sell?
   A: First, we need to categorize them into different cartons.
2. Q: How do I price the items?
   A: They were really cheap! It was a real bargain.
3. Q: Look at this refreshments menu. Tapas selection is amazing!
   A: Yes, they seem too tight. You need to rearrange them.
4. Q: I think we are short of experts on software engineering.
   A: Last year I was bombard with all kinds of questions.
5. Q: I would like to open a small retail shop on the Robson Street.
   A: Profanity should be banned for kids' movies.

Conversation Starters

Two students are having a conversation to have a garage sale. In your own words, complete the following conversation. (S1: student 1, S2: student 2)

Dialogue Practice

Roleplay preparing for a garage sale. Part 1 and 2 provide example questions for each role that may be used in the role.

Part 1 and 2: STUDENTS

1) Will you help me?	Sorry. I have a quiz on Monday.
2) What do I need to do first?	You need to collect items that you want to sell in the sale.
3) How should I price the items?	Normally it's 1/4~1/5 of the original price.
4) How about including two or three items with special bargains or at a really cheap price to get customers' attention?	That's a good idea.
5) What time does the garage sale start?	10 o'clock in the morning. Let's meet up at 9.
6) Why don't you get some paper cups?	Good. I can do that. I'm going to the grocery this afternoon.

Part 3: Read the questions in the left column and match the best answer from the right column.

1) Where should I start looking for items to sell?	a) Um...15 ones and 10 quarters should be okay.
2) Do you think someone will buy this item?	b) It looks old. If it is working, why don't you wipe it?
3) How much do you think we should prepare for changes?	c) You can try in your closet, attic, garage, or basement first. I think you will easily find out unwanted items.
4) What was the original price of this lamp?	d) As far as I remember, it cost over 60 dollars.

Useful Tips

A garage sale vs. a flea market

A garage sale, also known as a yard sale is an informal, irregularly scheduled event for the sale of used goods by private individuals. Popular motivations for a garage sale are "Spring cleaning" or the owner's move to a new residence, etc. The seller displays their wares to the passers-by or those responding to signs, flyers, Craigslist postings, Facebook updates, Twitter posts or newspaper ads. It occurs most frequently in suburban areas on good-weather weekends, and usually have designated hours for the sale.

On the other hand, a flea market or swap meet is a type of bazaar that rents space at a designated area to people who want to sell or barter cut-rate merchandise or secondhand goods.

Self-made Dialogues

Role-play: Given the role of A and B, make a short conversation.

Role A (student)

You are Hannah and are moving out to a new place soon. So you want to get rid of several things before you move.

Role B (student)

You are Hannah's friend, Paul and you suggest Hannah to join the garage sale this weekend. You plan how to prepare for the garage sale with her.

Role A	Role B
Say that you are moving out to a new place soon and you want to get rid of several things before you move.	
	Suggest having a garage sale this weekend and say you're going to help Hannah.
Ask Paul what to do first.	
	Say that she should collect and bring all the items.
Ask him how to organize the items.	
	Say that she should categorize them and put them in separate boxes.
Ask him how to price the items.	
	Say they should be 1/4 or 1/5 of the retail price.
Ask him how to advertise the sale.	
	Suggest her to make signs and ask how to attract people.
Advice to provide a special bargain and prepare refreshments.	
	Agree on them.
Ask him when to start the garage sale.	
	Say 9 o'clock and suggest meeting up a bit earlier to get ready
Agree with it and ask how much money and changes you should prepare.	
	Say changes of $100 should be enough.

Word in Use

Study how *change* can be used various ways in a sentence.

Verb: to become different

1-1. I really want to buy a new carpet, but I can't because my roommate doesn't like any change here.
[CHANGE+ adverb]

1-2. The sky started to change from grey to purple, but still he didn't arrive home yet.
[CHANGE + preposition]

1-3. In order to achieve my goal, I should start by changing my attitude.
[CHANGE + noun phrase]

Noun: the process of changing

2-1. My roommate doesn't like any changes made in this room.
[CHANGE + adjective]

2-2. Mary was fond of her changes in her fashion style from a baggy to a more professional looking.
[CHANGE + preposition]

Grammar Table

Review of grammar on *present tense* and *present continuous tense*

Present tenses for the future

Present simple tense can be used to talk about fixed timetables, programs, etc.

There *is* a garage sale in our neighborhood in this weekend.
What time does the film *begin*?
The train *leaves* Southampton at 12:30 and *arrives* in London at 2.

Present continuous tenses for the future.

Present continuous tenses can be used for activities that are already arranged or planned to do.

I'm moving to a new apartment next Saturday.
What *are* you *doing* on Saturday evening?
I'm not working this Friday.

Unit 3

TRANSPORTATION

- Section 1 **Understand public transportation schedule**
- Section 2 **Take a taxi**
- Section 3 **Buy a car**
- Section 4 **Maintain a car**
- Section 5 **Get or renew a driver's license**
- Section 6 **Drive a car**

A Map to Being an Excellent English Speaker

Section 1 Understand public transportation schedule

Main Dialogue

Situation: Mike is taking a bus to go to Main Library. The dialogue takes place at the bus stop to find the right bus. In the next dialogue, Mike asks the driver how to get to the target place. The last dialogue takes place at the newsstand with clerk. [M=Mike, D1=driver 1, D2=driver 2, P=passenger, C=clerk]

[at the bus stop]

M: Excuse me. Does this bus go to Main Library?

D1: No, you need to take a number 347 and then transfer to a 200 at Kream Street, about five stops from here.

M: How often does the 347 run?

D1: Every fifteen minutes.

M: Thanks

[on the 347 bus]

M: Excuse me. The smallest bill I have is five.

D2: Sorry, I cannot change it for you. (asking other passengers in the bus) Anyone has change for five?

P: Sure, I do.

M: Thanks.

D2: Get your changes from the slot.

M: I need to transfer.

D2: In that case, you'll have to pay 25 cents more.

M: Here you are. Would you tell me how to get to Kream Street?

D2: It will be announced, but where do you need to go?

M: Main Library of City University.

D2: This bus goes across Civic Park to Kream street. You should get off at the next stop and take bus number 200. The library is located at Main Square Station. It's three stops from Kream Streat.

M: How often does that bus come?

D2: It usually runs every 10 minutes. But you should check the time schedule. You can get one from the kiosk at the bus stop or on the website.

M: Thank you, sir.

D2: Here we are. This is Kream Street

M: Thanks. Have a nice day!

[at the newsstand]

M: Hi. Can I get a bus schedule for the Northwest route?

C: How many do you need?

M: One is enough.

C: The bus usually runs according to the timetable schedule, but sometimes it leaves one or two minutes earlier or behind the schedule.

M: I see and is it different during the weekend?

C: Yes. Schedules for weekdays and weekends are separated by colors. The Northwest bound is in blue and the schedules for holidays including Sundays are in red on the back of the paper.

M: How much is the schedule?

C: It's free. You can take as many as you need.

M: Really! Thanks.

Useful Expressions

Read the definition of useful expressions and the example sentences.

1. **transfer**: to change to a different vehicle during a journey

   A: Excuse me. Can you tell me where I can take the bus 11A?

   B: It doesn't stop here. You should take the bus number 8 and transfer at the next stop.

   A: I see. Thanks a lot.

2. **run**: to make buses, trains, etc., travel on a particular route

   A: Oh rat, it's so crowded! I can't even get in the train.

   B: Why don't you catch the next one? They run extra trains during the rush hour.

   A: Really? Oh, there comes the next one!

3. **slot**: a long narrow hole on a machine for inserting something (especially coins or papers)

   A: May I use this fax machine?

   B: Go ahead. Put your paper face down into the slot.

   A: Then should I press this button?

4. **kiosk**: a small shop, usually opens in the street where newspapers, drinks, candies, etc., are sold

   A: Did you read the paper yet?

   B: What are you talking about?

   A: Get a newspaper from the kiosk. There was a killing earthquake in Haiti.

5. **route**: a way or course for passengers from one place to another

   A: Which bus route is the fastest to our destination?

   B: Hmm, in this hour, the 431 is the best.

Additional Expressions

carpooling, transit, paratransit, tram, commute, auto maintenance, headway, fares, transit authority, transportation services

Exercise for Useful Expressions

Choose the one that has the most appropriate match between Q and A.

1. Q: Can I get a bus schedule for Northeast route?
   A: I'd love to pay for the bus schedule.

2. Q: Where is the coin slot?
   A: It seems we need two dollars for this.

3. Q: Excuse me. Where is the information kiosk?
   A: It's around the corner, across from this street.

4. Q: Do we have to transfer here to go to your place?
   A: It was cancelled. I felt terrible.

5. Q: Are all the buses running late because of snow?
   A: We have just moved into the new house.

Conversation Starters

A passenger and a driver are having a conversation at the bus stop. In your own words, complete the following conversation. (P : passenger, D1: driver 1, D2: driver 2)

[at the bus stop]

[on the bus]

Dialogue Practice

Roleplay having conversation about public transportation schedule. Part 1 and 2 provide example questions for each role that may be used in the role play.

Part 1: PASSENGER

1) Does this bus go to Main Library?	No, you should take 240, instead.
2) How often does the 347 run?	It runs every 30 minutes.
3) Would you tell me how to get to Kream Street?	You should take bus number 7 and go about 4 stops from here.
4) How much is the schedule?	You don't have to pay.

Part 2: DRIVER

1) Does a 2-1 stop here?	Yes, every fifteen minutes.
2) Do you have change for 5-dollar bill?	Sorry, I cannot change it for you.
3) Where do I get off to go to the Guildford Mall?	It will be announced.
4) Where can I get a bus schedule?	You can get it from the kiosk at the bus stop.

Part 3: Read the questions in the left column and match the best answer from the right column.

1) Is there another bus going to Herman Library?	a) It's one-fifty.
2) How much is the fare?	b) About 5 more stops to go.
3) How far is it from here to Soho station?	c) 270 and 450 pass that place.
4) How long do I have to wait for the next bus?	d) The buses run on the half hour.

Useful Tips

Passes

Various types of passes can be purchased from the designated places such as a subway station. There are a daily, a weekly, or a monthly pass, and a special pass for students or senior citizens. Some places may require a photo ID to buy the pass and some may not.
Public transportation is running according to schedule so that time for the bus and its frequency can be easily checked on the time schedule. The bus schedules are usually attainable at bus stops or on related web-sites.

Self-made Dialogues

Given the role of A and B, make a short conversation.

Role A (passenger)
You are Thomas and new to the big city. You are in the bus and want to know how to go to the main post office located in downtown.

Role B (driver)
You are Martha and give the passenger, Thomas, information about the bus transfer and its schedule.

Role A	Role B
Ask Martha if the bus goes to the main post office.	
	Tell Thomas that he needs to transfer to another bus after three stops.
Say you have only a 5-dollar bill.	
	Ask other passengers to change for five.
Thank her and ask which bus you need to transfer to.	
	Say he has to transfer to either 100A or 101C going toward downtown at the next stop.
Ask how often those buses run.	
	Say they run every 7 minutes and suggest him to check the bus schedule at the bus stop.
Thank the driver and get off the bus.	

Word in Use

Study how *run* can be used various ways in a sentence.

Noun

1. In the normal run of things, the only exercise I get is walking to the bus stop.
   [RUN + preposition + noun: way things happen]

Verb

2. The film festival will run even though it rains.
   [RUN + conjunction: to hold a competition or exhibit]
3. The professor runs summer courses for low-achieving-students.
   [RUN + noun: to offer]
4. The lease on my studio only has half year to run.
   [to + RUN : to continue for time]
5. She ran hot water into this huge bucket.
   [RUN + adjective: to receive]

Grammar Table

Review of grammar on *how often*

Questions with *how often*? or *how many times*? ask frequency and answers can be expressed from its upper to lower limits.

100%	nearly, always
	usually, normally
	often, frequently
	sometimes
	occasionally
	rarely, seldom
	hardly ever, scarcely ever
0%	never

How often does he come to his office?
He is *nearly* impossible to meet; he *rarely* comes to his office. He is *normally* running around between departments to make sure the project goes according to the plan.

Section 2 Take a taxi

Main Dialogue

Situation: The dialogue is between a taxi dispatcher and a customer who wants to call for a taxi to get to the airport. [T=transportation dispatcher, J=James (customer), D=driver]

T: Good morning, Red Cabs.

J: Hello. I need a cab to JFK Airport from my office today.

T: What's the address of your office, sir?

J: It's 1020 2nd Avenue. I need to get to the airport by 1 p.m., so please pick me up at around 11:30 a.m.

T: Sure. I'll have a cab waiting for you at 11:30 a.m. in front of your office and will call you when the driver arrives there. Can I have your name and phone number, please?

J: It's James Parker and my number is 633-1500. Do you charge a flat rate or the meter rate?

T: It's a flat rate, sir. It will cost you $80 including the 20% tip.

J: OK and how long does it usually take to get to the airport?

T: Are you departing from terminal 1 or terminal 2?

J: I need to get off at terminal 2.

T: Well, there is usually more traffic to that terminal. It will take about 40 to 50 minutes.

J: In that case, do you think 90 minutes is enough to catch the domestic flight?

T: Yes, I think so.

[in the taxi]

J: Hello.

D: Hello, sir. You're flying out from JFK International Airport, right?

J: Right. Please drop me off at terminal 2.

D: Okay. What time is your flight?

J: It's 1 p.m.

D: Don't worry. I'll take you to the airport safely and on time. Just in case, please put the seatbelt on for your safety. I will take route 80 and to Cannale Tunnel. It will take about 40 minutes.

J: Thanks.

[at terminal 2]

D: Sir, we're at terminal 2. It's $90.

J: Ninety dollars? But I was told that it will be $80 on a flat rate.

D: Of course I charge you a flat rate. It's $90.

J: I'm going to call the company to settle this.

D: Sure, go ahead.

J: Hello, this is James Parker. I called this morning to book a cab to JFK Airport, and I was told that the rate would be $80. But the driver says it's $90.

T: I'm sorry for your inconvenience, sir. May I have your phone number to check the reservation?

J: It's 633-1500.

T: Oh, I think the operator you talked made a mistake. The rate she gave you is for terminal 1. I'm sorry but the rate to terminal 2 is $90, sir.

J: Really! I don't' believe this. Never mind.

D: Sorry about the misunderstanding. Have a safe trip.

Useful Expressions

Read the definition of useful expressions and the example sentences.

1. **dispatcher**: a person whose job is to see certain kinds of transportation depart or leave on time

A: Do you know when the next train is coming?

B: I think it's coming in 20 minutes, but I'm not sure. You can check the schedule, or just ask a dispatcher standing over there.

2. **flat rate**: a single fixed fee charged for a service regardless of usage and situations

A: Hello. Z –plus Internet service. How may I help you?

B: Hi. I'd like to connect to the Internet. What's the monthly flat rate?

A: It'll be $45 for the basic service.

3. **depart**: to leave a place, mostly to start a trip

A: When does the train to Guildford depart?

B: Oh, it just left 5 minutes ago. The next one comes 25 minutes later.

4. **drop off**: to leave somebody at or deliver something to a desired place

A: Mom, can you give me a ride to school?

B: Sorry, I can't, but I can drop you off at the bus stop.

A: OK. Thanks.

5. **settle**: to solve a problem or to end a disagreement or argument

A: Hey, what's the result of the committee?

B: No need to worry. The affair was settled at no cost.

Additional Expressions

shortcut, baggage fare, tariffs, taxi stand, overcharge, fare system, late-night surcharge, fleet management, fare estimator, mobile booker

Exercise for Useful Expressions

Write True or False in terms of using the underlined words correctly.

1. You may borrow a dispatcher to check the bus schedule. ________

2. The plane to Chicago will depart 25 minutes earlier than its schedule. ________

3. Please drop off the meeting until he comes back. ________

4. Our committee wants to settle this financial dispute as soon as possible. ________

5. A taxi service in some cities offers a flat rate based on the zip code. ________

Conversation Starters

A taxi dispatcher and a customer are having a conversation on the phone. In your own words, complete the following conversation. (T: taxi dispatcher, C: customer)

Dialogue Practice

Roleplay booking a taxi. Part 1 and 2 provide example questions for each role that may be used in the role play.

Part 1: CUSTOMER

1) May I have a cab to JFK Airport, please?	Please tell me your address.
2) Do you charge a flat rate or the meter rate?	It's charged at a flat rate, ma'am.
3) How long does it take to get to the airport?	It usually takes less than 90 minutes about this time of day.
4) Do you think 90 minutes is enough to catch the domestic flight?	No, it may take about 2 hours considering the traffic jam.

Part 2: TAXI DISPATHCER

1) Should I be waiting outside for you?	We will call you when the driver arrives there.
2) What else should I tell you?	Please tell me your name and phone number please.
3) Do you know how long it takes to get there?	It will take about 40 to 50 minutes.
4) What happened to the cab which is supposed to be here now?	I'm sorry for your inconvenience, sir.

Part 3: Read the questions in the left column and match the best answer from the right column.

1) How much is the charge for late hours?	a) No, it is already included in the fare.
2) How much is the baggage fare?	b) We charge additional 5% of the rate.
3) Should I tip the driver?	c) It's $10 per bag.
4) What time do you want us to pick you up?	d) Washington Dulles International Airport, please.
5) Where do you want to be dropped off?	e) 1 o'clock sharp, please.

Useful Tips

Giving a tip to a taxi driver

It's a customary gratuity to tip for services in North America. Cab drivers, for example, heavily rely on the tips. It's reasonable to tip 15 to 20% of the taxi fare as a minimum to the drivers, and $1 or $2 extra for helping with bags. Leaving tips is necessary in restaurants, beauty shops, and any kind of services, even at a buffet for bringing drinks or cleaning up the table after the meal.

Self-made Dialogues

Role-play: Given the role of A and B, create your own dialogue.

Role A (customer)
You are Jin. You are going on a business trip and calling a cab dispatcher to book a taxi to go to the airport. You want to leave your home tomorrow at 6 in the morning to catch a 8:00 a.m. flight. Ask the cab dispatcher whether the fare is a flat rate or a meter rate. Tell the dispatcher that your home address is 1001 Bridge street in McKees Port and your phone number is 634-1638.

Role B (cab dispatcher)
You are Matt, helping the customer to book a cab. Ask the customer when and where she wants the cab to be ready. Also indicate that the fare is charged by meter. Thus, it may come to be about $65. Lastly, double check the customer's phonenumber.

Word in Use

Study how *settle* can be used various ways in a sentence.

1. My kids are having tough time settling into their new school.
   [SETTLE + preposition: to adjust oneself to the environment]
2. I settled myself comfortably in my favorite armchair.
   [SETTLE + pronoun: to be into comfortable position]

3-1. The matter is settled once and for all.
[Be-verb + SETTLEd + adverb: to resolve an argument or a problem]

3-2. Two countries managed to peacefully settle a dispute last week.
[SETTLE + noun: to resolve an argument or a problem]

Grammar Table

Review of grammar on *on time* vs. *in time*

on time	in time
If a man arrives *on time*, he is there at the correct time. He is neither early nor late. It also means punctual for a planned time. The flight from Shanghai will arrive *on time* according to the schedule. Mr. Smith wanted us to show up the meeting exactly *on time*.	If a man arrives *in time*, he is meeting a deadline. They were just *in time*. If you don't submit your project *in time*, you will be fired. In time also means early enough. Please come *in time* for dinner.

Section 3 Buy a car

Main Dialogue

Situation: The first dialogue is between two friends setting a date and the second dialogue is between a salesperson and a customer at a secondhand car dealer shop. [O=Orga, T=Tim, S=salesperson]

O: Could you recommend me a secondhand car dealer shop to buy a car at a reasonable price?

T: What kind of car are you looking for? I can think of two places: a place with good price but bad location and unsatisfactory service, or a good location with an excellent service. The second place is better if you want a passenger car.

O: I want a car which is a little more spacious than my old one. Let me start with the second place.

T: Do you know how to select a best secondhand car?

O: No. Actually, I have no idea about it. Would you help me find one?

T: Sure. When do you want to go?

O: How about this Friday afternoon?

T: How about after my last class on Friday? It will end at 1:00.

O: All right. Then, let's meet at around 1:00 at the lobby of Student Union building.

[at the secondhand car dealer shop]

S: Good afternoon, sir. How may I help you?

O: I'm looking for a SUV or midsize car.

S: Do you have any specific model in mind?

O: Well, how about GA or Hunda?

S: We have many Hunda and GA cars here. What about this one here? This is one of the most popular cars among Hunda products.

O: Yes, I've heard a lot of good things about Sorenson. Do you have any SUVs? They are better for camping.

S: Yes, indeed. How do you like this model? Its inside is spacious. Up to 6 adults can fit in the car. It has only 5,000 miles on it. GA launched this model last winter.

T: What's its gas mileage?

S: It has 15 miles per gallon.

T: That's an average. Then, what are the terms of warranty?

S: It remains up to 4 years or 20 thousand miles.

T: Has this car been in any accident?

S: No, here's a vehicle history report for you. This car is a real bargain.

O: Well, I'm interested in this car, but I don't have a firm belief on secondhand cars.

S: You don't need to worry. You can take it for a test drive.

O: I'd love to take it for a spin. But, how much is the car?

S: Since the resale on this model is still fantastic, this is a little expensive. It's $12,500.

O: Wow, that's much higher than I have expected. What do you think, Tim?

T: Engine sounds good, and there is no scratch on the outside. By the way, isn't the car too big for you?

O: I like a big car for safety.

T: I think $11,000 would be a more reasonable price.

S: No, that's too low. How about $12,000? That's the best I can offer.

O: How about 11,500?

S: Umm...Let me ask my boss. ... He said he can't go any below $11,800.

O: Well, I'll take it.

Useful Expressions

Read the definition of useful expressions and the example sentences.

1. **passenger car**: a type of car which carries people in general, such as a family car or a sedan

A: Tom, we should change a lane. This lane is for passenger cars only.
We are driving a truck, remember?

B: Seriously? I didn't see the sign.

2. **fit in**: to find or have enough space for somebody/something in a place or space

A: I'm moving this weekend, so I rented a big truck.

B: That's good. How big is it?

A: It has plenty of room that all my furniture can fit in the truck.

3. **launch**: to make a product available to the public for the first time

A: Hey, do you know when I can get the new version of Robot Z?

B: I think the new model will be launched in March.

4. **warranty**: a written agreement in which a company promises to repair or replace it if there is a problem with a product within a particular period of time, with free of charge

A: Hello, Quatro service center. How may I help you?

B: My CD player is broken It's still under warranty.

A: Could you tell me the model number?

5. **take for a spin**: to try to drive for testing

A: I bought the car that I've always dreamed of!

B: Wow, that's cool! Can I take it for a spin?

A: No way!

Additional Expressions

OBO(Or Best Offer), liability, full coverage, pick-up truck, conversion van, tune-up, paint-work, interior, records for the car, rock bottom price

Exercise for Useful Expressions

Write the letter that matches its best answer.

1. What does this sign mean?	______	a) Only passenger cars can park here.
2. How big is this car?	______	b) It's for launching her new business.
3. What's this party for?	______	c) At least 5 people can fit in.
4. Can I check the car before buying it?	______	d) Sure, you can take it for a spin.
5. Do they come with a warranty?	______	e) Yes, but the period is very short.

Conversation Starters

A salesperson, a customer, and his friend are having a conversation at a secondhand car dealer shop. In your own words, complete the following conversation.
(S: salesperson, C: customer, F: customer's friend)

[at the secondhand car dealer shop]

Dialogue Practice

Roleplay buying a car at a secondhand car dealer shop. Part 1 and 2 provide example questions for each role that may be used in the role play.

Part 1: CUSTOMER

1) What's its gas mileage?	21 miles per gallon.
2) What are the terms of the warranty?	The warranty lasts for one more year.
3) Has this car been in any accident?	No, it hasn't. It's almost a brand new car.
4) How much of a discount can you give?	At most 2%.

Part 2: CAR SELLER

1) How many people can ride in?	Up to 6 adults can fit in the car.
2) Is it possible to take it for a spin?	Yes, it is but go easy on the pedal.
3) Don't you think $15,000 is still too high?	That's the best I can offer. No less than that.
4) How do you check for the history of car accident?.	Here is a vehicle history report.

Part 3: Read the questions in the left column and match the best answer from the right column.

1) What's the mileage on the odometer?	a) It's about 4 years old.
2) What should I do to get a discount?	b) I can't drive a stick. I would like an automatic, please.
3) What year was that car manufactured?	c) It has 10,000 miles on it.
4) What type of car are you looking for?	d) I can give a 5% discount if your payment is made within a month.

Useful Tips

Kelly Book Price

Kelly Book Price is offered by Kelly Blue Book, headquartered in California and gives sources for new and used cars pricing and information. The book provides a generic car market value. If you register your zip code, you are introduced to specific information to your location. Here is the address of the web site: http://www.kbb.com

Self-made Dialogues

Given the role of A and B, make a short conversation.

Role A (salesclerk)

You are Shawn and work at a secondhand auto shop in Iowa. You have worked at this shop for 10 years and are trustworthy.

Role B (student)

You are Cathy and want to buy a secondhand car. You need a car in order to commute to school because you live far from it. You have to negotiate the price because you spent most of your money on moving to Iowa.

Role A	Role B
Ask Cathy how you can help her.	
	Tell Shawn that you are looking for a passenger car.
Ask what Cathy's preferred brand is.	
	Say you like to have a BMS.
Suggest her to check out the roomy family car and tell her that this model has launched a couple of weeks ago.	
	Ask about the mileage on the car.
Say it has 2,000 miles.	
	Ask how the engine runs.
Tell her it runs well even on the snow.	
	Ask how much it is.
Say it is $15,000.	
	Ask to give a discount of $2,500
Tell Cathy that it's not possible and you are not overcharging the car.	
	Say that you want to go for a test drive.
Agree and say you will get the key.	

Word in Use

Study how *launch* can be used various ways in a sentence

Verb

1. NASA announced that they are launching a satellite this month.
   [Be-verb + LAUNCHing + noun: to send something into the air or into the space]

2. E-head, a new headphone, was launched on the 28th of March.
   [Be-verb + LAUNCHed + preposition: to establish or introduce something]

Noun

1. The captain was on the deck of the launch, steadying a ladder.
   [preposition + LAUNCH: a large motor boat to carry people on rivers]

2. The launch of space shuttle was delayed due to the engine problem.
   [LAUNCH + preposition: a start]

Grammar Table

Review of grammar on *subjunctive verbs* used in noun *clauses*.

A subjunctive verb is to tell importance and urgency. It comes after certain expressions. They are to advise, to ask, to command, to demand, to desire, to insist, to propose, to recommend, to request, to suggest, and to urge. It's used in mainly dependent clauses before the main clauses. Its key feature is to use in a simple form, which means it does not have past, present, or future tense. There is no plural or singular form as follows.

The doctor *recommends* that she *drink* plenty of water. (NOT drinks)
Is it *essential* that we *be* here? (NOT are)
The students *demand* that the school *liberalize* its regulation on the hair code.
(NOT liberalizes)
The girl *advised* that he *not listen* to noisy music while people are sleeping at night.
(NOT doesn't listen)

Section 4 Maintain a car

Main Dialogue

Situation: This dialogue is between a mechanic and Shanti. Shanti wants an annual checkup for her car. [M=mechanic, S=Shanti]

M: Good morning, how can I help you today?

S: I think my car needs an inspection.

M: Did you make an appointment for today?

S: No, but can it be done today?

M: Umm, let's see. I think I can squeeze you in, but you have to leave your car and pick it up later.

S: Thanks a lot. My office is not far from here and I can take a bus.

M: I see that you need to renew the registration as soon as possible.

S: Yes. I need to change the sticker by April and I only have a few days left.

M: All right. Is that red car yours?

S: Right. It's that Bluick Laselle.

M: Okay, then it should be done by around 5 this afternoon. Call me around 1p.m. before you come to pick up the car, just in case something needs to be fixed.

S: Does it take that long?

M: About two and half hours because the state of New Jersey requires to get a full checkup.

S: I see. See you then.

[calling the mechanic]

S: Hello, Is this George's Garage?

M: Yes, it is.

S: I left my car this morning to get inspected, and you asked me to call you at around 1 p.m.

M: What kind of car is it?

S: It's red Bluick Laselle.

M: Oh, I see. Well, there are a few things that need to be fixed. We need to change air filter, and engine oil, and one of your head lights doesn't work.

S: Do they all need to be fixed at once?

M: If you don't, you can't pass the inspection.

S: How much would they cost?

M: The total amount will be $380.

S: I guess I don't have any choice. Please go ahead. Can I pick up the car this afternoon?

M: Come at around 5 p.m.

[in the afternoon]

M: Here is your key.

S: Thanks for rushing the work for me.

M: Everything seems okay. As we spoke on the phone, I changed air filter, engine oil, and the headlight. Your engine oil was dark. Have you changed the oil since you bought the car?

S: Maybe not. I don't know how to maintain a car.

M: You should check the engine oil, anti-freezer, and the air in the tire regularly. Try to change the oil every 3,000 miles.

S: Thank you for the tips.

M: Sure.

Useful Expressions

Read the definition of useful expressions and the example sentences.

1. **inspection**: a careful examination of something to find out anything wrong

A: It's time to get an inspection for our cars.

B: Right. I just hope that my car will pass the emission test.

2. **squeeze in**: to give time to somebody or something within a tight schedule

A: Hi, I'd like to make an appointment with Dr. Wang today.

B: Dr. Wang is not available today. If you come tomorrow morning, we can squeeze you in.

A: What time tomorrow?

3. **registration**: an official record of something or someone; a document showing that an official record has been made

A: What's wrong? You look blue.

B: I have to pay penalty fee for the late registration.

A: Gee...How much is it?

4. **garage**: a place where cars get repaired, serviced or parked

A: Oh, gosh. Tom got in an accident last night. His car was rear-ended by a truck.

B: That's terrible. How is he?

A: He's okay but the rear end of his car is totally smashed, so the truck towed it away to the garage.

5. **anti-freezer**: a chemical that is added to the water in the radiator of cars and other vehicles to stop it from freezing

A: What happens if I don't put anti-freezer in the car in winter?

B: The water in the radiator inside your car would freeze and it would cause mechanical problems.

Additional Expressions

license plate, dealer, odometer, manual car, automatic transmission, clutch, stick shift, accelerator, gas pedal, emission testing fee

Exercise for Useful Expressions

Write the letter that matches the word with its definition

1.inspection	______	a) chemical which prevents the radiator of cars from freezing
2. squeeze in	______	b) an official recording of items or names
3. registration	______	c) a building or indoor place where the cars are repaired or serviced
4. garage	______	d) a close examination for faults or errors of a car
5. anti-freezer	______	e) to fit into a small time span

Conversation Starters

A customer and a mechanic are having a conversation at a garage and later on the phone. In your own words, complete the following conversation.
(M: mechanic, C: customer)

Dialogue Practice

Roleplay having a conversation between a mechanic and his customer at a garage. Part 1 and 2 provide example questions for each role that may be used in the role play.

Part 1: MECHANIC

1) How can I help you today?	I have to get a car inspection.
2) Did you make an appointment today?	Unfortunately, not.
3) Which car is yours?	It's the yellow sports car.
4) Have you changed the oil after you bought the car?	Yes, every 5,000 miles.

Part 2: CUSTOMER

1) How can you get back to your office?	My office in not far from here.
2) When do you need the inspection?	I only have a few days left to change my sticker.
3) Is it okay to fix all parts needed for inspection?	Go ahead. I don't have any choice.
4) Did you change the air filter this year?	Maybe not.

Part 3: Read the questions in the left column and match the best answer from the right column.

1) When is the expiration date of your registration?	a) We have other cars to fix before yours.
2) Why does it take that long?	b) It's two weeks from now. I don't have much time.
3) When was the last time you change the oil?	c) Simple, check the tire air, oil, and anti-freezer regularly.
4) What are the tips for maintaining a car?	d) Um…I don't think I've ever changed it.

Useful Tips

Car Inspection

All vehicles are required to be inspected once a year and notify it to the Department of Motor Vehicle (DMV) in the USA. In passing the inspection, DMV will issue a registration card and an inspection sticker. The regulations may differ slightly state to state, but all states in the USA require car owners to keep the card in the vehicle and attach the stickers on the plate. The driver should remember the expiration date of the inspection and not to pass the due date. When the police catch a car with an expired registration, fine will be incurred.

Self-made Dialogues

Role-play: Given the role of A and B, create your own dialogue.

Role A (customer)
You are Ethan, and want to get an annual checkup of your car to get the registration card renewed. However, you haven't made a reservation. The mechanic says he will squeeze you in for this afternoon. You also ask for a rough estimate and when you should come back to pick up the car.

Role B (auto mechanic)
You are Jonas. Your customer wants to get his car inspected. Tell him that you will squeeze him in for this afternoon but next time, he needs to make an appointment in advance. Inform him that he may pay more than the estimate depending on the results of the checkup. Tell him to leave the car and the key inside the car now and pick it up at around 6.

Word in Use

Study how *inspection* can be used various ways in a sentence.

INSPECTION: a formal or official examination

1-1. She needs to get a quality inspection tomorrow.
[adjective + INSPECTION]

1-2. There was a strict inspection of all luggage in the airport.
[INSPECTION + preposition]

1-3. Our company president will make an inspection tour this afternoon.
[INSPECTION + noun]

Grammar Table

Review of grammar on the *relative pronouns* as prepositional complement

When the relative pronoun is used as prepositional complement, relative pronoun is fronted and the preposition may or may not go before reflective pronouns.

Tim is talking to a girl. I know her.
→ I know the girl *whom* Tim is talking *to*.
→ I know the girl *to whom* Tim is talking.

I slept in a couch last night. It was very cozy.
→ The couch (*which/that*) I slept *in* last night was very cozy.
→ The couch *in which* I slept was very cozy.

I went to a wedding. I wasn't invited to the wedding.
→ I went to a wedding *which* I wasn't invited *to*.
→ I went to a wedding *to which* I wasn't' invited.

Section 5

Get or renew a driver's license

Main Dialogue

Situation: The first dialogue is between two friends about taking a permit test and the second dialogue is between the Department of Motor Vehicle (DMV) officer and an examinee who is taking a driver's test. [A=Anna, J=John, O1=officer 1, O2=officer 2]

J: Hey, Anna, you asked me to help you renew the driver's license which is about to be expired. I called the driver's license center and found out that you don't need the road test. You just need to take a permit test.

A: Then how should I prepare for the test?

J: Why don't you go through the written test manual? I think I have a copy somewhere in my room. My sister took the test last month.

A: Is the written test difficult?

J: It's not that difficult. If you don't pass it, you can take it as often as you want, but not on the same day. Take your passport with you.

A: Thanks a lot. Can I take the test in Korean?

J: It may be possible in New York. In that case, when do you want to go?

A: How about this Monday?

J: I think the place is closed on Mondays. Let's go on Wednesday morning.

A: Okay.

[at the DMV]

A: Hi. I'm here to apply for renewing the driver's license.

O1: First, fill out this form. You need to take the vision test and then a written test. Please wait until you're called for the vision test.

[in the permit test section]

O2: Sit down in front of terminal 4.

A: How long do I have for the test?

O2: You can take your time as much as you want. Let me know if you have any questions.

A: Thanks.

O2: Go ahead. You can start now.

[an hour later]

J: Well, did you pass?

A: Yes. I got two questions wrong.

J: That's good. Now you need to get a doctor's signature from your family doctor. The DMV will send you a new license if you send this stamped form with the doctor's signature.

A: I don't have a family doctor.

J: Don't worry. I can take you to my family doctor. He will ask you a few questions. Then you can get the license in the mail. Afterwards, you will be permitted to drive. That's all.

A: Thanks again.

Useful Expressions

Read the definition of useful expressions and the example sentences.

1. **examinee**: someone who's taking an exam

A: I've heard the test was really difficult this year.

B: Yes, four out of five examinees said they totally bombed it.

A: I see.

2. **expire**: to be no longer valid because the period of time for which it could be used has ended

A: Oh my, I just drank milk with the expired date.

B: It's only one day passed. You'll be fine.

3. **permit**: a license given from one who has an authority after passing the first written exam for driving, it grants a permission to learn to drive

A: I have good news for you. I got a permit!

B: Congratulations! When is the road test then?

4. **vision test**: an eye examination performed by an optician

A: This is strange. The result of my vision test indicated that my visions are getting worse every year.

B: Really? Did you usually read books at night or in a bus?

5. **terminal**: a computer screen from which the data or desired information can be seen

A: What do I have to do to pass the test?

B: You should read the questions carefully and choose the best answer.

A: I'll do my best.

Additional Expressions

issue, individual state, commercial driver's license(CDL), vehicle registration plate, learner's permit, intermediate license, hit and run, tailgating, eligible age, driver's education

Exercise for Useful Expressions

Fill in the blanks with appropriate words from the list provided below. Use the words only once.

Jill went to DMV to renew her driver's license before it is ___________. An officer at the DMV said all ___________ should take off their glasses for the ___________. Afterwards, Jill put on her glasses back and sat down in front of the ___________ to take the ___________ test. However, the power went out. Thus, the officer asked her to move to the next seat. About thirty minutes later, the officer announced that she passed the exam.

examinees	pursue	permit	visual
terminal	expired	vision test	run

Conversation Starters

Two students are having a conversation about renewing a driver's license. In your own words, complete the following conversation. (S1: student 1, S2: student 2)

Dialogue Practice

Roleplay renewing a driver's license. Part 1 and 2 provide example questions for each role that may be used in the role play.

Part 1: EXAMINEE

1) How should I prepare for the permit test?	First, you have to study the manual.
2) Is it difficult?	It depends on whether you study or not.
3) Can I take the test in Korean?	I'm afraid that we don't have it in Korean.
4) What should I bring?	You need a photo ID such as a passport.

Part 2: OFFICER

1) What if I fail the exam?	If you don't' pass it, you can take it as often as you want.
2) Can I retake the test on that day?	You cannot take it on the same day.
3) What can I do to apply for the driver's license?	Fill out this form and you'll need to take a test.
4) How long am I given for the test?	You can take your time as much as you want.

Part 3: Read the questions in the left column and match the best answer from the right column.

1) I take the permit test for the first time. Is it difficult to pass?	a) You need to have a passport or I-20.
2) Can I take the test in another language?	b) There are only 3 chances for one testee.
3) Do I ever get the chance to take a test again?	c) The test is provided in several languages.
4) What should I take to DMV?	d) I don't think so. Just keep reading the test manual.

Useful Tips

DMV

DMV is an acronym for Department of Motor Vehicle. DMV is a place where people may visit once or twice a year, for example, to get a driver's license, renew a license, or register the car. Finding a closest DMV in the area is on the DMV website. In taking any tests related to driver's license, the person is required to accompany a valid photo ID.

Self-made Dialogues

Given the role of A and B, make a short conversation.

Role A (student)
You are Midori and need to renew your driver's license. You ask questions to Andrew to find out how you can renew your license.

Role B (student)
You are Andrew, a friend of Midori. You call the DMV for Midori and get the information on renewing the license to help her.

Role A	Role B
Greet Andrew and say you need help with renewing your driver's license.	
	Tell Midori that she needs to take a written test first, and advise her to study in advance.
Ask Andrew how difficult the test is.	
	Say it is not that difficult and tell her that she can take the test as often as she wants.
Ask him what to take to DMV.	
	Say that she needs to take a passport with her.
Ask whether you can take the test in Korean.	
	Tell her that it is possible in this state.
Thank him and tell him that you want to take the test on Monday.	
	Tell her that Mondays are closed and suggest to go on Wednesday morning.
Accept his suggestion.	

Word in Use

Study how *permit* can be used various ways in a sentence.

Noun

1. The government decided to grant an export permit.
   [noun + PERMIT: the act or document of giving permission or consent to]

Verb

2-1. If I am permitted a word, I would like to raise a few objections right now.
   [Be-verb + PERMITted + noun: to allow something to happen]

2-2. She permitted her daughter to drive at age 15.
   [PERMIT + noun phrase: to provide an opportunity to do something that normally isn't done before]

Grammar Table

Review of grammar on *help*

Help often follows *object+infinitive*. In British English, *to* is often omitted in the infinitive form, but this can be rather informal. Also, *help* can be followed by *an infinitive directly without an object.*

help + (object) + to-infinitive
I hope this book *helps* (you) *to broaden* your mind and thoughts.

help + (object) + bare infinitive
He will *help* (my little sister) *do* her assignment.

to + help
Would you like *to help clean* the room?

Section 6 Drive a car

Main Dialogue

Situations: The first dialogue involves a conversation between a customer and a gas station attendant and the second one is between a police officer and a driver who is stopped by the police. [A=Akiko, G=gas station attendant, P=police officer]

[at the gas station]

A: Excuse me, could you tell me how to put gas?

G: Sure. You should prepay first.

A: Should I pay in cash only?

G: No, you can pay with credit card.

A: How can I use the card?

G: Just insert your plastic and enter the PIN.

A: I want to pay with my Visa. (followed the procedure) Then, what?

G: First, choose the grade of gas you want, unleaded, plus or premium.

A: Which one should I put?

G: It is normally said in the manual or on the gas tank lid. For your car, unleaded should be fine.

A: I see. (pushes the button)

G: Then, pull the pump out and lift the nozzle up. Put the pump in the gas tank of your car and squeeze the lever. You can hold the lever or lock it if you want to fill the gas up. That's all.

A: Thank you. One more thing, sir! What is the closest highway to go to Irvine?

G: Well, you may want route 10 or 40. Forty may be closer from here, I think.

A: Then how do you get to route 40 from here? I couldn't find the way to highway.

G: Okay, if you go straight, about half a mile, you'll see a junction sign for the route. You cannot miss it. Make a left at the 5 way intersection. You'll be on Route 40. Connection to the route can be somewhat tricky.

A: I see. I must have made a wrong turn at the intersection.

[on the way home]

P: Ma'am, can I see your driver's license and registration?

A: Here. Do I need to get out of the car?

P: No, ma'am. Please stay in the car. Do you know why I stopped you?

A: No, sir. What did I do wrong?

P: You just drove through a stop sign. You had to come to a complete stop. Instead, you just slowed down and then drove away.

A: Did I? I thought I stopped completely.

P: According to your record, you were given a warning with the same problem in the last month. But you did it again.

A: Am I getting a ticket?

P: I have no choice in this time. From now on, you must stop completely at the stop sign.

A: All right, officer. Am I getting any points?

P: You have already accumulated 9 points. I will only give you a ticket this time. If you have one more violation, your license will be suspended for a period of time.

A: Really!

P: Ma'am, here is the ticket. One more thing, one of your break lights is out. You should get it changed as soon as possible. This is a warning. You can get a ticket again for that.

A: I will. Thanks for the info.

Useful Expressions

Read the definition of useful expression and the example sentences

1. **prepay**: to pay before using the service or product

   A: Hello, I would like to book a room for the 24th of December.

   B: You should prepay it with a credit card.

2. **PIN**: a personal identification number to have privilege to access one's account

   A: Okay, now all you have to do is just to press the PIN number.

   B: Wait. I wrote it down somewhere on the cell phone.

3. **nozzle**: a narrow short tube that is attached to the end of a pipe, or a tube to direct the stream of liquid, air, or gas passing through

   A: How can I fill up the gas from this?

   B: Insert the gas nozzle into the gas tank of your car and press the lever.

4. **accumulate**: to get or add something little by little and gradually over a period of time

   A: You have such a big bookshelf.

   B: Yes, people around me gave books away, and it accumulated enough to fill all these bookshelves.

5. **suspend**: to officially stop or end something especially for a short period of time; to prevent something from being active, used, etc. for a time period

   A: Okay, we have three drivers, so each can drive 4 hours in turn.

   B: Sorry guys, I can't. My license has been suspended lately.

Additional Expressions

hearing, proof of insurance, pedestrian crossing, school zone, yield, merge, no outlet, global positioning system(GPS), pull over, heavy foot

Exercise for Useful Expressions

Choose the most appropriate word for the blank.

1. The Business Commerce is considering imposing a __________ policy for gas stations.
   a) exchange b) fire c) terminal d) prepay

2. Online transactions are suspended if you enter wrong __________ more than three times.
   a) PIONs b) PNs c)PINs d)NPIs

3. You can put your finger over the __________ to produce a forceful spray.
   a) nozzle b) hole c) paper d) rubber

4. He seems to have __________ a lot of stamps collected from overseas.
   a) put b) broken c) accumulated d) written

5. Real estate sale will be __________ until all delinquent taxes are paid.
   a) started b) suspended c) busy d) introduced

Conversation Starters

The first dialogue is between a customer and a clerk at a gas station and the second one is between a driver and a police officer. In your own words, complete the following conversation. (C: clerk, D: driver, P : police officer)

Dialogue Practice

Roleplay being caught on the roadway. Part 1 and 2 provide example questions for each role that may be used in the role play.

Part 1: DRIVER

1) Do I need to get out of the car?	Just stay in the car and lower the window please.
2) What did I do wrong?	You ran through a red light.
3) Am I getting a ticket?	I'll just let you off this time.
4) Am I getting any points?	Yes, so you have accumulated 5 points.

Part 2: POLICE OFFICER

1) Didn't I slow down at a stop sign?	You had to come to a complete stop.
2) Are you giving me both a ticket and a point?	I have no choice in this time.
3) What happens if I get another point?	Your license will be suspended for a period of time.
4) Is it illegal not to change a broken tail light?	You can get a ticket for that.

Part 3: Read the questions in the left column and match the best answer from the right column.

1) Why do I need to pull over?	a) No, I can't do that. Show me your license.
2) What's the reason for stopping me?	b) You have 8 points so far.
3) Can you please let me go this time, sir?	c) You made an illegal turn.
4) How many points did I accumulate?	d) You didn't buckle your seatbelt.

Useful Tips

AAA (American Automobile Association)

AAA, read as "triple A," is one of the biggest auto clubs in the USA. It offers various services that are not provided by car insurance companies, such as travel guide and maps, roadside assistance, vehicle registration service, discounts at hotels and motels, and car insurance, etc. The annual membership fee is 50 dollars, and you can get a discounted rate for family members.

Self-made Dialogues

Role-play: Given the role of A and B, create your own dialogue.

Role A (driver)
Your name is Mijin. You are driving and really are late for the class. Suddenly a police officer asks you to pull over your car. You realized that you were driving at the speed of 65 in the 50 mph zone. Show him your driver's license and registration. Ask the police officer what happens if you violate the driving speed limit again.

Role B (police officer)
You are Chris. Announce Mijin to pull over the car. Tell her that she violated a speed limit. She exceeded the maximum speed limit of 50 mph restriction. Ask the driver to show you her driver's license and registration. Give a ticket and say that she has accumulated 7 points and the license may be suspended if she has one more violation with 3 points.

Word in Use

Study how *suspend* can be used various ways in a sentence.

SUSPEND: to stop or delay something or someone from working

1. Those who didn't play fairly at the match were suspended for 6 months.
   [Be-verb + SUSPENDed + preposition]

2. The sentence on a convicted person will be suspended until tomorrow.
   [Be-verb + SUSPENDed + adverb]

3. He will probably suspend immediate judgment on any words I say.
   [SUSPEND + adjective]

4. The judge will suspend a sentence of a convicted person.
   [SUSPEND + noun]

Grammar Table

Review of grammar on *auxiliary* verbs to express obligation

Have to, must, ought to, and *should* are used for necessity or compulsion. They all express obligation.

The negative form of *have to* can be either *do not have to* or *must not*. The former means something does not need to be done while the later means something should not be done. *Have to* changes its form to *has to* according to the subject.

I *have to* be there in time. / I *don't have to* be there in time
They *must* attend the seminar with me. / They *must not* attend the seminar with me.

Should and ought to express a necessity which may or may not be accomplished.
The criminal *should* be punished.
Mr. Simpson *ought to* call the cop.

The negative forms of *should* is *should not* while that of *ought to* is *ought not to*
Kids *should not* be left unwatched in the car.
Your mom *ought not to* sell her house, yet.

Unit 4

CAMPUS LIFE

Section 1 **Go to the library**

Section 2 **Get to know about the course**

Section 3 **Get a student credit card**

Section 4 **Look for a part-time job**

Section 5 **Register classes and pay tuition**

Section 6 **Get involved in extracurricular activities**

A Map to Being an Excellent English Speaker

Section 1 Go to the library

Main Dialogue

Situation: The first dialogue is between Sera and Amy at a university library. They both are freshmen, and the rest of the dialogues are between Sera and a librarian. [S= Sera, A=Amy, L=librarian]

[applying for a library tour]

S: Hey, what are you writing?

A: I'm filling out an application form for the library tour.

S: That's a great idea. Can I join you?

A: Sure, the tour begins at 4 o'clock and takes about 25 minutes. Fill out this form.

S: Hmm… this can be very informative. Before the librarian takes us through each floor and describes library resources and services, she will briefly talk about how to search through the school database.

A: Right. And what I like the most about the library is that it has several sessions each month giving special seminars on using the facility effectively and efficiently.

S: Really? What kind of seminars do they offer?

A: On using statistics, for example, SPSS, NVivo, etc.

S: Awesome! Do they also have seminars on improving writing skills?

A: No, but you can get help with that at the university writing center, located in Baker Hall.

S: Yeah, that's what I need.

A: You can make an appointment with them and they can help you improve your writing. I think the tour is about to begin. After this, I will take you to the writing center.

S: Great. Thanks.

[checking out books]

S: Excuse me. Can I check out this journal?

L: Sorry, the periodicals are not allowed to check out. You can use them only in the library.

S: I see. Do I need to get a card to photocopy this material?

L: It's more convenient. If you don't have the photocopying card, you can use coins. Otherwise, you can buy a $10, $20, or $30 card including the refundable card fee of $1.50. Whenever you need, you can add more value to your card.

S: Then I'll have a $20 card. And I'd like to check out these three books. How long can I borrow them?

L: You have 4 weeks.

S: That's quite long. Let me check them out.

L: Sure, your student ID, please.

[requesting interlibrary loan]

S: Excuse me. I need to find this thesis, but I can't find it in this library.

L: Let me check the database again. Oh, I see. It is located in another university. You'll have to request an interlibrary loan.

S: What's that?

L: We can borrow the resources from another place through this library and you pick them up here.

S: Wow, I didn't know I could do that.

L: If you want to request one, fill out this form. It should take about a week. I'll e-mail you when it arrives.

S: Thanks a lot.

Useful Expressions

Read the definition of useful expressions and the example sentences.

1. **take through**: to briefly explain and guide the place (or the product)

   A: Jen said this curator is really good. She could assume that he majored in European history and art.

   B: Awesome. We're very lucky to have him take us through here then.

2. **periodical**: a magazine or a journal, usually about professional subjects

   A: I couldn't find this periodical at the library.

   B: Is it a monthly magazine? Why don't you check out the online e-journal?

   A: Yeah, I think I'd better.

3. **refundable card fee**: the amount of money received for the value of the card when returning it to a salesperson

   A: Do you remember how much the refundable card fee was?

   B: It was 3 dollars. I'm graduating, so you can have my card.

4. **value**: the amount of money that something is worth

   A: Can I add value to the card later?

   B: Yes, just insert the card into the slot and add any amount of money you want.

5. **interlibrary loan**: borrowing any resources or receiving photocopies of documents to a library from another library

   A: Hello, I have requested an interlibrary loan about a week ago.

   B: Let me check if it arrived.

Additional Expressions

circulation desk, reference desk, library patron, library classification, online library, manuscripts archives, self-guided, overdue fine, extending the loan time, being on reserve

Exercise for Useful Expressions

Write the letter that matches the word with its definition.

1. take through	_______	a) magazines or academic publications issued at regular intervals
2. interlibrary loan	_______	b) the amount of money received for giving the card back
3. periodical	_______	c) an amount of money which is worth so that it can be exchanged for another thing
4. value	_______	d) a system in which a library borrows a book or audio-visual materials from another library
5. refundable card fee	_______	e) to explain something or guide someone

Conversation Starters

A student and a librarian are having a conversation at a library. In your own words, complete the following conversation. (S: student, L: librarian)

Dialogue Practice

Roleplay going to the library. Part 1 and 2 provide example questions for each role that may be used in the role play.

Part 1: STUDENT

1) Hey, what are you writing?	It's a form for the library tour.
2) Can I join you?	Of course, the seminar begins at 3.
3) What kind of seminars do they offer?	They offer sessions on how to access library database from outside the campus.
4) Do they also have seminars on improving writing skills?	Oh no, but on how to check grammatical or mechanical errors.

Part 2: LIBRARIAN

1) Can I borrow this periodical?	You can use them only in the library.
2) Should I prepay for making some copies from this book?	If you don't have the photocopying card, you can use coins.
3) Can you help me locate this book?	Oh, it is located in another university.
4) How can I ask for the interlibrary loan?	If you want to request one, fill out this form.

Part 3: Read the questions in the left column and match the best answer from the right column.

1) Where can I find a book about evolution?	a) Yes, it's 25 cents per each day overdue for each item up to a maximum of $25.00.
2) Do I pay for overdue fees?	b) As long as you have a valid library card.
3) Can the graduate check out the books?	c) They usually take about a week. I will email you when the books arrive.
4) How long does it take to receive interlibrary loans?	d) Look it up at the science section.

Useful Tips

University ID card

When a new student enters a university, the university issues an ID card to the student. Usually the student needs to submit his or her photo online in applying for the card. The card grants the student to access to university buildings and facilities, for example library, computer centers and school shuttle bus. The card also allows him/her to purchase goods and services at campus cafes, cafeterias, nearby stores, or photocopying centers. Discount rates of 10-20%, depending on the location, are given to students with their student ID card.

Self-made Dialogues

Given the role of A and B, make a short conversation.

Role A (freshman)

You are Junichi, an international student who is a freshman at a university. You were given a writing assignment which is due next week. However, you are worried about your poor writing and want to get help from someone.

Role B (junior)

You are Alex, a junior and meet Junichi at the library. You provide information that he needs about the writing center.

Role A	Role B
Ask whether Alex finished his writing assignment and say you are worried about it.	
	Say that you have finished your assignment and let Junichi know that there is a writing center.
Ask what a writing center is for.	
	Explain that it is to help students improve the writing style or check mechanical errors, and is located in Cannon Hall.
Ask its working hours and who works there.	
	Say that its working hours is 11 to 5, between Mondays and Thursday, and graduate students who majored in English are working at the center to help other students improve their writing.
Thank Alex.	

Word in Use

Study how *value* can be used various ways in a sentence.

Noun

1. We cannot easily estimate the value of this property.
   [VALUE + preposition: the amount of money that something is worth]
2. Fancy sports cars tend to hold their value well.
   [VALUE + adverb: the importance or usefulness of something]
3. The teenagers have completely different ideas of values and expectations.
   [VALUE + conjunction: beliefs]

Verb

4. I value your honesty.
   [VALUE + noun phrase: to think something is important]
5. They have a painting valued at $ 7million.
   [VALUE + preposition: to say how much something is worth]

Grammar Table

Review of grammar on *if / unless clause*

If and *unless* are adverb clauses of conditions.

1) *If*-clause describes a possible condition and the main clause shows the results.
   If it rains tomorrow, I won't go hiking.
   If you come to the party this weekend, everybody will be happy.
   I'll be really grateful *if* you take me to the airport.

2) *Unless*-clause means same as *if … not.*
   I'll go shopping *unless* it's hot. = I'll go shopping *if it's not hot.*
   I won't attend the meeting *unless* you come. = I won't attend the meeting *if you don't come.*
   He can't graduate *unless* he passes the exam. = He can't graduate *if he can't pass the exam.*

Section 2 Get to know about the course

Main Dialogue

Situation: Hannah just came to Spanish class and met a classmate and a professor for the first time. Hannah and her classmate sat next to each other and became project partners. [H=Hannah, J=Jane]

[in the classroom]

H: Hi!

J: Hello, you must be a freshman.

H: How can you tell? Everything's new to me. I'm so excited and nervous at the same time.

J: Nothing to worry about. By the way, I'm Jane and am a junior.

H: I'm Hannah. Nice to meet you, Jane. Are there any other books or reading packets to buy for this Spanish class?

J: No. You've got all. Sometimes you can get a second-hand book for a class if the professor is using the same book from the previous semester.

H: Where can I get the second-hand books?

J: You can find them in the bookstore. They sell both new and used books placed in the same shelf next to each other for all courses or through online from any major bookstores.

H: Is this a used book?

J: Yes, I paid $25 although it looks practically new.

H: That's an excellent idea! Why didn't I think of that? From next semester, I'm going to purchase my books earlier. Well, Jane, did you have lunch? Do you want to grab a bite?

J: Sure. Let's get out of here and talk about our project then.

H: Good. Is the cafeteria okay?

J: Perfect.

[in the cafeteria]

H: So what do we have to do for this project?

J: We need to do research on any topic related to Mexico and present it using Power Point.

H: Oh boy. What can I do? I'm not good at Spanish.

J: Professor Sarabia is a quite tough grader but if you try hard, you will survive. Hang in there. I'll help you out as much as I can. How many credits did you register?

H: 15 credits.

J: Are you taking Japanese for Bilinguals and Native Speakers? In that class, you will do lots of writing and speaking in Japanese. Professor Hayaku has high expectations from his students.

H: That's nice to know, but is there anything else I should know about this professor?

J: No, but as far as I know, you must be on time for his classes or appointments. He is an extremely punctual person. Also, when you work on any of his writing assignments, you should be careful not to plagiarize.

H: What? I didn't get that.

J: You shouldn't cut and paste or copy any part of others' work onto your paper, which you found from the Internet sites or other resources. If you copy seven or more words consecutively in a sentence from others' work, it is considered plagiarized. If you get caught doing that, you will get an 'F' from the class.

H: I better watch out for that.

J: Ya, you should do so. As you know, this is true in any class. Professors in America, unlike in other countries, don't tolerate that kind of behaviors from their students.

H: Thanks for all information. Sorry, but I have to go to my next class.

J: All right. See you later.

Useful Expressions

Read the definition of useful expressions and the example sentences.

1. **reading packet**: a collection of reading materials bound which is used as either supplementary to the textbook or main reading materials

A: Have you read those three articles for tomorrow?

B: What articles?

A: The articles on our reading packet! Didn't you check the syllabus?

2. **grab a bite**: an expression of 'Let's eat something'

A: I'm starving to death. Can we grab a bite before we get to work?

B: Sure. What would you like to eat?

A: Sandwich will do.

3. **credits**: a unit of study at college or a recording of the work students need to complete before graduation

A: How many credits are appropriate to take per semester in the States?

B: Well, it depends on the university. What about in your country?

A: Same here. In my case, I'm supposed to register 15 credits for each semester.

4. **punctual**: arriving at precise or exact time appointed

A: Sorry Rachel. I'm late again.

B: I can't put up with this anymore. You have never been on time for anything. Can't you be more punctual, please?

A: I'm sorry. My landlord came for the rent when I was about to leave the apartment.

5. **plagiarize**: to take or use someone else's idea as one's own without giving credit to the work

A: Hey! I took one of Shakespeare's poems and used it on my paper.

B: Good. I assume that you cited the info and put the reference on the back of your paper, right?

A: No. Should I?

B: Of course! If you didn't, you are plagiarizing, which is also considered a crime in our country.

Additional Expressions

course packs, plagiarism detector, citations, a literature response journal, summer reading list, copyright holders, royalty fees, GPA calculator, neuroscience, applied music

Exercise for Useful Expressions

Choose the most appropriate word for the blank.

1. __________ has lots of articles and materials to read for students as a course requirement.
   a) An album　　b) The student notebook　　c) A reading packet　　d) A calendar

2. I'm so hungry. Let's __________ before we go to our next class.
   a) go to park　　b) grab a bite　　c) take a rest　　d) take a nap

3. How many __________ are you taking in this semester?
   a) pictures　　b) cards　　c) books　　d) credits

4. It's difficult to be __________ if there is a traffic jam on the way to work.
   a) punctual　　b) penetrate　　c) late　　d) busy

5. Professors cannot tolerate when students __________ someone else's work.
   a) look after　　b) ask　　c) plagiarize　　d) help

Conversation Starters

Two students are having a conversation. In your own words, complete the following conversation. (S1: student 1, S2: student 2)

Dialogue Practice

Roleplay for the first day of class is shown below. Part 1 and 2 provide example questions for each role that may be used in the role.

Part 1: FRESHMAN

1) Is there anything I should know about the professor?

Not much, but you should be careful about being late for class.

2) Where can I find the second hand books?

It is in the Student Circle building.

3) Are there any other books or reading packets to buy?

I'd better check the schedule on the course syllabus.

4) Is this a used book?

No, it's published a few months ago. I couldn't find a used one.

Part 2: JUNIOR

1) What should we do first for our project?

We have to research on any topic related to Mexico.

2) What if I fail this class?

If you try hard, you will survive.

3) What do I need to keep in mind in doing our project?

You shouldn't copy any part of others' work onto your paper.

4) Where can I get the reading packet?

You can get it from the photocopying center.

Part 3: Read the questions in the left column and match the best answer from the right column.

1) Which classes did you sign up for?	a) I don't know. I haven't been assigned to one yet.
2) Who is your advisor?	b) We need to get it done by the end of this month.
3) When is our deadline for this project?	c) I signed up for Biochemistry and English 101 classes.
4) Where can I get the textbooks for our course?	d) You can purchase them from the bookstore or on line.

Useful Tips

Used or secondhand books

Many university students want to buy and sell used books since they cannot afford to buy many required textbooks for their courses; many of them can be pricey. If students try to buy used books, they should plan out their schedule in advance so that they can get the books in a better condition and save time searching the books they need. Checking the school forum and bulletin boards is helpful, because the students often put ads on these places to sell their books on their own. Always search online for books. The books can be cheaper than a college campus bookstore.

Self-made Dialogues

Given the role of A and B, make a short conversation.

Role A (freshman)
You are Jenny, a freshman, sitting in a college classroom. The first class is just about to begin. Ask a classmate who is sitting next to you whether you need to buy a textbook or not.

Role B (junior)
You are Chris, a junior. Tell Jenny that there are no required textbooks, but let her know that a reading packet is required for supplementary readings.

Role A	Role B
Ask about what the required textbooks are.	
	Say that there is no required textbook for this course but there is a reading packet.
Ask what a reading packet is.	
	Explain what a reading packet is.
Ask where and how to get a reading packet.	
	Suggest Jenny to get the packet from the university bookstore, but explain that it is for supplementary readings.
Thank him.	

Word in Use

Study how *punctual* can be used various ways in a sentence.

PUNCTUAL: happening at exactly the same time that has been arranged

1-1. My aunt is always punctual to the minute.
[PUNCTUAL + preposition]

1-2. My landlord expects punctual payments from us.
[PUNCTUAL + noun]

1-3. Paul has been reliable and punctual.
[conjunction + PUNCTUAL]

Grammar Table

Review of grammar on *what as noun clause*

A noun clause means a clause that acts as a noun in a sentence. In other words, *what* + subject + verb can act as a subject, a complement, and an object.

Subject

What I said is true.

What the English teacher said was really amazing.

Complement

Man is *what* he eats.

The great thing about my dog is *what* he can do for me.

Object

I like *what* I see.

Ask Bill *what* he wants for dinner.

The word *what* can be replaced with *the thing which.*

This is what I want. = This is *the thing (which)* I want.

Section 3 Get a student credit card

Main Dialogue

Situation: Eunji is from Korea and is a freshman at the university. She wants to get a student credit card. The first dialogue is between her and a sales person from a credit card company, and the second one is between her and a bank teller. [E=Eunji, S=sales person, B=bank teller]

[at a credit card concession]

S: Hello. How may I help you?

E: I want to get a credit card. Can I get some information about the kinds of cards you offer?

S: Of course. Are you over 21?

E: No, I'm 19.

S: In that case, your parents have to cosign your application.

E: That's not possible. They are in Korea.

S: Then do you have a guardian or an adult who could cosign the application?

E: No.

S: Sorry, but the law on student credit card for underaged has become much more strict since last year.

E: Okay, I see. Thanks.

[at the bank]

E: Can I apply for a credit card even though I'm underaged?

B: Sure, all you have to do is to fill out this form.

E: Really! I'm so excited. Can you explain possible cards I can get?

B: For students who are underaged, there is only one card. The credit limit on this card is only $300, but there is no membership fee. If your credit remains satisfactory for six months, then the company will increase your limit.

E: What's the interest on that?

B: It's 22% annually.

E: Wow, that's rather too high.

B: Not really, as long as you can pay the whole amount within a month, then there is no interest. If you pay the minimum amount indicated on the bill, there is no penalty either.

E: What? How much is the penalty?

B: It's $25 plus interest. If you pay in time, there is no problem. The card will come in handy especially in an emergency situation. When you don't have any cash at the moment, you can use the card. You have one month to pay the bill.

E: All right. I guess I need one, only for an emergency.

B: I need to photocopy your photo ID and your savings bankbook with your application.

E: I don't' have my bank book. Will you be working tomorrow?

B: Of course, I will. If you have any question, you can come and ask me.

E: I have one more question. Who issues the credit cards?

B: Banks do. Our card is issued by American Transitional Bank. Other banks will also issue a Visa card.

E: Thanks a lot for your information. Since I'm using Bank of Citizens to do all my bank transactions, I should find out if the bank also offers a credit card.

B: By all means, please do. If you decide to get the card from our bank, then you can come back.

E: See you, then.

Useful Expressions

Read the definition of useful expressions and the example sentences.

1. **concession**: a place to sell something, sometimes an area which is part of a larger building or store

A: Aren't you hungry? I need to grab a bite before having dinner.

B: How about hot dogs? Let's go to the concession stand and get some. I'm kind of hungry, too.

2. **cosign**: to sign jointly a document with another person who can be responsible for paying the debt

A: One of my friends asked me to cosign his loan.

B: You should be really careful on that. If you cosign for someone who is not really credible, you might end up paying for his debts.

3. **guardian**: a person who is legally responsible for the care of another person, especially an underaged person

A:You seem to do lots of things for your grandmother.

B:Yes, because I'm her legal guardian.

4. **come in handy**: to be useful especially when something is needed

A: No! Don't throw that used bicycle away. The wheels might come in handy later.

B: Do you think so?

5. **by all means**: used to say that someone is willing to give permission to have/do something

A: Do you think it's better to tell him the truth before he finds out?

B: Of course. Please do so by all means.

Additional Expressions

credit line, credit history, sponsor, asset, liability, APR(annual percentage rate), redemptions, fraud liability, rewards, secured visa card

Exercise for Useful Expressions

Choose the right word which has similar meaning as the underline word(s).

a. concession	b. by all means	c. come in handy	d. cosign	e. guardian

1) Keep those tissues, and they can be useful when you watch a sad movie tonight.

2) My friend promised me to sign jointly my bank loan documents.

3) My aunt was my protector after both of my parents passed away from the car accident.

4) I'd like to take a short break and get some food from the stall in that building.

5) A: Can I borrow your eraser?
   B: Sure, go ahead.

Conversation Starters

A student and a bank teller are having a conversation at the bank. In your own words, complete the following conversation. (S: student, B: bank teller)

Dialogue Practice

Roleplay having a conversation between a student and a bank teller. Part1 and 2 provide example questions for each role that may be used in the role play.

Part 1: STUDENT

1) Can I apply for a credit card although I'm underaged?	You need someone to cosign the application.
2) What's the interest on that?	It's about 12% to 19% annually.
3) How much is the penalty?	You should pay $26 including interest.
4) Who issues credit cards?	Any banks do that.

Part 2: BANK TELLER

1) What do I do to get a credit card?	All you have to do is to fill out this form.
2) In that case, can you raise my credit limit to $400?	The credit limit on this card is only $300.
3) How can I avoid paying the penalty?	If you pay the minimum amount indicated on the bill, there is no penalty.
4) What are some advantages of having a credit card?	The card will come in handy especially in an emergency situation.

Part 3: Read the questions in the left column and match the best answer from the right column.

1) Why do you need a student credit card?	a) It's my aunt, Hannah.
2) Who is your guardian?	b) I prefer Visa, please.
3) Which would you prefer, Visa or Master card?	c) I can get discounts at the school bookstore with the card.
4) Have you applied for a credit card and been rejected by any bank?	d) Not that I know of.

Useful Tips

Student credit cards

Banks offer various kinds of student credit cards. Since Federal laws impose restrictions regarding issuing credit cards to individuals under 21, students should research and read contracts carefully before they sign it. And very often the applicant needs to prove their independent ability to repay debt, or adult co-signers who agree to accept joint liability for the account. Student credit cards sometimes offer 3 – 5 % cash back on eligible purchases at drugstores, convenience stores, gas stations, and utilities (including cable).

Self-made Dialogues

Role-play: Given the role of A and B, create your own dialogue.

Role A (student)

You are Chris, an international student from Taiwan. You want to apply for a credit card, but you are underaged. Ask a salesperson from the credit card company the kind of cards you can get and if you need to have your application cosigned. Ask also about the interest rate and the penalty fee for late payments or having insufficient fund in your account. Tell her you don't have your photo ID with you.

Role B (salesperson)

Your name is Mary. You are a salesperson from a credit card company. Tell the student that if he is under 19, there is only one type of card he can get, but needs a cosigner to sign the application. Explain that the annual interest rate is 22% and the penalty fee is $27 plus interest. Ask him to come back later with his Photo ID.

Word in Use

Study how *cosign* can be used various ways in a sentence.

COSIGN: to sign jointly

1-1. I believe he'll cosign my loan no matter what.
[COSIGN+ noun phrase]

1-2. He foolishly cosigned for someone else, and ended up with huge debts.
[COSIGN + preposition]

1-3. Mary's parents had to cosign in getting a bank loan to pay for her tuition.
[to + COSIGN]

Grammar Table

Review of grammar on the *adjective clause pronouns*

Adjective clause pronouns are used to modify a noun phrase, and the head of the noun phrase is called the antecedent.

I have *a friend*. He is good at speaking Russian. [a person]
→ I have a friend *who is good at speaking Russian.*
The adjective clause pronoun *who* points back to the antecedent *friend* in the noun phrase.

The rose is my mom's favorite. It is in the garden.
→ The rose *which(that) is in the garden* is my mom's favorite. [a thing]
The adjective clause pronoun *which* points back to the antecedent *rose* in the noun phrase.

Section 4 Look for a part-time job

Main Dialogue

Situation: The dialogue is between a student, Sarah and a clerk at the university marketing office. Sarah is calling to find the information about a job and she is being interviewed later. [S=Sarah, C=clerk, I=interviewer]

[on the phone]

C: Hello, the university marketing office. How may I assist you?

S: I'm calling about an assistant manager position that was advertised in my school newspaper. Is it still available?

C: Yes, it is.

S: I'd like to get a little more information about the position. What type of work would I be doing? What's the monthly pay?

C: Well, an assistant manager will be doing the basic office work, organizing, collecting, and analyzing data. For this position you'll need to have some background on statistics, although you don't need any work experience. The starting salary is 1850 dollars per month. If you are interested in the position, you should send me your resume with a cover letter, and then we'll call you for an interview to discuss your qualifications more in detail.

S: Great. I'll send them within a few days. Thanks.

[at the office]

C: Hello, Sarah. I'm Christine. I spoke with you on the phone earlier.

S: Yes, Christine. Very happy to meet you.

C: Nice to meet you, too. I'll take you to the place for the interview. Please follow me.

[at the interview]

I: We are happy to have you here for the interview. Have a seat and just be yourself.

S: Thank you.

I: Let me start by asking about your reasons for seeking this position.

S: I know that I don't have much work experience in this field, but I have done lots of related work by helping out my professor with data collection and analysis. He got me interested in the market research area. I'd like to learn more and develop my skills in this field.

I: All right. Are you still a student?

S: Yes, I'm a senior and this is my last semester.

I: Your resume indicates that you have worked as an assistant manager in the customer service at Kaufmann's department store. What did you do there and why did you quit the work?

S: I was to oversee what was going on at the department and to write a summary report on it once a month to the manager.

I: I bet that was a big responsibility.

S: It was, and it was time-consuming. That was the main reason I quit working there. It involved so much time that I couldn't do both work and study at the same time.

I: I see. Why do you think we should hire you?

S: I really enjoyed doing the market research for my professor. Most of all, I enjoy working with people, and love the challenge that this job offers.

I: Well, you seem to be a very diligent and enthusiastic person. I will make my decision within a few days and let you know the result. Do you have any last minute question?

S: No, not now.

I: It was my pleasure meeting you. And, thank you for coming for the interview.

S: Thank you.

Useful Expressions

Read the definition of useful expressions and the example sentences.

1. **position**: an opening for a job or an employment

   A: Hello, I'm here for the interview for a secretarial position.

   B: Follow me. The manager is waiting for you.

2. **statistics**: the science of collecting and analyzing the gathered information in numbers

   A: Hey, listen. According to official statistics, 90% of people in that country don't know how to drive a car!

   B: That's a surprising fact. Do they ride a bicycle instead?

3. **cover letter**: a letter that explains briefly of one's abilities and experiences in writing which are outlined in the resume

   A: If you are interested in this job, send a resume and a cover letter to the human resource department.

   B: Thank you. Would you tell me whom I should address to?

4. **qualification**: a type of experience or skills for a particular position or profession

   A: Any other qualifications are needed for this job?

   B: Um... oh, you need at least 1 year of work experience in this field.

5. **indicate**: to point out or to show whether the evidence is true or not

   A: Hey, check this out. This table indicates that you're overweight.

   B: No way! I'm slim, don't you think?

Additional Expressions

fill out, vacancy, flexible working hours, personnel manager, openings, job hunting, replacement, recommendation, recruiting, underemployed jobs

Exercise for Useful Expressions

Fill in the blanks with appropriate words from the list provided below.

Everyone feels anxious when it comes to getting a job in their senior year in college. ___________ show that students have problems in writing a decent ___________ for the ___________ they want in the job market. Some students don't even know how to write a resume. Seniors in the university are so tied-up with meeting the ___________ required for the job that they do not have much time in constructing a good resume. Survey of the job market, however, ___________ that constructing a good resume should be the first step in getting a good job.

position	final letter	indicate(s)	statistics
location	cover letter	qualifications	

Conversation Starters

A student is taking an interview for a part-time job. In your own words, complete the following conversation. (I: interviewer, S: student)

Dialogue Practice

Roleplay taking a job interview. Part 1 and 2 provide example questions for each role that may be used in the role play.

Part 1: INTERVIEWER

1) Why are you seeking for this position?	I love spending time with children.
2) What did you do in your previous work?	I ran errands for my boss.
3) Why did you quit your previous job?	The job required me to work till late at night.
4) Why do you think we should hire you?	I have the appropriate experience from my previous job.

Part 2: STUDENT

1) What can I help you with?	I'd like to get more information about the position.
2) Will you send me your resume and a cover letter?	I'll send them within a few days.
3) What are you hoping to learn from this job	I'd like to learn more and develop my skills.
4) Could you tell me about your strong points?	I enjoy working with people and love the challenge that job offers.

Part 3: Read the questions in the left column and match the best answer from the right column.

1) How long does it take for you to commute?	a) About 5 hours a day.
2) Do you have any special qualifications?	b) I am skillful in operating Photoshop.
3) When would I be notified the results of the interview?	c) I'll let you know the results in a week.
4) How many hours would I be working?	d) No, there isn't.
5) May I ask if there would be any work on Saturdays?	e) It usually takes 45 minutes by subway.

Useful Tips

Part-time jobs

The majority of university students seek for part-time jobs because not only the tuition is very expensive but also being independent either financially or emotionally is part of being American. Students often use a bulletin board or a student service center in finding job advertisements. These job ads provide the descriptions which usually include job title, hours per week, wage, position description, how to apply, etc. A common part-time job for students is babysitting. Picking up a local newspaper and looking through the classified ads for "babysitters wanted" can yield some job leads. A babysitting job can also be found through online.

Self-made Dialogues

Develop the conversation by using prompt words in a bracket with a partner.

You are making a call to ask about a babysitting job which you found through online. You want to check out the details and set up an interview. [S: student, M: mother]

S: Hello. This is Christine. Did you post the babysitter position at the bestbabysitter.com?
M: ______________________________.

S: I'm calling to get some information about the position. What are the babysitting hours?
M: ______________________________.
(from Monday to Wednesday, 4 to 7)

S: That would be fine. How old are the kids?

M: ______________________________.

(2 children of 5- and 9-year olds)

S: Is there any special activity that I should engage in with your children?

M: ______________________________.

(reading books, playing with the children and making sure they brush their teeth.)

S: What's the overtime pay?

M: ______________________________. ($15 an hour, usually on weekends)

Do you want to set up the time for an interview?

S: Sure, I'd love to.

Word in Use

Study how *position* can be used various ways in a sentence.

Noun

1. There's no doubt that Mary will attain the position.

   [verb + POSITION: to get the job]

2. We are not in a position to help you.

   [preposition + POSITION: the situation that someone is in]

3. What's your position on nuclear power?

   [POSITION + preposition: an opinion about a particular subject]

Verb

4. Soldiers positioned themselves around the bank.

   [POSITION + pronoun: to put something or someone in a particular place]

Grammar Table

Review of grammar on *future progressive* vs. *simple future*

The most often used constructions to express future tense are *will*, *shall* and *be going to*. Among these, *will* is the most common expression. Simple future of *will* is used to express prediction while the future progressive *will/ shall + be+ -ing* describes an event that will be in progress at certain time in the future.

The weather *will* be nice tomorrow.
I am standing in front of the red telephone booth waiting for you. *I'll be standing* here until you come out.

Future progressive is especially useful to be more polite and tentative. The second example below using future progressive is more polite than the first example sentence using simple future.

When *will* you come to see me?
When *will* you *be coming* to see me?

Section 5 Register classes and pay tuition

Main Dialogue

Situation:The dialogue is between an advisor and a student, Minho, and it's taking place in the advisor's office and the financial office. [A=advisor, M=Minho, FC=financial office clerk]

[at the advising session]

A: Hello, Minho. How can I help you?

M: Well, I'll be a junior this year and I'd like to know what classes I'm supposed to take for my major.

A: Okay, let me look at your record ..., so you're finished with your liberal arts requirements, right?

M: Yes, and I've decided to major in Business.

A: I see, then you should declare your major and then take courses listed within the curriculum of the major. Look through the time schedule and select the courses that you want to take. You should select some required and obligatory elective courses from your department.

M: What do you mean?

A: Besides taking the required courses for your major, you also need to take several elective courses at different levels. You should take two from 100 levels and three from 200s.

M: Is it possible to drop a course after the registration period?

A: Yes, but only during the add/drop period. Make sure to check its dates.

M: Can I audit some classes, too?

A: Do you want to audit to get a pass/fail grade or just sit in the class?

M: Just to sit in, because I heard that macroeconomics is a difficult course to pass.

A: Yes, you can. But you should get the permission from the professor who's teaching the course.

M: Okay, I'll. Oh, I have one more question. Where is the new financial office?

A: The office is moved to Baker Hall. It's located right next to the registration office.

M: Thanks and bye bye!

[at the financial office]

FC: Hello, what can I do for you?

M: Hi, I've received a notice from the office of late tuition payment and about applying for financial aid.

FC: Please wait. Your record shows that as an international student, you have completed I-20 and the financial support form when you transferred from your previous school, but you should still apply for the aid.

M: Is it possible for international students to get the financial aid?

FC: Only if we find that you do not have the resources to fund your education during your study and have met academic standards.

M: In that case, I should apply for it. What forms do I need to submit?

FC: I'll get you the forms right now. Please wait.

M: Thank you.

FC: (came back with the forms) As soon as you complete these forms, bring them to me. You should also find out from your department if there are any research assistant positions open.

M: Why didn't I think about that before! Thank you for the information.

Useful Expressions

Read the definition of useful expressions and the example sentences.

1. **liberal arts**: subjects of study that develop students' general knowledge and ability to think rather than their technical skills

A: Hey, Brian. Which liberal arts courses did you take last semester?

B: British literature. It was great.

2. **obligatory**: mandatory, referring something that should be done because of the law, rules, etc.

A: Hey, there's a policeman. Put the seatbelt on.

B: Peter, I did it already. Wearing safety belts in Ohio is obligatory while driving.

3. **elective course**: a course that students can select and choose classes among alternatives

A: Jen, what are you taking for the elective courses this time?

B: Psychology maybe? I don't know, I haven't decided yet.

4. **audit**: to attend a course without taking any exams or receiving credits at a college or a university

A: Why are you taking this class? I heard the professor gives students lots of assignments every week.

B: I know, but he's very well-known in this field of study.

A: Then why don't you audit the class first?

5. **tuition**: the money charged to students to provide educational or learning experience

A: I think I should take a semester off from school.

B: What? Why?

A: I need to save money for the tuition.

Additional Expressions

full or partial refund, admission, waitlist, coursework, auditor, syllabus, transferring the credits, sign up, out-of-state tuition, administrative registration fee

Exercise for Useful Expressions

Choose the one that has the most appropriate match between Q and A.

1. Q: Isn't it obligatory to wear a safety helmet to drive a motorcycle?
   A: Yes, that's right. You don't have to.

2. Q: What liberal arts course do you recommend to take?
   A: You've got to be serious in taking liberal arts because you can not develop your technical skills for your major.

3. Q: Gosh, I can't afford to pay the tuition this year. What can I do?
   A: I know. It's very hard to get a nice tutor this year.

4. Q: May I audit your class, Professor Lopkin?
   A: Sure, you may as long as you submit all the assignments that students are required to do.

5. Q: Are you taking the contemporary literature class as an elective this semester?
   A: Yes, I'm supposed to. It's mandatory to take the class.

Conversation Starters

A student and an advisor are having a conversation at the advisor's office and financial office. In your own words, complete the following conversation. (S: student, A: advisor)

Dialogue Practice

Roleplay registering the class. Part 1 and 2 provide example questions for each role that may be used in the role play.

Part 1: STUDENT

1) Could I know what classes I'm supposed to take for my major?	Have a seat. Let's review the curriculum together.
2) Is it possible to drop some of the classes?	Yes, but I'd like to encourage you to go through.
3) How can I audit some classes?	You need to ask the professor first.
4) Where is the financial office?	It's on the second floor of this building.

Part 2: ADVISOR

1) What courses should I take if I change my major?	There are several required and obligatory elective courses from your department.
2) Could you tell me more about obligatory elective courses, please?	You need to take at least one class.
3) When can I add one more course?	You can do that during the add/drop period.
4) Is it possible to change the topic of our project now?	You should get the permission from the professor.

Part 3: Read the questions in the left column and match the best answer from the right column.

1) Did you sign up for this class?	a) Sure, but you need to fill out this form first.
2) Have you checked the add/drop period?	b) Yes, I did. This class is being offered only in spring semester.
3) Could I have your signature on the registration form, please?	c) No, I haven't. Is it over?
4) When can I check the course schedule for this semester?	d) You can check it on our website tomorrow morning.

Useful Tips

Three types of student loans

1) Federally subsidized loans: They allow students to defer interest accrual while they are in school.
2) Federally unsubsidized loans: Interest is accrued from the time students borrow money.
3) Private student loans: They are currently guaranteed a return on their investment due to legislatively enacted changes in 2005.

Student loans may be offered as part of a total financial aid package that may also include grants, scholarships, and/or work study opportunities. The Federal Work-Study program provides a great opportunity for students to earn money from part-time jobs while Federal government pays a portion of students' wages and their campus employer contributes the rest toward the tuition payment. Off-campus jobs must be local.

Self-made Dialogues

Role-play: Given the role of A and B, make a short conversation.

Role A (sophomore)

You are Tom, a sophomore who decided to major in accounting. You ask your friend, Jessie how many credits you should take and which professor she recommends.

Role B (senior)

You are Jessie, a senior majoring in accounting. Answer Tom's questions about the accounting major.

Role A	Role B
Say Jessie that you changed major to accounting and ask what her major is.	
	Tell him that it is accounting.
Ask her how many credits she took from the accounting department.	
	Say you took 21 credits.
Ask her which subjects you should take first.	
	Tell him to take Economics and Finance first, and Information Systems for Accounting Majors later.
Ask which professor she would recommend for economics.	
	Respond by saying that Professor Woz and Professor Thurman would be great.
Ask her reasons for recommending them.	
	Say that their classes were challenging but helpful in firmly developing the concepts of economics.
Tell her that you think you should audit some classes before taking them.	
	Tell him that it is possible but he needs to get the permission from the professors first.
Thank her and say it was a great help.	
	Say you'll see him next semester.

Word in Use

Study how *audit* can be used various ways in a sentence.

Verb: to attend a course without expecting to receive formal credit

1. You cannot audit the class unless you have the permission from the professor.
   [AUDIT + noun]

Noun: a formal examination of an organization's accounts

2-1. The audit revealed the company had misled investors.
   [AUDIT + verb]

2-2. You need to submit the audit plan by tomorrow.
   [AUDIT + noun]

Grammar Table

Review of grammar on the *adjective clause pronouns as the object*

Adjective clause pronouns used as the object of a verb

This is the man. I met him yesterday.

→ This is the man *who(m)* I met yesterday.

Who(m) is used as an object of a verb *met*.

An adjective clause pronouns used as an object can be omitted.

The pen was stolen. I bought it at the store.

→ The pen *(which(that))* I bought at the store was stolen.

Which is used as an object of a verb *bought*.

Adjective clause pronouns used as the object of a preposition

This is the man. I played tennis with him.

→ This is the man *with whom* I played tennis.

→ This is the man *who(m)* I played tennis *with*.

→ This is the man I played tennis with.

Preposition can come before adjective clause or after the subject and the verb of adjective clause.

Section 6

Get involved in extracurricular activities

Main Dialogue

Situation: Hannah is a newly appointed resident assistant (RA) from Ireland. She is invited to the new RA initiation at the party. First dialogue takes place at the RA office and next one does at sorority club. [H=Hannah, S=Shelly]

[at the RA office]

S: Hello, congratulations on becoming an RA.

H: Thanks.

S: I'm Shelly. Are you a freshman?

H: Hi, I'm Hannah. You can tell, huh? It's my first year. I'll be knocking on your door for help quite often.

S: Well, I'll be glad to help you out.

H: For a starter, what kind of work will I be doing?

S: You need to check whether students are conforming to the dorm policy or not. Here is the guideline. Make sure to read page 12 and remember the ten rules. If students break any of those rules for more than three times, they will be kicked out of this dormitory.

H: I see.

S: If you have any other questions, you know what to do. By the way, are you a member of any clubs?

H: No, but I've been wanting to join a sorority club. I think I signed up to become a Phi Delta Sigma member on the orientation day.

S: Wow, I am a member of that sorority club.

H: That's great, but I don't know if I will be picked as a member of that club.

S: Don't worry. I will strongly recommend you to my club members. Speaking of it, let me call my friend to find out whether they have finalized the new member list.

[at sorority club]

H: Hey, Shelly.

S: Congratulations, and I'm so happy that you are a member of this sorority.

H: Thanks. I'm so excited. Do you know how long I have waited for this moment?

S: I can't imagine! Now I can tell you things you'll have to do for the initiation. A biggest part of the ceremony is to volunteer at an orphanage on a Saturday and at a senior care center on a Sunday.

H: Really? That's the initiation? It sounds great. I really enjoy playing with children.

S: Well, we choose our members mainly based on the voluntary experiences, besides the minimum GPA requirement of 3.2.

H: I see. I'm really happy to be a member of the club. How often do we do the voluntary work?

S: Once a month. All members are divided into groups of 5 or 6 and go to an assigned center. We rotate by going to several different centers each month.

H: Will I be assigned to specific work?

S: The captain will arrange the work based on your preference which you have indicated in the application form.

H: If I get to be sent to an orphanage, I want to help children with their math skills. I really enjoyed doing that in my previous voluntary work place.

S: That sounds great. We need someone like you. Don't get the wrong idea that that's all we do. We also have parties almost every Saturday evening. Members usually have a blasting time. However, you need to keep in mind to maintain your GPA. If you don't for two consecutive semesters, your membership will be terminated. So much for the introduction, let's get back to the crowd.

H: Very well. Let's talk more later.

Useful Expressions

Read the definition of useful expressions and the example sentences.

1. **RA**: (abb. resident assistant) a person who supervises dormitory at college or university
   A: I'm not sure whether I can adjust to college life well in the first year.
   B: Don't worry. I got lots of help from other RAs with my school work, and made lots of friends.

2. **sorority**: a club for a group of female students at an American college or a university
   A: I had a serious argument with my sorority sister last night.
   B: Why did you? Sorry I couldn't help you out because I was so stoned at that time.

3. **finalize**: to complete a plan, trip, project, etc.
   A: Did you hear how the meeting went?
   B: No. The committee just met to finalize the contract.

4. **initiation**: the act of someone becoming a member of a group, often with a special ceremony
   A: Is there an initiation fee for joining this club?
   B: No, but make sure to participate in the initiation ceremony this Friday evening.

5. **consecutive**: following one after another in a series without interruption
   A: Did you watch the contest last night? Who is the winner?
   B: Peter Thompson. He won the three contests consecutively.

Additional Expressions

custodian, fraternity, refreshment stand, community assistant/advisor, counselor, chapter house, church outreach, habitat for humanity, yearbook staff, residential community

Exercise for Useful Expressions

Write True or False in terms of using the underline words correctly.

1) R.A. is the supervisor in the dormitory. ________

2) The new handsome member of the sorority club who Mary met in the orientation was my ex-boyfriend. ________

3) To finalize the work means to start from scratch. ________

4) The new members were introduced in the initiation ceremony last night. ________

5) I had a stomachache for three consecutive days last week so I couldn't do anything since Friday. ________

Conversation Starters

An RA and a student are having a conversation about joining a sorority club. In your own words, complete the following conversation. (R: resident assistant, S: student)

Dialogue Practice

Roleplay being involved in extracurricular activities. Part1 and 2 provide example questions for each role that may be used in the role play.

Part 1: NEW STUDENT

1) What kind of work will I do? — You'll work on the advertisement.
2) How often do you do the voluntary work? — At least twice a month.
3) Will I be assigned to a specific work? — It depends on the leader of our club.
4) What else should I know about being a member of this club? — Just keep your balance between study and club activities.

Part 2: RESIDENT ASSISTANT

1) What are my responsibilities here? — You need to check whether students are conforming to the policy.
2) What if students break the rules a lot? — They will be kicked out of the dorm.
3) How can I be picked as a member of that club? — Don't worry. I'll strongly recommend you.
4) What happens if I fail to maintain my GPA? — Your membership will be terminated.

Part 3: Read the questions in the left column and match the best answer from the right column.

1) What's my duty as a member of this club?
2) Why don't you sign up for the volleyball tryout?
3) What if I failed in entering Rotary club?
4) What are some requirements in order to join the activity?

a) You can get in next time.
b) Do you think I can make it?
c) You'll do the voluntary work as a tutor.
d) We need a student with a long-term commitment.

Useful Tips

Fraternities and sororities

The word fraternities or sororities come from Greek. Fraternity means brothers while sorority means sisters. Fraternities and sororities have begun late 18th century and the purpose of these Greek organizations is the personal development of their members. Social and cultural fraternities or sororities have intimate bonds of brotherhood or sisterhood. As members, they share friendship, knowledge, loyalty, academic achievement and intellectual development. They learn, grow and experience through their core value of community service, friendship, leadership and scholarship. Some fraternities and sororities select members based on objective criteria refer to nondiscrimination policies.

Self-made Dialogues

Create your own dialogue according to the following situation.

Mendi is a freshman and Sherry is a senior in college. They both are RAs and they met at the RA initiation for the first time. Mendi says she wants to join the sorority club, Phi Delta Sigma. After Mendi finds out Sherry is a member of the club, she asks about how to become a member and what they do as a member. Sherry explains that they do voluntary work twice a month and have a lot of parties. She also warns her that members of the club should maintain a high GPA. She promises that she will strongly recommend Mendi to the club members and tells her the initiation will be held at 6 in the evening on this coming Friday.

Word in Use

Study how *finalize* can be used various ways in a sentence.

Finalize: to make something final or to complete

1-1. When did they finalize the contract?
[FINALIZE + noun]

1-2. Paul said the adoption was finalized.
[Be-verb + FINALIZEd]

1-3. They will meet to finalize the terms of the treaty.
[to + FINALIZE]

1-4. I couldn't finalize the deal until my boss arrived.
[auxiliary verb + FINALIZE]

Grammar Table

Review of grammar on *verb infinitive* vs. *verb + gerund*

Forget + infinitive means to forget something that needs to be done in the *early future*.
Don't *forget to take* your umbrella before you go out.

Forget + gerund means to forget something that happened in the *past*.
I *forgot taking* my umbrella, so I got all wet on the way home.

Try + infinitive means to *make an effort* to accomplish something.
I *tried to complete* my task in time, but I failed.

Try + gerund means to do a *tentative or experimental* action.
If your coffee is bitter, *try putting* some sugar in it.

Verbs such as *forget, remember, try*, and *regret* can be used either with infinitive or gerund, having different meaning.

Unit 5

AT THE BANK

A Map to Being an Excellent English Speaker

Section 1

Open or close a bank account

Main Dialogue

Situation: The dialogue is between the bank teller and the customer at the bank. Heanny is at the bank to set up a new bank account and asks questions that he doesn't understand. [H=Heanny Lee, B=bank teller]

B: May I help you?

H: I'd like to open a bank account.

B: Savings or checking account, sir?

H: I need both.

B: Do you have a photo ID with you?

H: I have a passport. Is it okay?

B: Sure, that'll be fine. In the meantime, would you fill out this form?

H: Hmm… I don't have a home phone number.

B: Do you have any contact number? Is there any number you can be reached at?

H: I've been here in Seattle for less than a week. I am going to install the home phone in a week. Can I bring the number then?

B: That'll be fine. Are you finished with the form?

H: Yes, here it is.

B: Will you be depositing any money today?

H: $2,500 in the savings account and $1,750 in the checking account, please.

B: All right. I'll take care of this.

H: I have a few questions about the checking account.

B: Yes, go ahead.

H: How do I write a check?

B: You have to write the date, the amount you are writing for and to whom the check is for. The last thing you would have to do is to sign the check. Be careful with the number of zeros you are writing. One more important thing is to write a memo in the check and keep a memo of its usage in your checkbook.

H: I see. What happens when I don't have enough money in my account and deposit it too late? Would I be charged for having nonsufficient fund (NSF)?

B: It depends. If the person you wrote the check for already tried to cash the check from your NSF account, then you will be charged for $25 for bouncing the check. As long as you balance your checkbook and check it regularly, you shouldn't have much problem. If not, you can always ask for the balance at the counter whenever you come to the bank.

H: I see.

B: If you have any questions, just call or come to the bank for help. All right, Mr. Lee, the bank will give you a few checks, but you'll have to order your own books. Here is the catalogue. You can select the style and design that you want.

H: Uhm... I'd like to order this IS290 with blue background. How long will it take?

B: It will take about a week.

H: One more question. I have a regular bill every month. Is it possible to set up an automatic wire transfer to another account?

B: I'm sorry, but our bank doesn't have such a system.

H: Really? It's going to be such a hassle, but I guess I'll have to write checks every month.

B: I'm afraid that you'll have to do that. Anything else you would like to do?

H: Can I use a debt card to withdraw money from an ATM?

B: Yes, of course.

H: That'd be all.

B: Okay, here are your savings and checking account books. Thank you and have a nice day! Next in line, please.

Useful Expressions

Read the definition of useful expressions and the example sentences.

1. **account**: a contract between a customer and a bank that allows to keep money in or withdraw it from the bank

A: I just opened a bank account for our son, Dave.

B: That's good. Now he can learn how to manage money, right?

A: Exactly.

2. **deposit**: to put money into a bank account

A: I'd like to deposit $300 into my account.

B: You would need to fill out a deposit slip.

3. **bounce**: having insufficient money in the account at time someone tries to cash the check

A: I have just received a bounced check with the monthly bank statement .

B: Oh, no. How much are you supposed to pay for the penalty?

A: It says $25.

4. **balance**: a total amount of money left in a bank account

A: I'd like to check the balance of my checking account.

B: Sure. Here is the balance written on a piece of paper.

5. **set up**: to open or establish something

A: What are you going to do after you finish studying?

B: I'm going to set up a business this coming summer.

Additional Expressions

late payment, PIN, account holder, safety deposit box, individual account, joint account, Internet banking, bankruptcy, covering the check, money order

Exercise for Useful Expressions

Write the letter that matches its best answer.

1. What kind of account do you want to open?	______	a) Of course, what's your account number?
2. Can I make a deposit here?	______	b) None, it's for free.
3. What would happen if I got a bounced check?	______	c) Into which account, sir?
4. Could you check my balance?	______	d) I want to open a cash deposit with fixed rate.
5. How much does it cost to set up an automatic transfer to another account?	______	e) You'll have to pay a fine.

Conversation Starters

A customer and a bank teller are having a conversation at a bank. In your own words, complete the following conversation. (C: customer, B: bank teller)

Dialogue Practice

Roleplay having a conversation between a bank teller and a customer. Part 1 and 2 provide example questions for each role that may be used in the role play.

Part 1: BANK TELLER

1) Do you have a photo ID?	Here is my passport.
2) Is there any number you can be reached at?	I will give you my cell phone number.
3) Are you finished with the form?	Almost finished. Give me a few more minutes.
4) Will you be depositing any money?	No, I'll just pay the bills today.

Part 2: CUSTOMER

1) Can you tell me your home phone number please?	I will install the home phone in a week.
2) How much would you like to deposit into each account?	$2500 in the savings account and $1750 in the checking account, please.
3) Have you decided on the design of your check book?	I'd like to order this IS290 with blue background.
4) What would you do since we don't have an automatic transfer system?	I'll have to write checks every month, then.

Part 3: Read the questions in the left column and match the best answer from the right column.

1) Do you want to deposit any money now?	a) It will take 3 to 4 working days.
2) What happens if there's not enough money in my checking account for the check I wrote?	b) No, not today.
3) How long will it take to get my check book?	c) Sure. Do you want to set it up now?
4) Can I set up an automatic wire transfer to another bank?	d) You may be charged for the bounced check.

Useful Tips

Bank accounts

In the United States, two most often used bank accounts are savings account and checking account. Savings account will pay interest on the money which may be a term account for a specific period of time. On the other hand, people get paid by checks so it is necessary to open an account. Checking accounts are also used as a primary instrument for withdrawing money. With a checking account, paying bills, making purchases and transferring money are possible. Banks usually don't give interest for having money in this account.

DATE	DESCRIPTION	WITHDRAWALS	DEPOSITS	BALANCE
03-10-16	ATMW	**21.25		**474.11
03-10-16	ATMF	**1.50		**472.61
03-10-20	DEBP	**2.99		**469.62
03-10-21	WEBP	**300.00		**169.62
03-10-22	ATMW	**100.00		**69.62
03-10-23	DEBP	**29.08		**40.54
03-10-24	DEBR		**2.99	**43.53
03-10-27	TELP	**6.77		**36.76
03-10-28	PYRL		**694.81	**731.57
03-10-30	WEBT		**50.00	**781.57

Please refer to the back cover for the list of common transaction codes.

Please verify your account activity regularly. If there is an error, notify the bank within 45 days.

NSF: NSF is an acronym of Non-Sufficient Funds. When the checking account balance is less than the amount to cover the checks the customer issued within a period of time, the bank returns these checks to the customer with the monthly statement. NSF is also called a returned check, a bounced check, a bad check, or a rubber check.

Self-made Dialogues

Given the role of A and B, make a short conversation.

Role A (bank teller)

You are Kelly. You help Johan to close his checking account.

Role B (customer)

You are Johan and you want to close the bank account due to limited locations of the bank. Also the bank service is unsatisfactory.

Role A	Role B
Greet the customer and ask how you may help him.	
	Say you want to close your checking account.
Ask what led him to close his account.	
	Answer that there are not enough locations as well as the poor customer service.
Say sorry and ask for his photo ID.	
	Ask the teller if a driver's license is fine.
Say it's okay and give him a form to fill out.	
	Give the completed form and ask what you should do with your bounced check.
Say he will be charged $20 for it.	
	Ask her if you need to pay it now before closing the account or pay later if possible.
Reply by saying that he can pay it later and ask if you can help him with anything else.	
	Tell her you're fine and thank her for the help.

Word in Use

Study how *order* can be used in various ways in a sentence.

Noun

1. He couldn't ignore teacher's order to remain seated.
   [ORDER + infinitive: telling somebody to do something]

2. Kevin, could you put your books in order?
   [preposition + ORDER: arranging properly]

Verb

3-1. He ordered that we should sit down quietly and pay attention to him.
   [ORDER + conjunction: to tell somebody to do something]

3-2. Mom ordered us to make our room tidy.
   [ORDER + pronoun: to tell somebody to do something]

4. We ordered hamburgers and French fries.
   [ORDER + noun: to ask for something]

Grammar Table

Review of grammar on *present perfect with since* and *for*

The preposition *since* is used with the time when the action started and followed by a particular time.

I have been here *since* five o'clock.
Jamie hasn't eaten meat *since* he was 23.
Ken has been my best friend *since* we were eight.

The preposition *for* is used with a period of time and followed by a duration of time.

We have been here *for* three weeks.
Paul has worked for the government *for* more than nine years.
He hasn't been to the museum *for* ages.

Section 2 Deposit or withdraw money

Main Dialogue

Situation: The first dialogue is between the bank teller and the customer, Sumin. Sumin is asking how to cash in checks and withdraw money. The second dialogue is between Sumin and her friend, Holly, talking about how to read the bank statement. [B=bank teller, H=Holly, S=Sumin]

[at the bank]

B: Next in line. Good morning! How may I help you?

S: Yes, I have traveler's and personal checks that I'd like to cash in.

B: Sorry, ma'am. You can't cash personal checks today. You will need to deposit them in your account and wait for the checks to be cleared. The earliest you can cash them is tomorrow after 12 p.m.

S: Sure, let me deposit them in my checking account now.

B: Please endorse these checks.

S: Excuse me?

B: Sign your name on the back of them. (finishing the process) Okay, here is your receipt. Anything else I can help you with?

S: I also need to withdraw some money from my checking account. How do I do that?

B: You should write "cash" in the check payable section, today's date, the amount you want to cash, and then sign your name on the back. Also, I need to see some kind of a photo ID.

S: Here is my student ID card.

B: Sorry, but it's not a proper ID. You'll need an ID card issued by the government, such as driver's license or passport.

S: Oh, I see. Here is my passport.

B: Thank you. Can you endorse the check on the back?

S: Sure. (signs the check)

B: How would you like your money?

S: Can I have five 20's, seven 5's, and ten 1's?

B: Sure. Here is five, four, three, two ... (counting money to the customer)

S: One more thing I need to do. I need to transfer $175 from my savings to the checking account.

B: You'll need to fill out this withdrawal slip for your savings account and the deposit slip for the checking account. Do you have your savings account book with you?

S: Here you are.

B: (finish all the transactions) Well, you are all set. Have a nice day!

[asking Holly, her friend, how to read the bank statement]

S: Holly, would you help me understand this bank statement?

H: Sure, what seems to be the problem?

S: What does NSF mean in this checking account statement?

H: It means you did not have enough money in your account at the time someone was trying to cash your check. Luckily, the bank did not charge you any fee for that. When you receive your monthly statement, you should make sure whether all checks have been cashed or not, check the beginning and the ending balances and compare them with the balance of your checking account book.

S: What do I do if the balances don't match?

H: Then you should go through the voucher and check each one of them, checking the charge fees and the checks that have not been cashed. If you subtract them from the final balance of the statement, then this amount should match the final balance of your checkbook.

S: I see. It's so much easier to understand it now. Thanks.

Useful Expressions

Read the definition of useful expressions and the example sentences.

1. **clear**: to give or get official approval for something to be done

   A: How long does it take to cash this check?

   B: To clear the check, you need to deposit it in your bank account first and wait for about 3 days.

2. **endorse**: to sign on the back of a check

   A: Could you endorse the check on the back?

   B: Sure. Can I cash the money now?

   A: Not today. It will be available after 2 p.m. tomorrow.

3. **slip**: a small piece of paper, especially one for writing on or with something printed on

   A: Can I get a sales slip for this purchase?

   B: Here it is.

4. **transaction**: a business deal that is done between people, especially when buying and selling something

   A:I didn't write the check to Peabody Pools.

   B: Why don't you check the monthly statement for the transaction?

5. **subtract**: to take some away from something, usually a number in calculation or to withdraw

   A: Son, if you subtract 5 from 9, what do you get?

   B: I get 4. Am I right?

   A: Well done.

Additional Expressions

passbook, bankbook, transaction account, certified check, commission rate, remittance, futures transaction, countersign, charge a commission, transaction summary

Exercise for Useful Expressions

Write the letter that matches the word with its definition.

1. clear	________	a) to sign a name on the back of a check for being paid into a bank account
2. endorse	________	b) a piece of paper that indicates the payment is made for the purchase
3. slip	________	c) to get or give official permission
4. transaction	________	d) to take away
5. subtract	________	e) activities related to bank services

Conversation Starters

A customer is talking to a teller at the bank. In your own words, complete the following conversation by filling in the blank bubbles. (C: customer, B: bank teller)

Dialogue Practice

Roleplay having a conversation between a customer and a bank teller at the bank. Part 1 and 2 provide example questions for each role that may be used in the role play.

Part 1: BANK TELLER

1) Can you endorse the checks on the back?	All of them?
2) Anything else I can help you with?	Yes, I need a withdrawal slip.
3) How would you like your money?	Ten 20s, please.
4) Do you have your savings account book with you?	Yes, I've got mine here.

Part 2: CUSTOMER

1) What can I do for you?	I have traveler's and personal checks that I'd like to cash in.
2) Do you want to cash the checks?	Let me deposit them in my checking account for now.
3) Is there anything else?	One more thing I need to do. I need to transfer $175 from my savings to the checking account.
4) Do you have an ID with you?	Here you are.

Part 3: Read the questions in the left column and match the best answer from the right column.

1) When can I have a debit card for my account?	a) If it's less than $100, it will be $2.
2) How much is the service fee for withdrawing money from ATM on weekends?	b) The bank will charge you fees.
3) What happens when the balances don't match?	c) It will be delivered to your place within a week.
4) Can you tell me what NSF means?	d) Oh, that means your account doesn't have enough money when somebody wants to cash your check.

Useful Tips

Bank statement

Many countries use only a bank book to record all transactions occurred. In addition to using a bank book, banks in the USA provide a bank statement. They send the statement to the account holder, usually once a month. These days, banks send it through email or to cell phones in the form of electronic statement.

FIRST BANK OF WIKI
1425 JAMES ST, PO BOX 4000
VICTORIA BC V8X 3X4 1-800-555-5555

CHEQUING ACCOUNT STATEMENT
Page : 1 of 1

JOHN JONES
1643 DUNDAS ST W APT 27
TORONTO ON M6K 1V2

Statement period	Account No.
2003-10-09 to 2003-11-08	00005-123-456-7

Date	Description	Ref.	Withdrawals	Deposits	Deposits
2003-10-08	Previous balance				0.55
2003-10-14	Payroll Deposit - HOTEL			694.81	695.36
2003-10-14	Web Bill Payment - MASTERCARD	9685	200.00		495.36
2003-10-16	ATM Withdrawal - INTERAC	3990	21.25		474.11
2003-10-16	Fees - Interac		1.50		472.61
2003-10-20	Interac Purchase - ELECTRONICS	1975	2.99		469.62
2003-10-21	Web Bill Payment - AMEX	3314	300.00		169.62
2003-10-22	ATM Withdrawal - FIRST BANK	0064	100.00		69.62
2003-10-23	Interac Purchase - SUPERMARKET	1559	29.08		40.54
2003-10-24	Interac Refund - ELECTRONICS	1975		2.99	43.53
2003-10-27	Telephone Bill Payment - VISA	2475	6.77		36.76
2003-10-28	Payroll Deposit - HOTEL			694.81	731.57
2003-10-30	Web Funds Transfer - From SAVINGS	2620		50.00	781.57
2003-11-03	Pre-Auth. Payment - INSURANCE		33.55		748.02
2003-11-03	Cheque No. - 409		100.00		648.02
2003-11-06	Mortgage Payment		710.49		-62.47
2003-11-07	Fees - Overdraft		5.00		-67.47
2003-11-08	Fees - Monthly		5.00		-72.47
	*** Totals ***		1,515.63	1,442.61	

Self-made Dialogues

Develop the conversation by using prompt words in a bracket with a partner.

You are a bank teller having a conversation with a customer about some bank services at the bank. [B: bank teller, C: customer]

B: Good morning, how may I help you?
C: Hello, I want to deposit two checks to my accounts. I want the $200 check into my checking account and $320 into the savings account.

B: ______________________________. (endorse)
C: Can I withdraw $400 in cash now?

B: ______________________________. (No, need to be cleared)
C: OK, I can wait until then.

[next day]
B: Good afternoon, how may I help you, sir?
C: I'd like to withdraw $400 from my checking account.

B: ______________________________. (withdrawal slip)
C: Here you are.

B: ______________________________. (How)
C: Two one hundreds, two fifties and ten tens please.

B: Here you are. Have a nice day.

Word in Use

Study how *check* can be used various ways in a sentence.

Verb: to examine something

1-1. Please make sure you check your e-mail by 9 a.m.

[CHECK + noun phrase]

1-2. I just wanted to check whether she was right or not.

[CHECK + conjunction]

1-3. Let's check out new Chinese restaurant in downtown.

[CHECK + adverb]

Noun: a piece of paper that has the same value as cash

2. What he gave me last week was a bad check.

[adjective + CHECK]

Grammar Table

Review of grammar on *passive* and *past forms of infinitives*

Passive infinitive is used in the form of *to be + past participle* to explain what happens to people and things, like what is done to them.

He has lots of work *to be done*.

I didn't expect *to be invited* at this party.

Past-passive infinitive is used in the form of *to have been + past participle* to talk about past events with present results.

He is so lucky *to have been accepted* as a T.A in the university.

Your thesis is supposed *to have been written* in English.

Section 3

Solve problems related to banks

Main Dialogue

Situation: The dialogue is between the bank teller and the customer. They are having a conversation about problems related to reissuing a bank statement and a credit card. [C=customer, B=bank teller]

[at the bank]

B: Next in line. Good morning! Can I help you?

C: Yes. I need to get a copy of my bank statement for last month.

B: Do you need an official or an unofficial one?

C: The official one, please. My loan agency wants a copy to check my credit and for a record.

B: Since we sent you the statement about a week ago, you will need to pay the fee for reprinting.

C: How much is it?

B: It's $2.50.

C: No problem. Here you are. (giving the money)

B: Okay. Here is the copy. Anything else?

C: I have a question about the checking account statement. How much do you usually charge for bounced checks?

B: For each check you bounce, the bank will charge a $25 fee and it will also charge an overdrawn fee of $25 to the person that you wrote the check to.

C: Really? I guess I'll need to balance the check book regularly and check the balance more often.

B: You can also check the balance of your account online at any ATM or go to any branch office. Moreover, a bank statement will be sent to your home every month.

C: I see. I'll keep an eye on that. I have one more question about this statement. In my paycheck voucher, the total of my pay was $185, but this statement indicates that I have deposited $105. Could you check this? Here is a copy of the voucher.

B: Let me check this. Please wait. (coming back a few minutes later) I am sorry. There has been a mistake on this deposit slip. You wrote it as $105 as you see in this slip.

C: I guess we both made a mistake. The number“8” looks like a “0.” it's hard to distinguish them.

B: The difference will be added to your checking account.

C: Thanks.

[on the phone]

C: Excuse me. I lost my credit card.

B: Do you know your card number?

C: No. I wrote the number down somewhere, but I don't remember the place.

B: It's okay. What's your name and Social Security Number?

C: My name is Abdul Ahad. I don't have an SSN yet, but am getting it next week. My Visa card was issued by this bank.

B: It should be fine. Looks like no one has used your card yet. Thus, I stopped the card and it can't be used by anyone anymore. We'll issue you a new card and send it to you by mail.

C: How long will it take to get the new card?

B: About 5 to 7 working days. It will be sent to you as a registered mail, so someone should be at home to receive the card.

C: All right. Thanks.

Useful Expressions

Read the definition of useful expressions and the example sentences.

1. **bank statement**: a monthly summary statement of all transactions occurred in a bank account

   A: I've found my bank statement!

   B: Great! Let's start analyzing the statement to figure out why this check was bounced.

2. **loan agency**: a consultant who provides services for people in getting a loan

   A: I guess I need to get a bank loan for my tuition.

   B: You do? Then why don't you use the loan agency at the student center? I heard they provide students with a reasonable interest rate.

3. **overdraw**: to draw money from a bank more than the balance of the account

   A: I am going to buy the new O-Box for this weekend.

   B: But, you said you are overdrawn by $500 from your account!

4. **issue**: to become available or be brought to public notice by authority

   A: My passport is about to expire.

   B: When was that issued?

   A: 5 years ago.

5. **registered mail**: a mail or a parcel recorded in a post office to make sure it is treated with special care

   A: Honey, are you going to the post office today?

   B: Yes. I'm ready to send my applications.

   A: Why don't you send them by registered mail to make sure that someone receives them?

Additional Expressions

magnetic strip, charge-offs, debit card, wallet protection toolkit, negative balances, nonpayment of items, monthly maintenance fee, online application, transaction history, collection agency

Exercise for Useful Expressions

Fill in the blanks with appropriate words from the list provided below. Use the words only once.

Sam: Gosh, did you go shopping again, Alice?

Alice: Yup. I was passing by a department store on the way home and saw a pair of these lovely red shoes in the show case and well, I heard them whispering, "Take me, take me!"

Sam: You told me last week that you had been ___________ from your account by over $400!

Alice: I know…I think I might have to get a loan. Do you know where a nearby ___________ is?

Sam: Wake up, Alice! Getting a loan for shopping?

Alice: What should I do then? I wish I were rich.

Sam: Don't be stupid. You need to check your ___________ first. Can I see it?

Alice: Wait a moment. I remember getting a ___________ from my bank a couple of days ago. Here.

Sam: Now I see why the bank didn't ___________ a check to you.

overdrawn	transact	issue	record	bank statement
bounce	loan agency	registered mail	overdraft	

Conversation Starters

A customer and a bank teller are having a conversation at a bank. In your own words, complete the following conversation by filling in the blank bubbles. (C: customer, B: bank teller)

Dialogue Practice

Roleplay having a conversation about problems related to a bank. Part 1 and 2 provide example questions for each role that may be used in the role play.

Part 1: BANK TELLER

1) Can I help you?	Yes. I'd like to cash this cashier's check.
2) Do you need an official one or an unofficial one?	I need an unofficial one, please.
3) Do you know your card number?	No. I don't. What can I do?
4) Would you like to receive your new card by mail?	Sure. Please make sure that it is a registered mail.

Part 2: CUSTOMER

1) Would you tell me your card number?	Yes. I wrote the number down somewhere.
2) Your name and SSN, please?	I don't have SSN yet, but am getting it next week.
3) How do you want to receive your new card?	I'd like to get the card by mail.
4) Is Friday okay with you to get a registered mail?	All right. Thanks.

Part 3: Read the questions in the left column and match the best answer from the right column.

1) What if I don't have a SSN yet?	a) No, I check my bank account every week.
2) Have you ever had your checks bounced?	b) If you have a savings account, you should be fine.
3) How often do you send a bank statement?	c) We charge you $30 per check you bounce.
4) How much do you charge the nonsufficient account fee?	d) We send it to you every month.

Useful Tips

SSN

SSN means social security number and is a nine-digit number issued by Social Security Administration. It is issued to U.S. citizens, permanent residents and temporary residents. Its main purpose is to track individuals for tax. For international students, Social Security does not assign them a number just because they are enrolled in a school or a university. If the school authorizes the students to work either on or off campus, and they meet all regulations required by the Social Security Administration, then they can apply for the number.

Self-made Dialogues

Develop the conversation by using prompt words in a bracket with a partner.

You lost your savings account bank book. You go to the bank and ask to a teller whether you can have the new book with the same savings account number. [B: bank teller, C: customer]

B: Hello. How can I help you?

C:____. (lost my bank book)

B: Okay then, do you want to make a new savings account?

C: ________________________________. (a new book with the same account number)

B: It is possible but I think it's better to make a new savings account number for the security reason. You can make it now, if you want to.

C: ____. (yes)

B: Okay, please fill out this form. Do you have your photo ID with you?

C: ____.(yes and would like to make a new check card)

B: Okay, then please fill out this form. Is there anything else I can do for you?

C:____. (need to withdraw money)

B: Sure, please fill out this slip.

C:____. (okay)

Word in Use

Study how *cause* can be used various ways in a sentence.

Verb: to make something happen

1-1. This hot weather and unhealthy food can cause a heart problem.
[CAUSE + noun phrase]

1-2. I didn't mean to cause you a trouble.
[CAUSE + pronoun + noun]

1-3. The damage to Rome was caused by the event.
[Be-verb + CAUSEd + preposition]

Noun

2-1. I didn't understand the cause for complaint because the food and wine were exquisite.
[CAUSE + preposition: a reason for something]

2-2. Wars have various causes that contribute to enmity.
[CAUSE + relative pronoun: a reason for something]

3. The school raised $150,000 for their cause this month.
[CAUSE + pronoun: a group of people's aim or principal]

Grammar Table

Review of grammar on *passive*

The passive form is used when the emphasis is on the action. Thus, the passive forms are used if the thing receiving the action is more important and should be emphasized. Also the passive form can be used when who is doing the action is not known or not important. The basic form is *be* + *past participle*.

Right now, the address *is spoken* by Paul.
The project *will be finished* by team A before tonight.
This sonnet *is written* by the famous, Shakespeare.
Bill *was offered* the project by Helen.
English *is spoken* in many countries.

Section 4 Transfer or wire Money

Main Dialogue

Situation: The dialogue occurs at the bank relating to bank transactions and involves conversations between a customer, a bank teller, a manager, and a security guard. [C=customer, B=bank teller, M=bank manager, S=bank security guard]

[calling to the bank]

B: Good afternoon. Trans America Union Bank. How may I help you?

C: I need to wire transfer the money internationally. What type of documents should I prepare?

B: In that case...you would need information about the sender and the beneficiary. For the sender, you need name and address of your bank, account number, and savings account book that you are sending money from. You also need beneficiary's name, phone number or contact information, name and address of a bank or branch office, bank account number, and swift code or Bank Identifier Code (BIC). When you prepare all this information, you can come to the bank and wire transfer the money.

C: What is a swift code or BIC?

B: They are the code to identify the bank. Each bank is assigned with a code. It's like a SSN of a person. Your beneficiary's bank should be able to provide the information without much problem.

C: Thanks.

B: Oh, make sure to check the full names of both the sender and the beneficiary. The names should match the ones on the passport.

C: I got it.

[at the bank]

C: Excuse me, should I stand in this line for wiring money internationally?

S: No, you don't have to wait in line. The line is for the customers with typical bank transactions. The bank manager will assist you.

M: Hi! How can I help you?

C: I need to wire money to South Korea and I have all the documents that I have been asked to prepare.

M: Then, let's start the process by filling out this form. Jot down all the information I have marked on this form, including the amount. And, you know there will be a wiring fee of $18 for the amount less than $10,000. If the amount is more than that, then the fee will be higher.

C: No problem. What's the exchange rate these days?

M: Well, it's not bad. Today's rate has gone down a little. It was 1,155 won per dollar yesterday, but it's 1,140 today.

C: That's good. I would like to send $3,500 today.

M: In that case, you will need a total of $3,518. Let me see… Hold on for a minute… Will you withdraw the money from your account?

C: Yes. It will be from my savings account and here is my bank account book. I've also finished filling out the form.

M: You'll have to fill out the withdrawal slip.

C: (complete the form) Here.

M: (return a few minutes later) Please read the form and sign your name here…
(the customer signs the form) Okay. This is your copy and you are all set. Thank you.

Useful Expressions

Read the definition of useful expressions and the example sentences.

1. **wire**: to send money overseas to a person through online

   A: Hi, this is Sam. I have not received the refund from my insurance company.

   B: I'll arrange to wire the money today.
   (cf. wire transfer: a method of transferring money from one person or institution to another, made from one bank account to another bank account)

2. **beneficiary**: a person who is legally entitled to receive money or property from someone

   A: I'd like to ship this box to Shanghi.

   B: You forgot to write the beneficiary's P.O. Box. Who is receiving this box?

   A: Oh, my mom. Her P.O. Box is 13579-2.

3. **assign**: to allow someone to have or use something

   A: Which rooms are assigned for today's conference?

   B: For us, room A and B.

4. **jot down**: to write something quickly

   A: Amy, if you are not doing anything this Saturday, would you like to go out?

   B: Great! What is your number?

   A: Wait a second, why don't you jot down my number on this napkin?

5. **exchange rate**: the value or amount of the currency of a country for the purpose of conversion into the currency of another country in exchange

   A: What's the exchange rate from dollar to yuan?

   B: The exchange rate is six yuans per dollar.

Additional Expressions

currency, silver dollar, routing number, advanced fee, internet fraud, vault, investing account, payee, adjustment, compound

Exercise for Useful Expressions

Choose the most appropriate word for the blank.

1. Jamie is in Italy traveling right now, but he called and asked me to __________ some money to him yesterday.

   a) tire b) wire c) fire d) hire

2. When you want to send money to someone, you should spell the name of the __________ correctly.

   a) benefit b) beneficial c) beneficiary d) beneficence

3. Our English teacher __________ a task on Shakespeare which is too difficult for our group to complete.

   a) resigned b) cosigned c) signed d) assigned

4. I had to __________ what the teacher said quickly before the bell rang.

   a) come down b) jot down c) get down d) go down

5. What's the __________ for won to dollars? I need to know how much cash I should prepare for my trip to Las Vegas.

   a) daily rate b) postal rate c) exchange rate d) birth rate

Conversation Starters

A customer, a receptionist, a manager, and a security guard are having a conversation at the bank. In your own words, complete the following conversation.
(C: customer, B: bank teller, S: bank security guard, M: bank manager)

[at the bank]

Dialogue Practice

Roleplay having a conversation at the bank. Part 1 and 2 provide example questions for each role that may be used in the role play.

Part 1: CUSTOMER

1) What type of documents I would need for that?	None. Just bring your ID with you.
2) What is a swift code?	It's a code to identify the bank.
3) Should I stand in this line for wiring money internationally?	Yes, please go to the second counter from the left.
4) What's the exchange rate these days?	You mean dollars to pounds?

Part 2: BANK TELLER

1) Here are all the documents you mentioned. Is there anything else I should check again?	Make sure to check the full names of both the sender and the beneficiary.
2) Is there something I should be aware of?	The name should be matched the name on your passport.
3) How much does it cost to send a wire transfer to South Korea?	There will be a wiring fee of $18 for the amount less than $10,000.
4) Which form should I use to withdraw money from the account?	You'll have to fill out the withdrawal slip.

Part 3: Read the questions in the left column and match the best answer from the right column.

1) Where is the place for international wiring money?	a) It's $20 for the amount less than $10,000.
2) Which account are you withdrawing money from?	b) Please go to the 2nd floor.
3) How much is the wiring fee to South Korea?	c) From my savings account.
4) Can I wire the money first and then bring the missing document later?	d) In that case, you should come back later with all your documents.

Useful Tips

Different types of money

Currently, there are six denominations of paper money in the USA: one-dollar bill featuring a portrait of George Washington, two-dollar bill featuring Thomas Jefferson, five-dollar bill featuring Abraham Lincoln, ten-dollar bill featuring Alexander Hamilton, twenty-dollar bill featuring Andrew Jackson, fifty-dollar bill featuring Ulysses S. Grant, and one hundred-dollar bill featuring Benjamin Franklin. Ten- or twenty-dollar bills are most often used and one hundred-dollar bills are not as much used as other bills. Two dollar bills are considered as luck for their rarity.

Self-made Dialogues

Create your own dialogue according to the following situation.

A: You are Yumiko Tada. You are at the bank and want to wire transfer $3,000 to Japan. The money will be withdrawn from your savings account. Provide all information requested by the bank teller. For example, Michiyo Tada is the beneficiary, and her address is 142-552 Jungsi, Moritz, Tokyo. Also ask the teller about today's exchange rate.

B: You are a bank teller. Your customer, Yumiko, wants to wire the money to Japan. Get all the information necessary to complete the transaction, such as information relate to the sender and the beneficiary, the amount, the swift code or BIC. If she does not know what a swift code or BIC is, then explain them to Yumiko.

Word in Use

Study how *start* can be used various ways in a sentence.

Start: to take a first step to do something

1-1. Why don't you start your work right now?
[START + noun phrase]

1-2. I will start swimming from tomorrow.
[START + gerund]

1-3. When does water start to become gas?
[START + infinitive]

1-4. We didn't start until the rain stopped.
[START+ conjunction]

2. This writing is awful. I need to start all over.
[START + adverb: to begin again]

Grammar Table

Review of grammar on *each* and *every*

Each and *every* are both determiners and only singular nouns and singular verbs are followed after them.

> *Every student was* absent from school today.
> *Each painter is* great.

The difference in meaning *is* that both can be used without much difference, but *each* is better to use when we think of people or things separately or individually, one at a time. On the other hand, *every* is closer to all, thinking of people or things together, one in a group or in total

> I gave *each* student a pencil to write. (This means I give pencils to students one by one.)
> I gave *every* student a pencil to write. (This means I give pencils to all the students.)

Unit 6

AT THE HOSPITAL

Section 1 **Find a good doctor and make an appointment**

Section 2 **Have a health interview**

Section 3 **Perform CPR and give a simple first aid**

Section 4 **Identify an appropriate department**

Section 5 **Go to the drugstore**

Section 6 **Discuss how to work out**

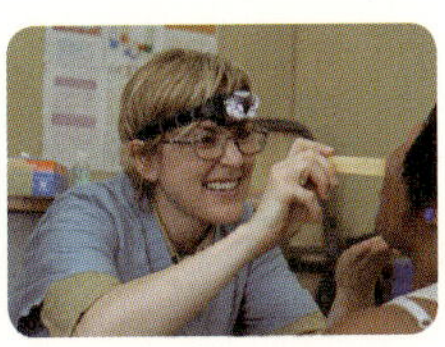

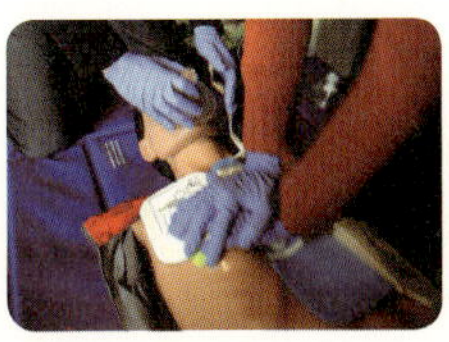

A Map to Being an Excellent English Speaker

Section 1

Find a good doctor and make an appointment

Main Dialogue

Situation: The dialogue is between Kelly and Helen who is sick. Helen is an exchange student from Korea. Kelly helps her out and she makes an appointment with a doctor. [K=Kelly, H=Helen, N=nurse]

[at home]

K: Hey, what are you eating?

H: Well… It's porridge, a Korean style. My mom used to make this when I was sick.

K: Are you feeling okay now?

H: No, I haven't been feeling very well these days and often had stomachaches.

K: Is that because of the upcoming exams?

H: I'm not sure. I used to have a severe stomachache during, you know, PMS. But this time is different. The symptoms are worse. I also have migraines and backaches. It's been over a week.

K: Oh… that sounds awful. Why don't you go see a doctor?

H: Well, I've heard that I should pay a lot for visiting a clinic. And I'm not sure if my insurance will cover this.

K: But you'd better go see a doctor and have him check you out. Otherwise, the problem may last longer and get worse.

H: I couldn't agree with you more!

K: My sister often had similar problems, so my mom took her to the doctor. If she had waited another month, she would have had a surgery. Do you want to try the same place my sister went?

H: Why not? Do you have the number?

K: I'll ask my mom. You can also find a doctor by going through the Yellow Page. There is a list of all OBGYN doctors.

H: If there are so many names, I would not know whom to choose.

K: I know. I feel the same way. Let me get the number for you. Wait. Here is the name, the phone number and the address. And I think you should find out from your insurance agent on the coverage again.

H: Yeah. I just did while you were on the phone with your mom. I called the student information center and they said my insurance will cover that.

K: Great! Make an appointment as soon as possible.

H: Thanks.

K: No problem. His name is Dr. Peterson.

H: Thank you.

[calling the doctor's office]

N: Good morning. Dr. Peterson's Clinic. May I help you?

H: Hello, I'd like to make an appointment.

N: Okay. Is this your first visit to this clinic?

H: Yes.

N: We have 10 and 3 o'clock available on Friday. And the rest of this week is all booked.

H: 10 o'clock would be better for me.

N: Okay, your name, please.

H: It's Helen Park. My last name is spelled P-A-R-K.

N: Well, Helen, Dr. Peterson will see you at 10 o'clock on Friday.

H: Thank you. Bye.

Useful Expressions

Read the definition of useful expressions and the example sentences.

1. **porridge**: a dish usually served as breakfast made by boiling oatmeal with milk or water

   A: Hey, Jean. Why are you having porridge for lunch?

   B: My mom made it for me because I had an indigestion last night. It's like a chicken soup in your country.

2. **upcoming**: going to happen soon

   A: Peter, you look nervous. What's wrong?

   B: Because of the upcoming presentation of my thesis.

3. **PMS**: (abb. premenstrual syndrome) physical and emotional problems that many women experience before their period

   A: Where is Jane?

   B: She's not coming today. She just called in sick.

   A: What? Why?

   B: PMS, you know. She must be suffering from the pain.

4. **symptom**: a change in the body or mind which shows unhealthiness

   A: What are the symptoms?

   B: I have such a severe sore throat that I can't even drink water.

5. **OBGYN**: (abb. obstetrics & gynecology)
   obstetrics: the branch of medicine concerned with the birth of children
   gynecology: the medical practice dealing with the health of the female reproductive system

   A: Susan, did you hear that Hyewon is pregnant?

   B: Really? Wow, that's a good news.

   A: Yes, I called her last night and she said she was looking for an excellent OBGYN doctor.

Additional Expressions

dry heaves, pap smear, cervical check, regular physical checkup, pre-existing conditions, department of surgery, internal department, physicians, surgeons, diagnosis

Exercise for Useful Expressions

Choose the one that has the most appropriate match between Q and A.

1. Q: Are you feeling okay? You look terrible!
   A: No, I've felt nauseous and had a terrible headache all day long. The symptoms are getting worse.

2. Q: Would you recommend me a great female OBGYN doctor?
   A: All I want was information which is hard to access.

3. Q: Is gaining weight one of the symptoms of PMS?
   A: The worst moment was when he showed up at the front door.

4. Q: Do you know any delicious porridge recipe?
   A: Oh yes. My grandma used to make a great lemon cake.

5. Q: Where can I find information regarding the upcoming movies?
   A: Well, for the third year in a row, I went to the seminar.

Conversation Starters

Two students are having a conversation to find a good doctor. In your own words, complete the following conversation.(S1: student giving advice, S2: student who is sick)

Dialogue Practice

Roleplay having a conversation about health problems. Part 1 and 2 provide example questions for each role that may be used in the role play.

Part 1: ADVISOR

1) What are you eating?	I'm having chicken soup.
2) Are you feeling okay now?	I don't feel right.
3) Why don't you go see a doctor?	I'm supposed to.
4) Do you mind if I find a doctor for you by going through the Yellow Page?	No, I don't. I would be happy if you do so.

Part 2: PATIENT

1) You look sick. What's the matter?	The symptoms are getting worse.
2) Why don't you do something about it instead of staying home and do nothing?	I know, but I've heard that I should pay a lot for visiting the clinic.
3) Do you want me to grab a Yellow Page to find a good doctor?	No, you don't have to because I wouldn't know whom to choose.
4) Where can we get some financial help to go see a doctor?	The student information center said my insurance will cover that.

Part 3: Read the questions in the left column and match the best answer from the right column.

1) Are you feeling not well?	a) The best day and time will be Fridays after one o'clock.
2) Have you seen a doctor?	b) Not yet. Maybe I should.
3) When will you be available for a dentist appointment?	c) I think I'm coming down with something.
4) How do you feel after taking the medicine?	d) Much better. Thanks for asking!

Useful Tips

White page & Yellow page

In the North America, there are two phone directories in every region, a White Page and a Yellow Page. A White Page is a telephone directory of a local area with a list of all phone numbers of residences who are registered under the phone number with their addresses. The numbers are listed in alphabetic order by name. A Yellow Page is mainly a business directory, categorized alphabetically according to the type of products or services. This book includes phone numbers, maps, and email addresses of local business. The book also contains lots of advertisements inside.

White page

Yellow page

Self-made Dialogues

Given the role of A and B, make a short conversation.

Role A (resident)
You are Judy, a local resident in a small city in the U.S. You are a friend of Christina. You get a call from her.

Role B (patient)
You are Christina, and have recently moved to the same city where Judy lives. You are pregnant for the first time. You call Judy to get a recommendation for a good doctor.

Role A	Role B
Answer the phone.	
	Say who you are.
Ask how Christina is doing these days.	
	Tell her the news about your pregnancy.
Congratulate her and ask her about health and symptoms these days.	
	Tell her that you have a morning sickness every day and it's been worse.
Suggest her to see a good OBGYN doctor.	
	Say you don't know anyone in particular as you have just moved to this area and ask to recommend a good doctor.
Tell her that Dr. Brian is your OBGY doctor since you were a child and is excellent. Suggest to make an appointment.	
	Thank her and ask her his number and address.

Word in Use

Study how *cover* can be used various ways in a sentence.

Verb

1. My brother covered his big belly with an extra large shirt.
   [COVER + noun phrase: to put something upon something]

2. I will be out for a moment. Could you cover for me if the boss asks me where I am?
   [COVER + preposition: to provide an excuse to cover something or someone up]

3. He tried to cover up all his guilt as much as possible at the court.
   [COVER + adverb: to keep the secret]

Noun

4. Kevin, could you find some place to take cover? It's raining too hard.
   [verb + COVER: to look for the safety]

Grammar Table

Review of grammar on *used to*

Used to expresses when something has been done quite often in the past but it doesn't happen any longer in the present. A root verb is always followed after used to.

> I lived at the orphanage when I was young. I don't live there anymore after I graduated from high school. I *used to* live at the orphanage.
>
> There was a big tree next to the lake. The city council decided to cut up the tree. There *used to* be a big tree next to the lake.

Section 2 Have a health interview

Main Dialogue

Situation: The dialogue is taking place at the Dr. Sims's office among a patient, a nurse, and a doctor. A week later the patient visited his office again. [P=patient, N=nurse, D=Dr. Sims]

P: I have an appointment with Dr. Sims at 10, and this is my first visit.

N: In that case, would you fill out this form?

P: What's this for?

N: I need information on your medical history whether you or any of your family members had a history of any kind of cancer or major health problems. I also need information on your health insurance. Do you have Blue Cross and Blue Shield or Medicare?

P: I have the student insurance that my school provides.

N: That will be okay.

P: Excuse me. I don't know some of these names and I have never heard of them before.

N: If you haven't heard about them, then you may not have had the problems. Are you allergic to penicillin?

P: I don't think so.

N: Just fill out the form as best as you can.

P: All right.

N: (a few minutes later) Dr. Sims is ready to see you. You can go in.

P: Thanks.

D: Good morning. Let's see. What seems to be the problem?

P: I'm not sure whether it's a problem. It may be just a severe PMS.

D: So what are the symptoms?

P: I have migraines and backaches. Sometimes it's mild and sometimes it gets severe. It's been over a week.

D: Hmm.. Please lie down here. I will gently push my fingers on your stomach. Please tell me if it hurts. Okay? Does it hurt?

P: Oops, there! It hurts! And there, too.

D: You need to have an ultrasound and run the urine and the blood tests.

P: Is it a serious problem?

D: Not sure, yet, but I need more information. Please follow this nurse. After all tests are done, I should be able to give you the definite answer. The results will be out within a week. In the meantime, I will prescribe you something to soothe your pain. Take it twice a day, in the morning and in the evening after meal.

[a week later]

D: The results of tests show negative.

P: Whew. I'm happy to hear that.

D: Everything seems okay. Have you changed the environment or diet? Are you under lots of stress?

P: Well... I'm a graduate student, and I have recently moved from Seoul to Austin. It's not easy for me to adjust to Western style meals. On top of that, I sleep only a few hours a day because midterms are around the corner.

D: I see. Do you still get pains?

P: Not any more after having the medicine you have prescribed.

D: I suggest that you do something to relieve your stress and have enough sleep.

P: Okay, Dr. Sims. Thank you.

D: That's all for today.

Useful Expressions

Read the definition of useful expressions and the example sentences.

1. **allergic**: having your body reacts to something
   A: Wow, this chicken soup is like my mom's cooking. You've got to try this.
   B: Sorry, I'm afraid I can't. I'm allergic to chicken.
   A: Oh no. Then let me get you something else.

2. **run**: to do a test; to check on something
   A: I hate injections. Do I really need to do this?
   B: I'm afraid you should. The doctor needs to run some more tests on your blood samples.

3. **urine**: (a medical term of 'pee') the waste liquid that collects in the bladder from the kidneys
   A: How did the test go? What did the doctor say?
   B: I had a urine test and the test shows that I may need a further medical exam.

4. **soothe**: to make a tensed or painful part of someone's body feel more comfortable
   A: Nurse, do you have anything to soothe pain in my burned arm?
   B: Here it is. You should not apply this gel too much.

5. **negative**: not showing any evidence of a particular substance or medical condition
   A: Did you get the result from the doctor?
   B: Yes, the doctor said it's negative. He says it's okay for now, but I need to improve my eating habits.

Additional Expressions

chapped lips, blisters, bump, stitches, stuffy nose, cramps, bruises, rash, scab, influenza

Exercise for Useful Expressions

Choose the most appropriate word for the blank.

1. Paul has never had any __________ reaction to peanut butter.

    a) alliance   b) allowance   c) allergic   d) alternative

2. A few more tests need to be __________ to find out whether you have diabetes or not.

    a) hold   b) run   c) determine   d) cast

3. The doctor checked the result of a __________ test.

    a) urine   b) urinate   c) ureter   d) urethra

4. Amy mentioned that she used organic oils to __________ shoulder pain naturally.

    a) console   b) keep   c) inject   d) soothe

5. It was strange for Sally to skip her period, so she took a pregnancy test at home but the result was __________ .

    a) negative   b) manageable   c) opposing   d) bleak

Conversation Starters

A patient and a doctor are having a conversation at the doctor's office. In your own words, complete the following conversation. (D: doctor, P : patient)

Dialogue Practice

Roleplay having a conversation at the doctor's office. Part 1 and 2 provide example questions for each role that may be used in the role play.

Part 1: DOCTOR or NURSE

1) Would you fill out this form?	Okay, I will. I'll ask if I have some questions.
2) Are you allergic to penicillin?	Yes, I am. I need to be careful about taking a certain type of medicine.
3) What are the symptoms?	I have bad lower back pain.
4) Do you still get pains?	No, I feel much better. Thank you.

Part 2: PATIENT

1) Can I help you?	I have an appointment with Dr. Sims at 10.
2) What's the problem?	I have migraines and backaches.
3) How long have you been aching?	It's been over a week.
4) Are you still in pain after taking the medicine?	Not any more after having the medicine you have prescribed.

Part 3: Read the questions in the left column and match the best answer from the right column.

1) How did you sprain your ankle?	a) I just stepped on an uneven ground.
2) What can I do for you?	b) At least three times a day.
3) How often do you feel pain?	c) I've been overworking recently.
4) Have you been under lots of stress lately?	d) I'm here for my vaccination.

Useful Tips

Medical insurances in USA

1. Blue Cross and Blue Shield Association

The Blue Cross & Blue Shield Association (BCBSA) is an association which is composed of 38 separated health insurance organizations and companies. They provide health insurance to nearly 100 million Americans.

2. Medicare

Medicare is a social insurance program which is run by the U.S.A government. People aged 65 and over get the health insurance benefits.

3. Student Secure® International Student Insurance

Student Secure® international student insurance provides the health coverage for students who are studying outside of their home country around the world. Students on the F-1 or J-1 visa are eligible for this coverage which meets all school and government requirements. The coverage comes with a worldwide network of doctors and medical facilities, which offers a comprehensive care.

Self-made Dialogues

Develop the conversation by using prompt words in a bracket with a partner.

You got sick after you ate a peanut butter sandwich, and you are at the clinic to see a doctor. [D: doctor, P: patient]

D: What are the symptoms?

P: ____.

(fever, headache, or whole body itching)

D: I need to run the blood and the urine tests.

P: ____.

(Ask the doctor to soothe your pain or make it stop.)

D: ____.

(Ask whether the patient is allergic to peanut butter)

P: I don't really know what I'm allergic to.

D: ____.

(Ask what the patient ate within 2 days)

P: I ate a peanut butter sandwich for lunch.

D: I think that seems to be the problem. Take this pill 30 minutes after a meal.

P: ____.

(Thank doctor and ask when to come again.)

Word in Use

Study how *lie* can be used various ways in a sentence.

1. You had better lie down on the bed to get relaxed.
   [LIE+ adverb: to rest in a horizontal position]

2. The building you are looking for lies between the store and the bookstore.
   [LIE + preposition: to be located in a place]

3. Ever since you didn't come to the company, the machine has lain idle.
   [LIE + adjective: to remain in a certain state]

Grammar Table

Review of grammar on *whether* and *if*

Among interrogative words (what, who, whose, which, where, when, whether, etc.) *whether* and *if* lead indirect yes-no questions but only *whether* can be directly followed by *or not*.

> Have you heard *whether* Nick will come or not?
> I don't know *if* new medicine will do good or not.
> *Whether* or not Rob found his wallet was all she thought about.
> Do you know *if* or not he called her? (X)

Section 3

Perform CPR and give a simple first aid

Main Dialogue

Situation: The dialogue is between Sally and Mike at Sally's house. They are having a conversation about cardiopulmonary resuscitation (CPR) and dealing with a problem giving first aid. [S=Sally, M=Mike]

S: Hey, I heard you've learned how to perform CPR, right?

M: Yes, I'd learned that when I was like… 10th and 11th grade. Why do you ask?

S: The CPR test is tomorrow and I need to review and practice more with someone.

M: Well… I'm not sure, but I can try.

S: Great! I really appreciate your help.

M: Let's use this doll to practice. Do you remember the first step?

S: Hmm… Open the victim's mouth?

M: Before that! The first thing you should do is to check pulse by pressing two fingers gently on the side of patient's neck and feel it.

S: Like this way?

M: Yes. You then try to wake the victim up by gently rubbing the sternum.

S: I see. And then?

M: Perform the chest compression five times. Now open the victim's mouth and listen to his breathing or check whether the victim moves or shows any sign of aliveness.

S: I hope he doesn't have a garlic breath.

M: Sally, be serious!

S: Oh, sorry, go on. So what do I do if nothing happens?

M: If you think the victim is not breathing, then tilt the head and give a mouth-to-mouth resuscitation by blowing one breath into his mouth. Check the chest rising and falling. If nothing happens, give another one and repeat this process.

S: It's not that difficult.

M: Well, you should practice on this doll several times. Knowing and doing may be different. Or, you can practice on me.

S: What?

M: Just kidding. (a few minutes later) Ouch!

S: What happened?

M: I cut my finger.

S: You are bleeding a lot! Come here and use this towel to put pressure on the wound. I'll get the first aid kit.

M: I think it stopped.

S: Okay, now go wash the wound with the tap water. Hurry!

M: It hurts! Should I use the soap?

S: No, you don't have to. Soap doesn't do much on germs anyway. Oh, you're still bleeding a little. I found antiseptic and a few bandages in the first aid kit. Here, use this sterilized gauge for dressing.

M: Thanks. The wound looks better.

S: Let me help you. Don't move your finger and hold it still.

Useful Expressions

Read the definition of useful expressions and the example sentences.

1. **CPR: (abb. cardiopulmonary resuscitation)** an emergency procedure to restore breathing and blood circulation on people who are unconscious

   A: Did you hear the news that Eric got a car accident last night?

   B: Oh, my goodness. So how is he? Is he okay?

   A: It was a close call. Someone gave him CPR until the ambulance arrived.

2. **chest compression**: applying pressure to the chest during CPR to keep it from expanding

   A: Could you show me how to perform the chest compression?

   B: Sure. First, you should put both hands on the chest, one on top of the other one.

3. **antiseptic**: a substance which kills harmful germs or bacteria, usually for hygiene on wounds

   A: Oh my, I've got a paper cut. I hate this.

   B: You need to put antiseptic first on the cut.

4. **sterilize**: to make something totally clean and free from bacteria, germs, etc.

   A: I pierced my ears by myself.

   B: I hope you used a sterilized needle!

5. **dressing**: a piece of soft covering over a wound to protect it from its exposure

   A: What happened to his foot?

   B: He had that scar when he was in the incubator. The wound was so severe that the doctor had to change the dressing everyday to keep the wound from infection.

   A: How did it happen?

Additional Expressions

artificial respiration, unresponsive, medical specialists, primary care, general practitioner, safety training, emergency response supplies, gasping, airway, brain function

Exercise for Useful Expressions

Write True or False in terms of using the underline words correctly.

1. When someone has a broken leg, you need to do CPR ASAP. ________

2. For CPR, You need to use two-thumb chest compressions for babies instead of using palms. ________

3. Dressing on your wound is followed by putting antiseptic. ________

4. If you want to sterilize jars for jam before using them, put the jars in the oven for about 20 minutes. ________

5. A dressing is used to cover the wounds and prevent further harm. ________

Conversation Starters

First three boxes are a conversation between two students about how to CPR. The rest of the conversation is about giving simple first aid. In your own words, complete the following conversation. (S1: student 1, S2: student 2)

Dialogue Practice

Roleplay having a conversation about problems related to CPR and first aid. Part 1 and 2 provide example questions for each role that may be used in the role play.

Part 1: STUDENT

1) Have you learned how to perform CPR?	Yes, I took the course in first-aid.
2) What's the first step?	You should feel on the side of the neck to see if the victim has a pulse.
3) What has to be done after rubbing the sternum?	You need to check whether a patient is breathing or not.
4) What do I do if nothing happens?	Repeat the process again.

Part 2: INSTRUCTOR

1) Do you know anyone who can give me a CPR lesson?	I'm not sure but I can try.
2) How can I check the victim's pulse on his neck?	Press two fingers gently on the side of the patient's neck and feel it.
3) How do I know if the patient's breathing or not?	Check the chest rising and falling.
4) Can I practice CPR on you?	You should practice on this doll several times.

Part 3: Read the questions in the left column and match the best answer from the right column.

1) When do Korean students learn how to do CPR?	a) On the person who got drowned in the pool.
2) Have you done CPR to a victim before?	b) Call 911 as soon as possible.
3) What if there's no sign of aliveness?	c) Almost never because it's not mandatory.
4) How many times does pumping have to be done?	d) About 30 times will do.

Useful Tips

Cardiopulmonary resuscitation (CPR)

It is an emergency operation which carries out in an effort to manually preserve intact brain activities until further measures are taken. There are three simple process of doing CPR using the CPB steps.

1. First check the victim if he/she is unresponsive. Call 911 if the person is not breathing normally. While waiting for the arrival of a rescue team, perform CPR on the victim if you know how and/or are certified.

2. Start with chest compressions if the victim is not breathing normally. Push down in the center of the chest and pump as hard and fast as you can. Do a set of 5 first.

3. If there is no sign of breathing, tilt the head back and lift the chin to perform mouth-to-mouth resuscitation. Close nose and do cover blow the wind into victims' mouth until the victim's chest rises. Give 2 breaths and each needs to take one second to check the sign of breathing.

Self-made Dialogues

Given the role of A and B, make a short conversation.

Role A (student)

You are Kevin, and you are with your friends in the swimming pool. One of your friends has a cram on a leg and got drowned, and he seems unconscious.

Role B (paramedic)

You are Sean, and you receive an emergency call from Kevin.

Role A	Role B
Call 911 and say your friend was drowned in the swimming pool. Ask to send an ambulance as soon as possible.	
	Ask Kevin to check if his friend is breathing or not.
Say your friend is not breathing.	
	Request him to apply CPR right now.
Ask him how to do it.	
	Tell Kevin to follow his instruction by first checking his friend's neck and waking him up by rubbing sternum.
Ask him the next step.	
	Ask to start with chest compression and then open his friend's mouth and blow breath into his mouth several times.
Say his friend moves a little.	
	Tell him to wake his friend up and say you are almost there.

Word in Use

Study how *practice* can be used various ways in a sentence.

1. Saying is much easier than putting it into a practice.
   [preposition + PRACTICE: an action]

2. It takes lots of practice to become a professional golfer.
   [PRACTICE + infinitive: doing something constantly for improving a skill]

3. Your ideas are opposed to the usual Korean practice.
   [adjective + PRACTICE: a custom of something]

Grammar Table

Review of grammar on *determiners: the, a, an*

Indefinite article *a/an* is used within the discourse to refer to a particular thing or person in general, without specifically referring to a particular one. On the other hand, definite article *the* is used when the speaker/writer assumes that the listener/reader knows what the topic of talk is or to refer to a specific thing or person.

I want *an* apple.
We really want to have *a* kid.
They have a son and a daughter, *the* son is sweet but *the* daughter is mean.
I finally bought *the* bike that I've dreamed of!

Section 4 Identify an appropriate department

Main Dialogue

Situation: The first dialogue is between Shaun and Molly. Shaun is suffering from back pain and he is trying to find out whether to go. The second dialogue happens in the hospital room. [S=Shaun, M=Molly, N=nurse]

[at Shaun's house]

S: Hey, do you know which department I should go for back pain?

M: Well, I think you should go to the Orthopedics & Sports Medicine or Chiropractics Department. They offer services related with the hips, back, knees, neck, feet, and ankles. Do you feel pain when you stand up or crouch?

S: It's painful and interferes my daily activities.

M: I think you need to consult a doctor before attempting any kinds of exercise.

S: I will.

M: Can you stand straight, sit down, and walk back and forth? The pain may be from your poor posture.

S: Maybe you are right. Let me consider your suggestion and see if it helps.

[at the hospital]

S: Excuse me. I'm looking for the Gastroenterology Department.

N: It is on the 3rd floor.

S: Thank you.

[in the hospital room 301]

M: Shaun, what happened?

S: I was nauseated and vomiting with severe headaches for several days continuously last week. And my doctor told me to get some tests.

M: How are you feeling?

S: Well, I've been here for two days and going through lots of tests. Now I'm waiting to take MRI and gastroscope tests. I've never taken MRI before and am a bit nervous.

M: So you didn't eat dinner yesterday?

S: And breakfast in this morning! So hungry and have no energy.

M: Let me buy you a huge meal after you are finished with the tests.

S: Thanks. My doctor said that I am not allowed to have steaks for a while, but what I'm really craving for is an enormous rib eye steak and a glass of Merlot wine.

M: Let me make you a really healthy but still tasty meal when you are out. I've searched the recipes on the Internet all morning! I'll bring it in the next visit.

S: That's so sweet of you. Thanks, but I think I should go on a special diet, the doctor's order. By the way can you ask a nurse how long the MRI and gastroscope will take?

M: I already did. The nurse told me that it usually takes about 40 minutes to run the tests. You should take some kind of liquid and lie on the machine. Once you are on the machine, you are not allowed to move much. Nothing's painful. You will hear all kinds of weird sounds, but not to worry, the tests will be over soon. At least you don't need to get shots.

S: That's good. I hate needles.

M: When will you get the results?

S: Don't know yet.

Useful Expressions

Read the definition of useful expressions and the example sentences.

1. **chiropractics**: the treatment of injuries by pressing and moving people's joints, especially of the spine

   A: I've tried everything to cure my back, but it's not getting better.

   B: Did you try chiropractic adjustments? It worked for me.

2. **crouch**: to lower the body close to the ground by bending legs below

   A: Look at the cat in the grass! It's couching and about to jump now.

   B: It looks so creepy.

   A: What? Don't you like cats?

3. **consult**: to get information or advice from an expert or a knowledgeable, experienced person

   A: I'm so concerned about my major and my future. What should I do?

   B: Have you consulted your father about it?

   A: No way. He won't understand me if I say I want to be an actor.

4. **posture**: the position in which people hold their body when standing or sitting

   A: My daughter is having a backache.

   B: Tell her to sit properly and keep good posture at the desk.

   A: Will she get better then?

5. **gastroscope**: a medical instrument for examining the interior of the stomach

   A: Ooh, I'm nervous. Have you ever had a gastroscope for your stomach examination?

   B: No, but a friend of mine told me that having the gastrocope might cause a sore throat.

Additional Expressions

oral hygienist, pediatrician, cardiologist, optometrist, psychiatrist, dermatologist, lab technician, physical therapy, crutch, cast

Exercise for Useful Expressions

Fill in the blanks with appropriate words from the list provided below. Use the words only once.

Many students and white-collar workers suffer from back and shoulder pain. The pain usually occurs due to poor ___________. It's very important to learn and exercise healthy ways to move. Many studies show that stretching exercises are critical including repeating back ___________ and straightening up exercises. Some say that ___________ can be reliable although it is a part of an alternative medicine industry. If the pain gets severe, you should ___________ a doctor ASAP.

poster	crouching	behavior	catastrophic	consult
posture	console	confess	conserve	chiropractic

Conversation Starters

A student and a patient are having a conversation at the hospital. In your own words, complete the following conversation. (S: student, P. patient)

Dialogue Practice

Roleplay visiting a friend(student) in the hospital. Part 1 and 2 provide example questions for each role that may be used in the role play.

Part 1: STUDENT

1) How are you feeling?	Not so well. Thank you for coming.
2) How do you feel when you stand up or crouch?	It is not too painful.
3) Can you stand up straight?	I don't think I can. It hurts a lot.
4) Didn't you eat dinner yesterday?	No. I'm not allowed to eat anything before the tests.

Part 2: PATIENT

1) How's your neck?	It's painful and interfere my daily activities.
2) Have you taken any x-ray or MRI?	I've never taken MRI before.
3) What's your next test?	I'm going to take a gastroscope.
4) Do you want me to buy you steaks for dinner?	My doctor said that I'm not allowed to have steaks.

Part 3: Read the questions in the left column and match the best answer from the right column.

1) What's the matter?	a) Perhaps my posture is bad.
2) Why don't we grab something to bite before you go through the MRI?	b) No, but I should make a dental appointment ASAP.
3) You seem to have a lot of cavities. Don't they hurt?	c) I'm not supposed to eat anything before the test.
4) What do you think are the causes of your back pain?	d) I broke my leg.

Useful Tips

Tips for visiting hospitalized patients

1. Take some books or magazines for presents, which can reduce the patients' boredom. Flowers can also be a good present. Any drinks/food are prohibited.
2. Should not stay too long so that a patient doesn't have to entertain visitors.
3. Should use encouraging and comforting words like 'Things will go well' might make patients feel positive.
4. Should not visit patients anytime, possible only during the visiting hours.
5. Should not take any young children, under age 5, unless absolutely necessary.

Self-made Dialogues

Develop the conversation by using prompt words in a bracket with a partner.

A chiropractor is seeing a patient who is old, around the age of 70. His grandson is sitting beside him, watching the treatment. [C: chiropractor, P: patient's son]

P: Is my grandfather okay?

C: ____.

(Say yes)

P: ____.

(Tell the chiropractor that your grandfather may have tripped over something on the ice, and ask him what you should do)

C: I didn't find any problems from the X-ray.

P: Is there anything I need to know in order to make him feel comfortable at home?

C: ____.

(feel pains when crouching; needs to sleep in good posture)

P: ____.

(Thank him and ask him what you should do when your grandfather is dizzy, time to time.)

C: It may happen when he gets up too quickly from sitting. Why don't you consult the family doctor first?

P: Okay, thank you.

C: ____.

(Say he's all set)

Word in Use

Study how *consult* can be used various ways in a sentence.

CONSULT: to go to somebody for information or advice

1-1. I got into an accident and have to consult my lawyer for the damage.
[CONSULT + noun phrase]

1-2. It is not him but I am the one who needs to be consulted.
[Be-verb + CONSULTed]

1-3. You should have consulted with me about your investment on that new town area.
[CONSULT + preposition]

2. I looked up my high school buddy by consulting this website and gained access to his address.
[CONSULT + noun phrase: to look in or at something to get information]

Grammar Table

Review of grammar on the *let*, *make*, *have* and *get*

Causative verbs such as *let, make, have* and *get* have the same meaning which is something or somebody causing things to change or happen. Only simple form of verb is followed after *let*, *make*, and *have* while *get* is followed by infinitive.

Let me *see* your picture.
My mom *lets* me *wash* the dishes.
I *made* my brother *clean* the house.
I *had* repairman *fix* the sink in the bathroom.
I *got* my friends *to carry* all the books.

Section 5 Go to the drugstore

Main Dialogue

Situation: First conversation is between Hannah and her doctor, Dr.Lashivia, at the doctor's office. The second one involves Hannah and a pharmacist at a drug store. [H=Hannah, L=Dr. Lashiva, P=pharmacist]

[at the doctor's office]

H: Dr. Lashivia, why do I need to take MRI and the blood test?

L: Your doctor sent you here to get a closer examination of your thyroid gland. He felt a small lump in that area. He thinks there is a possibility of tumor or cancer. In this case, You need a further test like getting a biopsy.

H: Really? Is it something serious?

L: Let's get the test results first and then I can give you a better answer. In the meantime, you don't need to worry too much about it. Even if you have that, a tumor is a less serious type and the procedure of removing it is usually much simpler.

H: Are you sure?

L: Even if it is found to be in the later state, there is about 95% chance of survival.

H: Really? After taking the MRI scan, how long do I have to wait for the results?

L: About a week. Don't worry too much. Hold on, let me see your neck... It might be just a small lump. I can feel it here. Let me scan this area.

[a week later]

H: So Dr. Lashiva, did you get the test results back? Do I have a cancer?

L: No, Hannah. I didn't find any kind of cancer tumor. You are fine. It was only from a tissue contraction.

H: Are you sure? I was so worried about the test results. Now I feel better. However, I still have headaches and nausea.

L: It might be from stress. Let me prescribe you some medicine. Are you allergic to any kind of medicine, like penicillin?

H: No, doc. Not that I know of.

L: This medicine will make you somewhat drowsy. You should not drive for a few days.

H: But I have to drive to work and school.

L: In that case, take the marked ones only at night.

[at the drug store]

P: Hello. Who's next in line?

H: Hi. Please fill this prescription.

P: Sure. Would you like the generic or regular drugs?

H: Generic drugs are fine.

P: It's going to take about 15 minutes. You can come back after you finish shopping.

H: Also, could you refill this prescription?

P: Ma'am, this is not refillable.

H: Then, what do I do?

P: You can call your doctor to have him call me or another drug store, and give the prescription again over the phone.

H: No problem. I'm sure he has reasons for the prescription to be non-refillable. I should go and see my doctor again for the refills.

Useful Expressions

Read the definition of useful expressions and the example sentences.

1. **thyroid gland**: a small organ at the front of the neck which produces hormones and controls the way in which the body grows and functions

A: This tiny butterfly-shaped organ is called thyroid gland.

B: Right, it is the key to metabolism and hormone regulation.

2. **tumor**: a mass of cells growing in or on a part of the body where they should not, usually causing medical problems

A: So, what's the result?

B: I'm afraid that the tumor in your stomach turned out to be malignant.

3. **biopsy**: the removal of tissue from the body of someone who is suggested to have further tests for serious disease

A: I had a biopsy done last year and found nothing from the test. Why do I need to redo this?

B: It's because the blood test shows something again.

4. **nausea**: feeling sick and uncomfortable, with an urge to vomit

A: When I travel by car, I have a severe motion sickness which makes me nauseated.

B: What do you do in that case?

5. **generic drug**: a drug which contains similar active ingredients as the original formulation, rather than using a manufacture's or brand name and without advertising, selling at a lower than the market price

A: Excuse me. We are out of this medicine, but we have the generic drugs.

B: Is there any difference in its effectiveness?

A: No, not at all.

Additional Expressions

medical form, health certificate, dose, remedy, antipyretic, refrigerant medicine, nature medicine, experimental and molecular medicine, hospital reservation system, uncompensated care

Exercise for Useful Expressions

Write the letter that matches the word with its definition.

1. tumor ______
2. biopsy ______
3. nausea ______
4. thyroid gland ______
5. generic drug ______

a) a drug which is identical as the original formulation but sold at a lower price

b) a radical growth of malignant tissue

c) a butterfly-shaped organ, located near Adam's apple. It releases hormones into the bloodstream.

d) a sensation of uneasiness and discomfort in the stomach with an urge to vomit

e) a medical test by taking a sample of tissues to test for any serious disease

Conversation Starters

First three boxes are a conversation between a doctor and a patient at the doctor's office. The rest of the conversation is between the patient and a pharmacist at a drug store. In your own words, complete the following conversation. (D: doctor, P: patient, Ph: pharmacist)

[at the doctor's office]

[at the drug store to refill the prescription]

Dialogue Practice

Roleplay having a conversation at a doctor's office and a drug store. Part 1 and 2 provide example questions for each role that may be used in the role play.

Part 1: PATIENT

1) Why do I need to take MRI and the blood test?	Because x-rays are not enough to diagnose your case.
2) Is it something serious?	Nothing is 100 percent sure, yet.
3) How long do I have to wait for the results?	You will get the results by this Friday.
4) Are you allergic to any kind of medicine, like penicillin?	Yes. I am allergic to Sulfa drugs.

Part 2: DOCTOR or PHARMACIST

1) What is my next test?	Your doctor sent you here to get a closer examination of your thyroid gland.
2) Should I be worried about my symptoms?	Let's get the test results first and then I can give you a better answer.
3) How long should I wait?	It's going to take about 15 minutes.
3) How can I give you the prescription?	You can call your doctor to have him call me.

Part 3: Read the questions in the left column and match the best answer from the right column.

1) Do you have all results now?	a) Here you go.
2) May I have your prescription?	b) 30 minutes after each meal.
3) When do I take the medicine?	c) We are still waiting for the lab results.
4) What are the symptoms of a drug allergy?	d) It varies from a mild to a life-threatening effect.

Useful Tips

How to fill prescription

The prescription starts in the doctor's office or at the health clinic. Doctor is told if the patient is on any medications — even 'over-the-counter' or 'herbal medicines'. With some medications, there's a danger that one medicine may cause problems with the other (known as an interaction in the medical profession).

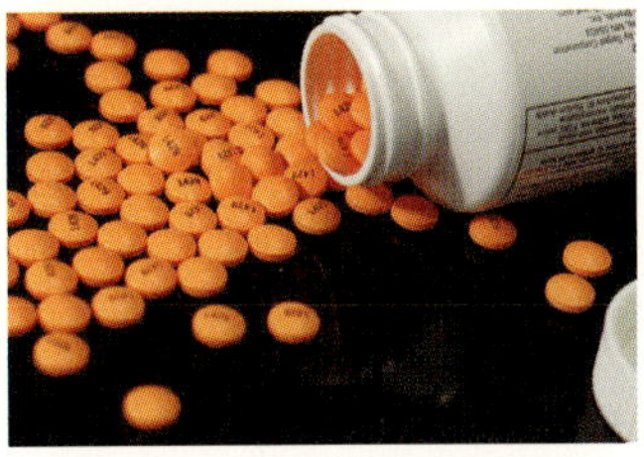

1. Over-the-counter drugs (OTC)

Unlike prescription drugs, OTC can be bought anywhere without prescription. The ingredients are safe and effective and it is selected by a regulatory agency. Examples of such drugs are the ones for headaches (Tylenol, Aspirin, etc.), stomachaches, cold medicines, etc.

2. Herbal medicine

It is also called botanical medicine because it is made from plant seeds, berries, leaves, or flowers. This conventional medicine becomes more popular in quality and effectiveness of disease. For example, tansy and winter savory are helpful to repel insects, Korean Mint, also known as hyssop is good to alleviate headaches and fatigue. Catnip is used for stopping excessive blooding or for cold symptoms such as fever.

Self-made Dialogues

Given the role of A and B, make a short conversation.

Role A (doctor)

Your name is Sarah, working for a general hospital located in the Eastern United States.

You are on break and met Kelly at a cafeteria.

Role B (doctor)

Your name is Kelly, a friend of Sarah. You are also a doctor working at the same hospital as Sarah. You met Sarah at a cafeteria before your work starts.

Role A	Role B
Say Kelly that she looks worried and ask her if she has any problem.	
	Tell your friend that you feel nauseated and often have a headache.
Ask to describe the symptoms more specifically.	
	Describe a situation of a cancer patient you are treating.
Ask her to tell you more about her patient's condition.	
	Tell her about a lump of 1 cm on the X-ray results of the thyroid gland.
Ask how serious it is.	
	Say the patient was treated with a tumor on the breast about a year ago.
Tell her about having a biopsy and console her.	
	Tell her that you are waiting for the result.
Ask her whether she told the patient and her family about it.	
	Say yes or no, and hope that it will work out well.

Word in Use

Study how *fill* can be used various ways in a sentence.

1-1. Students quickly filled the auditorium.
[FILL+ noun: to make something full of something]

1-2. David is filling the cup with salt instead of sugar.
[Be-verb + FILLing + noun: to make something full of something]

2. My sister will fill in for me while I'm away for a week.
[FILL+ preposition: to do somebody's job for a short time while they are not there]

3. The meals at my school never fill me up.
[FILL + pronoun + preposition: to give somebody lots of food]

Grammar Table

Review of grammar on *adverbs with comparative*

Adverbs such as *much, a lot, a bit, a little, slightly, even, far* and *still* can be used before the comparative adjective or adverb to emphasize the meaning of comparative phrase.

Let's use fork instead of chopsticks. It is *much* easier.
Can you speak *a bit* loudly?
Your dad's illness is *far* more serious than he thought.
The little boy ran *slightly* farther than his friends.

Section 6 Discuss how to work out

Main Dialogue

Situation: The dialogue is between Helen and Jessica at the cafeteria, and they are talking about exercising and how to do it well. Helen is about to start exercising and Jessica is advising her. They are friends from the university. [H=Helen, J=Jessica]

H: Hey, Jessie, do you work out these days?

J: Of course, I began jogging regularly since I came to this school. I run around the campus every other day. If it rains, I go to the track at the indoor gym. It's located right next to the dorm.

H: Hmm...

J: Why? Are you thinking about start exercising?

H: Yes, seriously. To be honest, I hate exercising but I feel I need to these days. In the last 3 months, I've gained 5 pounds!

J: It's not much.

H: For me, it's a big deal. I feel really uncomfortable. I can see why I gained that much. During those months, I sat in front of the computer all day long. I didn't have much time to move around, except moving from one class to another one.

J: Hahaha. I know. We all do the same during the semester. We are always in the library, stuck to the desk.

H: Jessie, what time of the day do you usually jog and how long do you do that?

J: Usually around 6 o'clock in the morning for about 50 minutes. I stretch first for about 10 minutes before I start moving, walk fast for 10 minutes, and then run for 30 minutes. Doctors recommended to run at least 20 minutes for your heart.

H: How fast do you run?

J: You don't have to run fast. You need to set your own pace. Don't forget to stretch again at the end. Jogging really helps me lose weight. You should work out, Helen. It feels great and you will feel your whole body changing.

H: I can see that from you. You are in such a great shape and so slim. How do you maintain that shape so well? Do you do something else?

J: Thanks. I also lift weight at the gym. You shouldn't lift heavy things. You'll get big muscles like a man. This kind of exercise will burn fat and increase the metabolism.

H: How do you keep up with the workout? You must be so dedicated.

J: Sometimes I don't feel like running, but I push myself and think about how amazing I would feel after working out. I also think about the moment that I'll be able to fit into a size-4 jean which I wore in high school and has been hanging in the corner of my closet.

H: Ya, me too! I've always wanted to be able to fit into those size jeans. By the way your skin looks so fair.

J: Well, I don't do anything but jogging and lifting weights regularly and sweat a lot from the exercise. I guess the working out makes my skin look fair and clean. So, no more clogged pores. Anyway, did you know that there is a free yoga class in the gym?

H: Are you kidding me? You mean free for students?

J: Yes, it was in our school newspaper. The classes will be only on Fridays though. Do you want to check that out?

H: Sure. I heard yoga is a health-enhancing exercise. Are you going to sign up too?

J: Definitely. I've always wanted to take a yoga class.

H: Awesome, let's do it together!

Useful Expressions

Read the definition of useful expressions and the example sentences.

1. **work out**: to train the body by physical exercise
   A: Do you work out these days? You look awesome.
   B: Of course I do. I work out five times a week. What about you?
   A: I don't. I'm totally out of shape these days. I should exercise.

2. **dedicated**: spending a lot of time and effort doing a particular activity
   A: My friend, Eric, is so dedicated that he never skips the Korean class.
   B: Why is he so dedicated?
   A: He said he wants to be a singer in Korea.

3. **fair**: light tone color
   A: Look at your face. You have such a fair skin!
   B: It takes a great effort to maintain such kind of skin.

4. **clogged pore**: tiny spots or holes in the face skin, blocked by dirt
   A: Do you have any idea to how I can avoid from getting clogged pores?
   B: Why don't you use good cosmetics? It's time to change them to better ones.
   A: Then do you think it can solve the problem?

5. **enhancing**: improving value, quality, or attractiveness of something
   A: I really don't know what to do. I've tried everything that I can to motivate myself to exercise.
   B: Perhaps it may be due to not having enough energy. Why don't you drink coffee before exercising? It can be an enhancing drink to boost your energy.

Additional Expressions

diet, calories, cut down, anemic, obesity, outdoor activities, trim down, mental fitness, burn off, substitute food

Exercise for Useful Expressions

Choose the right word which has similar meaning as the underline word.

1. It is so difficult to <u>work out</u> to burn the calories.
   a) eat　　b) calculate　　c) exercise　　d) happen

2. University presidents should be more <u>dedicated</u> in drawing funds.
   a) desecrated　　b) devoted　　c) uneducated　　d) protected

3. To make your skin look <u>fair</u>, drink lots of water and avoid long exposure to sunlight.
   a) clear　　b) foul　　c) complexion　　d) ordinary

4. These problems are caused from <u>clogged</u> pores and squeezing blackheads.
   a) blocked　　b) slot　　c) flushed　　d) blinded

5. When you want to keep your hair color, mask your hair over with a color <u>enhancing</u> conditioner.
   a) enlarging　　b) compounding　　c) imposing　　d) improving

Conversation Starters

Two students are having a conversation about exercising. In your own words, complete the following conversation. (S1: student 1, S2: student 2)

Dialogue Practice

Roleplay having a conversation about problems related with being sick. Part 1 and 2 provide example questions for each role that may be used in the role play.

Part 1: STUDENT 1

1) Do you work out?	Yes, three times a week.
2) How long do you jog?	I usually jog about 50 minutes.
3) How fast do you run?	I've kept pace around 12 to 13 minutes per mile.
4) How do you keep up with the workout?	I look at pictures of famous models.

Part 2: STUDENT 2

1) Why do you exercise?	The exercise will burn fat and increase the metabolism.
2) How fast do I need to walk first?	You need to set your own pace.
3) What do you think about lifting a 4-pound dumbbell for a warm-up exercise?	You shouldn't lift heavy things.
4) Do you do something else to make your skin glow?	I guess the workout makes my skin look fair and clean.

Part 3: Read the questions in the left column and match the best answer from the right column.

1) How do you exercise?	a) I know a great one. Jenny Moore. She's awesome.
2) Can you tell me about your diet?	b) I eat carbohydrates only once a week.
3) Do you take any supplements?	c) Yes, I take a daily dose of protein powder.
4) Would you recommend me a good yoga teacher?	d) I swim every day at seven in the morning.

Useful Tips

University gym

University campus has a gym. There can be several gyms around the campus for different purposes, for example fitness area, racquetball courts, basketball courts, tennis courts, swimming pools, etc. A gym usually has locker rooms and shower facilities.

Any current students, faculty and employees are eligible to use the facilities for free during the designated hours. Some universities give out their family members a privilege to use these facilities, but may need to pay a certain amount of fee to join the membership. Lockers can be reserved by renting them. Students can find out the rental period and rates on the school website. In using the gym, students should always check the website in reserving the space, because classes maybe conducted during at certain times and facilities are mostly operated on a "first come, first served" basis. The website information can include hours of operation, reserved time of basketball courts, schedules for various programs, etc. When students use any school facilities, a student ID is often required at a front desk.

Self-made Dialogues

Develop the conversation by using prompt words in a bracket with a partner.

You have seen a celebrity who recently lost a lot of weight and now is in good shape. You are talking about the celebrity with your friend. [S1: student 1, S2: student 2]

S1: ____?
(You ask your friend whether she knows Beyoncé on TV nowadays)

S2: Yeah, she's so glamorous. She must have lost a lot of weight.

S1: I read news on the Internet that she dedicated herself on working out so hard in the last 6 months.

S2: ____.
(Tell your friend that you are surprised and amazed by how Beyonce's skin looks fair. Encourage your friend to work out together.)

S1: ____?
(Suggest a type of exercise such as yoga, pilates, or jogging, and tell your friend that doing it for an hour a day will help much.)

S2: Also sweating from exercising will set us free from clogged pores!

S1: Of course! Let's start from tomorrow. I can't wait to see myself in shape.

S2: ____.
(Before putting into action, you suggest your friend to ask a trainer whom she may know about the rules for exercise first.)

S1: What for?

S2: ____.
(You say it is the first step toward enhancing your life and stay healthy, and not to get hurt.)

Word in Use

Study how *work out* can be used various ways in a sentence.

Verb

1. Recently, I started working out at the gym with my sister.
   [WORK OUT+ preposition: to train the body through physical exercise]

2. The project has worked out so well that we might finish everything on time.
   [WORK OUT + adverb: to have successful result come out]

3-1. I couldn't work it out with her on what she wanted for her birthday.
   [WORK + pronoun + OUT+ preposition: to comprehend someone's character]

3-2. I don't have cash with me right now, so can we work it out later?
   [WORK + pronoun+ OUT + adverb: to calculate something]

4. Can you work out what these squiggles mean?
   [WORK OUT + clause: to find the answer to something]

Noun

5. She does a 30-minute workout every morning.
   [WORKOUT + determiner: a period of physical exercise]

Grammar Table

Review of grammar on *during, while* and *for*

During [a preposition]

During means any time or period of a given time, but doesn't tell us how long something happens. There should be a noun phrase form after *during*.

> My grandfather was born *during the Second World War.*
> We have lots of snow here *during the winter.*

While [a conjunction]

While is usually used when two things happen at the same time; thus, it is used to join two clauses together, having the main clause followed by the "*while-*" part as the dependent clause.

> The cat came back home *while I was taking a bath.*
> A burglar broke in *while I was sleeping.*

For [a preposition]

For means a length of time, and often used with a period.

> Blair hasn't spoken to him *for a month.*
> Ben has been sleeping *for 9 hours straight.*

APPENDIX

Main Dialogue 번역

이미지 출처

ANSWER SHEET

Unit 1

Section 1. Book a ticket

상황: 다음은 예약 접수 담당자와 고객이 나누는 대화로 고객이 티켓 예매를 확인하려고 담당자에게 전화하는 것으로 시작합니다. [S=Susan Morris, 예약 접수 담당자, P=Park Jiyeon, 고객]

S: 안녕하세요. Mavis Airlines입니다.

P: 제가 며칠 전에 Seattle행 온라인 티켓을 예약했는데, 예약을 확인하려고 전화했어요.

S: 먼저 예약하셨는지 확인해보고 도와드리겠습니다. 예약번호가 어떻게 되나요?

P: 네, T96PR21이예요.

S: 파일이 업로드되는 동안 잠시 기다려 주세요. 확인하려고 하는데요. 성함이 어떻게 되시나요?

P: Park, Jiyeon입니다. Park은 저의 성이고요, 철자는 P-A-R-K, 그리고 Jiyeon의 철자는 J-I-Y-E-O-N이예요.

S: 네, 좋습니다. 5월 14일에 Shanghai에서 Seattle로 가는 티켓을 한 좌석 예약하셨네요. 고객님이 타게 될 비행기는 MA404이고 20시 30분에 출발합니다. 예매는 잘 되었습니다.

P: 고맙습니다.

[며칠 후, 항공사로 다시 전화함]

S: 안녕하세요. Mavis Airlines입니다. 무엇을 도와 드릴까요?

P: 네, 제가 5월 14일에 출발하는 Seattle행 온라인 비행기티켓을 예약했는데요. 그런데 급한 일이 생겨서 이번 주 내로 Seattle로 가는 방법을 찾아야 합니다. 도와주실 수 있으신가요?

S: 저희 웹사이트를 확인해보겠습니다. 몇 분이 함께 여행하실 건가요?

P: 저 혼자예요. 제가 웹사이트를 통해 확인했을 땐 모든 티켓이 예약된 상태였어요.

S: 경유하는 것도 괜찮으시다면 제가 자리를 마련할 수 있을 것 같아요. 몇 분 전에 Los Angeles를 경유하는 티켓 한 장이 취소되었거든요.

P: 잘됐네요. 티켓 날짜가 어떻게 되나요?

S: 4월 27일이에요. 19시 15분에 출발하는 비행기입니다.

P: 왕복티켓 금액은 얼마인가요?

S: 1,643달러입니다.

P: 학생을 위한 할인 티켓이 있나요?

S: 만약 학생 ID 카드의 복사본을 제출할 수 있다면 20% 할인을 받을 수 있어요.

P: 그럼, 그 날짜에 티켓을 예약해도 될까요?

S: 물론이죠. 성함을 말씀해 주시겠어요?

P: 제 이름은 Park, Jiyeon입니다. Park이 저의 성입니다.

S: 잠깐만요…… 고객님도 아시겠지만 미환불 티켓을 구매하셨군요. 이럴 경우 날짜를 변경하는데 과징금을 내셔야 해요.

P: 과징금이 얼마인가요?

S: 티켓 요금의 10%를 내야 하므로 164달러가 되겠네요.

P: 제게 선택권이 없으니 추가금을 더 내도록 하겠습니다.

S: 결재는 어떻게 하시겠어요?

P: 과징금까지 포함해서 모두 비자 카드로 결재할게요. 카드번호는 5555-7878-4444-1000이고 만료일은 7월 10일 2021년입니다.

S: 네. 보안코드는 어떻게 되지요? 카드 뒷면에서 찾을 수 있는 세자리 숫자입니다. 서명 칸에 있는 네 자리 숫자 다음에 있습니다.

P: 네, 알겠어요. 보안코드는 4-2-5이예요.

S: 네, 고객님의 예약이 완료되었습니다. 제가 더 도와드릴게 있나요?

P: 아니요. 괜찮습니다.

S: 고객님의 출발 시간은 4월 27일 19시 15분이며 항공기 번호는 MA404이고 Pudong Airport에서 출발하여 같은 날짜의 15:20분에 Los Angeles 공항에 도착합니다. 이후에 Seattle로 가는 다른 항공편으로 환승하며 출발 시간은 17시 42분이고 20시 25분에 Washington 공항에 도착합니다. 고객님의 티켓번호는 MX235701입니다.

P: 네, 감사합니다.

S: 고객님께서 이메일을 통해 e-티켓을 받으시면 여행일정표를 꼭 확인하세요. 감사합니다. 좋은 하루 되세요.

Section 2. Check in at the airport

상황: 다음은 접수담당자와 고객이 공항 탑승 수속 창구에서 나눈 대화입니다. [R=접수담당자, C=Cathy, S1=보안요원1, S2=보안요원 2, S3=보안요원3]

[탑승 수속 창구에서]

R: 다음 분 오세요…... 어서 오십시오. 탑승권과 여권 보여주시겠습니까?

C: 여기 있어요.

R: 창가 쪽 자리로 드릴까요 아니면 통로 쪽으로 드릴까요?

C: 통로 쪽으로 주세요.

R: 네. 가방은 몇 개 부치시나요?

C: 두 개요.

R: 다른 누군가가 가방을 싸주었거나 가방에 접근했나요?

C: 아니요, 제가 혼자 쌌어요.

R: 가방을 저울에 올려주세요…... 이 가방은 30kg이므로 3kg이 초과되었습니다. 가방에서 짐을 조금 빼거나 아니면 추가비용을 내셔야 합니다.

C: 초과 비용은 얼마를 내야 하나요?

R: 킬로그램당 항공료의 2%여서, 승객님은 53달러를 내셔야 합니다.

C: 네, 그럼 초과비용을 낼게요. 카드로 계산 가능한가요?

R: 그럼요.

C: 여기 있어요.

R: 혹시 기내수화물 가지고 계신 것 있나요? 이것 또한 규칙을 따라야 해서요.

C: 방침이 무엇인가요?

R: 수화물은 10kg을 넘으면 안되고요. 크기도 22 x14 x 9인치의 크기로 가장 큰 가방의 사이즈는 45인치입니다. 승객님의 가방은 괜찮아 보이네요. 여기 탑승권이 있습니다. San Francisco행 출발시각은 16:45분이시니까 7번 탑승구로 15:45분까지 가시면 됩니다.

C: 실례합니다만, 직항 항공권을 가지고 있는데 저는 어디에서 가방을 세관 검사하나요?

R: 승객님의 모든 가방들을 받으신 뒤 입국 관리 사무소가 있는San Francisco공항에서 세관 검사를 받으실 겁니다.

C: 감사합니다.

R: 별말씀을요. 준비 다 되셨고요. 즐거운 여행되세요.

[보안검사 통과하기]

S1: 신발, 벨트, 전자기기, 금속물체를 바구니에 넣고 보안경계선을 지나가세요. 노트북과 핸드폰도 꺼내시고 선반에 올려놓으세요.

C: 네.

S2: (한 명씩 유심히 살피며) 다음 분.

S3: 팔을 평행으로 올려주세요. (금속탐지기로 확인하며) 다 되셨어요. 소지품 챙기시고 저를 따라오세요.

C: 네.

S3: 이 가방을 좀 열어주시겠어요? 이것은 무엇인가요?

C: 제 화장품인데요.

S3: 어느 것이든 액체 50ml가 넘는 것은 기내 안으로 가져가실 수가 없어요. 여기에 두셨다가 돌아오셔서 찾아가시거나 또는 기내에 탑승하지 않는 누군가에게 가져가달라고 부탁해야 합니다.

C: 네, 알겠습니다. 여기에 두고 가야겠네요.

S3: 네, 이제 출입국관리소에 가시면 됩니다.

Section 3. Get services in the plane

상황: 다음은 승무원과 승객의 대화입니다. 비행기를 타는 순간부터 내릴 때까지의 대화입니다. [F= 승무원, C=Cathy, P=승객]

[비행기에서]

F: 탑승권을 보여주시겠습니까?

C: 여기 있어요.

F: 승객분의 자리는 23-C 입니다. 오른쪽 통로에 있습니다. 가방은 머리 위에 있는 짐칸이나 발 밑에 넣어 두시겠습니까?

C: 제 가방을 짐칸에 넣는 것을 도와주실래요?

F: 물론이죠.

C: 고맙습니다. 그리고 물 한잔 가져다 주시겠어요? 지금 약을 먹어야 하거든요.

F: 잠시만요…… 여기 있습니다.

C: 고맙습니다.

[몇 분 후]

C: 실례합니다. 좌석을 바꿀 수 있을까요? 이 좌석은 너무 불편하고 멀미가 나네요. 그리고 여긴 화장실 바로 옆이잖아요.

F: 빈 좌석이 있는지 알아보도록 하겠습니다. (몇 분 뒤) 죄송합니다만 남아있는 빈 좌석이 없네요. 아마도 승객분께서는 앞 좌석에 계신 신사분과 자리를 바꾸셔야 할 거 같습니다.

C: 이런…… (그 남자에게 질문) 실례합니다. 혹시 저와 자리를 바꿔 주실 수 있겠습니까?

P: 죄송합니다만, 저도 같은 어려움에 처해 있습니다.

[식사 시간 중에]

F: 좌석을 세워주시고 팔걸이를 내려 주시겠습니까? 음료는 무엇을 드릴까요? 주스와 탄산음료, 맥주와 와인이 있습니다.

C: 오렌지 주스로 할게요.

F: 네. 알겠습니다. 치킨과 미트로프가 있습니다. 어떤 걸로 하시겠습니까?

C: 미트로프가 맛있겠네요.

F: 여기 있습니다. 맛있게 드세요.

C: 설탕과 함께 커피 좀 주시겠어요?

F: 네. 이 통로에 계신 승객님들께 음식을 제공하는 동안 잠시 기다려 주십시오…… 여기 있습니다.

C: 감사합니다. 그런데 비행 시간이 얼마나 남았나요?

F: 앞에 있는 스크린을 통해 확인하실 수 있습니다. 여기에 보시면, 9시간 45분 남았네요.

[출입국 신고서 작성]

C: 출입국신고서를 작성하는 것을 도와주시겠어요?

F: 물론이죠. 먼저 개인 신상 정보를 적어주세요.

C: 9번 문항은 무엇을 말하는 건가요?

F: "당신이 탑승한 도시"의 뜻은 승객님이 떠났던 곳이므로 서울이 되겠네요.

C: 이 질문은 무엇이죠?

F: 음, 이 질문은 승객분이 채소나 육류 또는 현금을 가지고 왔는지를 묻고 있네요. 신고하실 것 있으신가요?

C: 아니요. 없습니다.

F: 이런 경우에는 "no"라고 표시되어 있는 모든 칸에 체크해 주시고 여기에 서명해주시면 됩니다.

[착륙하기 전]

F: 승객 여러분은 자리로 돌아가 앉아 주시고 착륙 준비를 해 주십시오. 좌석을 똑바로 세워 주시고 모든 가전제품은 반드시 전원을 꺼주십시오.

C: 화장실 가도 될까요?

F: 네. 하지만 서두르셔야 합니다.

Section 4. Go through the customs

상황: 다음은 세관 관사와 승객, Tony의 대화입니다. 세관 통과소에서 서류나 비자에 도장을 받을 때 일어나는 대화입니다.
[O=세관 관사, T= Tony]

[세관 통과소에서]

O: 여권하고 입국 카드 보여주세요. 어디로 여행가십니까?

T: Seattle에 갑니다.

O: 방문 목적이 어떻게 되십니까?

T: Washington 대학교에 공부하러 왔어요.

O: 전공이 뭐에요?

T: 산업 공학입니다.

O: 미국에 얼마나 계실 건가요?

T: 공부를 마치려면 2년이 걸릴 것으로 생각됩니다.

O: 어디에 머무르실 건가요?

T: Seattle 북동부에 위치한 Madison Park에서 사는 제 호스트 가족과 함께 머무를 겁니다.

O: 미국 방문이 처음이신가요?

T: 아니요, 두 번째입니다.

O: I-90 서류는 어디 있나요?

T: 잠시만요……. 여기 있습니다.

O: 승객님의 비자가 만료되었습니다.

T: 네? 그건 전에 있던 비자고요. 일주일 전에 새로 비자를 갱신했어요. 다음 페이지에 보면 있을 텐데요.

O: 네. 좋아요, 모든 서류가 된 거 같습니다. 가셔도 됩니다. 즐거운 여행되세요.

[세관사무소 통과하기]

O: 신고하실 거 있으세요?

T: 아니요.

O: 여권하고 세관 신고서 좀 볼 수 있을까요?

T: 물론이죠. 여기 있어요.

O: 이 선으로 서주시겠어요? 승객님의 가방들을 검사해야 하거든요.

[가방 확인하기]

O: 짐들을 전부 테이블에 올려놓으신 후 열어주시겠어요? 농산물이나 육류, 액체 같은 것을 가지고 계시나요?

T: 아니요.

O: 이것들은 무엇입니까? 액체가 든 병들이 너무 많이 있는데요.

T: 저희 엄마가 싸주신 간장과 참기름입니다.

O: 이것은 무엇입니까?

T: 그건 말린 고사리인데요. 이 물품들을 가지고 가는데 문제가 되나요?

O: 네. 이러한 물품들을 해외에 가지고 가실 수가 없습니다. 특히 이 말린 고사리 같은 경우는 전염을 일으킬 수 있는 곤충들을 동반할 수가 있기 때문이에요. 죄송합니다만, 이것들은 제가 가지고 가야겠습니다.

T: 그렇지만 이것들은 완전히 햇빛에서 말린 것인데요. 전 이것이 필요해요.

O: 여전히 위험합니다. 다음에는 꼭 규정 사항을 주의 깊게 읽어주세요.

O: 그러겠습니다. 이제 가도 되나요?

T: 네.

Section 5. Report for the baggage lost

상황: 첫 번째 대화는 승객과 공항 안전 요원과의 대화이고 두 번째는 승객과 항공사 접수 담당자와의 대화입니다. 승객이 수화물 찾는 장소를 알아보러 가는 순간부터 수화물 분실신고서를 작성할 때까지의 내용입니다. [C=고객, S1=안전요원 1, S2=안전요원 2, R=접수 담당자]

C: 죄송한데요, "수하물 찾는 곳"이 어디인기요?

S1: 네, 이층에 있습니다. 서점이 보이실 때까지 직진하시면 가게 맞은 편에 엘리베이터가 보이실 거에요. 그걸 타고 이층에 내리시면 "수하물 찾는 곳"에서 고객님의 비행기 번호에 따른 수하물 컨베이어벨트를 보실 수 있을 것입니다.

C: 죄송하지만, 제가 방향을 정확히 이해하지 못했네요.

S1: 저를 따라오세요. 제가 모셔다 드리겠습니다.

C: 감사합니다.

[승객 수하물 찾는 곳에서]

C: 실례합니다. 제 짐을 찾을 수가 없어서요. 어디에서 찾을 수 있을까요?

S2: 수하물 분실 청구 섹션으로 가셔야 해요. Section D 앞에 사무실이 있습니다. 그곳에서 짐들의 위치를 찾아줄 거에요. 저기 사무실이 보이세요?

C: 네, 감사합니다.

[수하물 분실 청구 사무소에서]

R: 안녕하세요. 무엇을 도와드릴까요?

C: 네, 제 가방들을 찾을 수가 없네요. 수하물 컨베이어벨트에서 약 30분 가량 기다렸습니다. 제 가방을 좀 찾아주시겠어요?

R: 어느 항공편을 이용하셨나요?

C: Katthy Airlines요.

R: 고객님의 클레임을 진행하겠습니다. 걱정 마세요, 이런 일이 일어날 수 있습니다. 특히 중간기착지 사이에서 시간이 충분하지 않을 때 발생하더라고요. 비행기 번호가 어떻게 되세요?

C: KA402 입니다.

R: 확인하겠습니다. 비행기표와 여권을 보여주시겠어요?

C: 여기 있어요.

R: 가방은 몇 개 체크인 하셨나요?

C: 2개요.

R: 컴퓨터에 따르면 고객님의 가방은 여전히 Los Angeles에 있네요. 다음 비행기에 싣고 내일 Seattle에 도착할 것입니다.

C: 오 이런. 어떻게 된 거지요?

R: LA에서 아마 잘못된 비행기에 실린 것 같아요. 고객님께서 직접 가져가시겠어요, 아니면 집으로 배송해 드릴까요?

C: 제 집으로 배송이 가능한가요?

R: 물론입니다. 고객님이 이 용지에 작성하시면요. 반드시 Seattle에 있는 정확한 주소와 연락처를 기입해주세요.

C: (완성한 용지를 건네며) 여기 있어요.

R: 시간은 내일 9시에서 12시 사이, 기사가 배송을 해드릴 것입니다. 반드시 기사가 배송하기 직전 전화를 드릴 때 꼭 누군가는 전화를 받아주셔야 합니다.

C: 네 알겠습니다. 저 끝났나요?

R: 네, 모든 것이 끝나셨습니다.

C: 도와주셔서 감사합니다.

Unit
2

Section 1. Make dinner

상황: Cathy는 미국인 호스트 가족과 함께 살고 있는 학생입니다. 어느 주말, 호스트 아줌마가 추수감사일을 위해 미국 전통 음식을 준비하기로 결정했습니다. 이 대화는 무엇을 요리할지 이야기하는 순간부터 요리를 대접하기까지의 대화입니다. [C=Cathy, L=호스트 아줌마]

C: 안녕하세요, 아줌마

L: 오, 안녕. 오늘은 학교에서 일찍 왔구나.

C: 네. 아줌마가 요리하는 거 보고 싶어서요. 제가 집에 돌아가면 이 경험을 저의 가족에게 얘기해 줄 수 있잖아요.

L: 그거 좋구나! 칠면조 먹어 본 적 있니?

C: 아니오. 아직이요.

L: 명절에 칠면조를 요리하는 게 우리 가족의 전통이야.

C: 정말 기대가 되요.

L: 좋아. 오늘의 메뉴는 칠면조와 함께 그레이비 소스, 칠면조 안에 들어갈 스터핑, 깍지콩 캐서롤이야. 디저트는 블루베리 파이고.

C: 맛있겠는데요. 벌써 음식 냄새가 나는 거 같아요.

L: 자, 칠면조를 제외하고 대부분 음식은 내가 이미 다 준비해놨어.

C: 알겠어요. 재료가 뭔가요?

L: 먼저, 칠면조, 1/4 컵의 올리브 오일, 가금류 시즈닝, 양파, 당근, 감자, 마늘 그리고 로즈마리랑 타임 몇 잎이 있으면 돼.

C: 알았어요. 이 칠면조로 제가 뭘 하면 될까요?

L: 먼저, 우리가 고기를 다듬어야지. 목, 장기들 그리고 지방을 제거해야 돼. 그리고 안쪽과 바깥쪽을 잘 씻고 종이 타월로 두드려 말려줘야지. 올리브 오일 좀 건네 줄래?

C: 여기요.

L: 고마워. 올리브 오일 대략 1/4 컵을 가져와서 가금류 시즈닝이랑 잘 섞어. 칠면조를 시즈닝으로 잘 문질러. 그런 다음 안쪽과 바깥쪽에다 허브도 뿌려줘야 하지.

C: 제가 도와드릴게요.

L: 야채들을 먼저 잘라주지 않을래? 양파, 당근, 감자랑 마늘을 잘게 잘라줘.

C: 네. 야채들은 뭐에 쓰이죠?

L: 칠면조 안에다가 넣을 거야. 그리고 나머지 야채는 시즈닝이랑 잘 섞은 다음에 고기 주변에 둘러줘야지. 칠면조 고기를 씻기 전에 오븐을 350도로 예열하는 거 잊지 마라.

C: 네. 아줌마께서 말씀하신 대로 했어요.

L: 이제 칠면조를 오븐에 넣을 준비가 된 거 같은데.

C: 맞아요. 된 거 같네요.

L: 칠면조 가슴 부분을 위쪽으로 가게 놓고 올리브 오일을 칠해야 해. 버터를 써도 된단다. 자, 다 됐구나.

C: 왜 고기에 버터를 칠해야 하나요?

L: 그래야 껍질이 마르지 않는단다.

C: 알았어요. 걱정 마세요. 제가 고기 잘 보고 있을게요. 요리되는 데 얼마나 오래 걸리나요?

L: 칠면조의 크기에 따라 다른데 이건 큰 게 아니라서 한 2시간 정도 걸릴 거야. 요리가 다 될 때까지 30분 마다 오일이나 버터를 칠해주는 거 잊지 마라.

C: 빨리 완성됐으면 좋겠어요!

Section 2. Watch TV

상황: 이 대화는 호스트 가족의 거실에서 일어난 Terry와 그의 친구인 Peter 간의 대화입니다. TV 프로그램에 대해서 얘기하고 있는 중입니다. [T= Terry, P= Peter]

T: 야, 나 숙제 때문에 어제 밤에 "Lost Forever" 5번째 에피소드를 놓쳤어.

P: 너도 그 프로그램 봐? 내 주변 사람들 대부분이 그거 보는 거 같더라고.

T: 그 프로그램 좋아하지 않아? 요즘에 제일 인기 있는 프로그램 중에 하나잖아.

P: 음, 나는 아니야. 계속 보기에는 너무 이해가 안 가더라. 나는 인내심이 없어서 등장 인물들한테 무슨 일이 일어날지 알려고 다음 에피소드를 계속 보는 게 안돼. 아무 것도 해결된 게 없잖아.

T: 그러니까 사람들한테 인기가 있는 거지.

P: 난 그런 드라마 류는 좋아하지 않아. 절대 안 끝날 거 같은 생각이 들어.

T: 그럼, 네가 제일 좋아하는 드라마는 뭐야?

P: 너 채널 21에서 하는 "Blue Books"라는 거 알아?

T: 들어는 봤는데 보지는 않았어. 내용이 뭔데?

P: 서점 주인하고 그 사람의 친구 2명에 관한 거야. 서점 주인은 술 마시는 것을 좋아하고 손님들을 싫어해. 게다가 책을 너무 아껴서 책을 파는 걸 어려워해.

T: 하하, 어떻게 그래?

P: 걔 친구들은 더 웃겨. 주인의 조수는 되게 착한데 서점 주인은 그냥 그 조수가 거기 있다는 자체로 벌을 준다니까.

T: 재미있겠는데!

P: 매주 금요일 밤 10시에 21번에서 해. 한 번 봐.

T: 그럴게. 인터넷으로 이전 에피소드 볼 수 있어?

P 그럴걸. 하지만 돈을 내야 할거야. 첫 번째 시리즈는 DVD로 가지고 있어. 내 꺼 빌려도 되고.

T: 고마워! 그런데 어제 "Young and the Sleepless" 봤어?

P: 아니. 나는 연속극은 안 봐.

T: 그럼 다시보기로 봐야겠다. 너 오늘 밤에 영화 채널에서 "Shinning of the Dead" 하는 거 알아?

P: 진짜? 그거 되게 웃기다고 들었는데. 좀비들한테서 살아남는 거 맞지?

T: 맞아. 같이 볼래?

P: 좋아. 그거 R등급이야?

T: 아마 PG 13일걸?

P: 그렇다면 내 친구하고 그 애의 여동생을 초대할래. 다 같이 볼 수 있겠다.

T: 좋아. 몇 시에 내려갈까?

T: 영화가 9시 30분에 시작하니까 영화 시작하기 10분 전에 거실로 내려와.

P: 그래. 내가 팝콘 만들게.

T: 좋은데! 내가 음료수 몇 개 챙길게.

Section 3. Have a family reunion

상황: 첫 번째는 Tom과 그의 친구 Olivia가 전화로 나누는 대화입니다. Tom은 자신의 가족 행사에 Olivia를 초대하고 있습니다. 두 번째 대화는 Tom의 집에서 일어납니다. [O=Olivia, T=Tom]

T: 안녕, Olivia. 나야, Tom.

O: 안녕, Tom. 무슨 일이야?

T: 이번 주 토요일에 시간 괜찮아? 우리 가족 행사가 있는데 올래?

O: 하지만 그건 너희 가족들만을 위한 거잖아.

T: 문제될 건 없어. 매년 크리스마스에 가족 모임 파티를 하는 게 우리 집 전통인데 너를 파티에 초대하고 싶어서.

O: 아, 그래? 재미있겠는데! 나 미국에서 지내면서 그런 파티에 초대되어 본 적이 없어. 너의 파티에 간다면 기쁘겠다.

T: 정말 재미있을 거야. 전 세계에서 온 내 친척들도 만날 수 있고 또 모든 사람들이 크리스마스 트리 아래에 선물도 놔두거든.

O: 흥미롭겠는데!

T: 하루 종일 영화도 좀 보고 게임도 하고 그러는 거지. 그럼 오후에 한 2시쯤 올래?

O: 그래. 내가 뭐 가져가거나 도와드릴 게 있을까?

T: 그냥 와서 재미있게 보내면 돼. 그럼 그때 보자. 안녕.

O: 그때 보자.

[탐의 집]

O: 안녕하세요. 메리 크리스마스!

T: 메리 크리스마스! 들어와. 가족을 소개해줄게. Olivia, 여긴 엄마, 아빠, 그리고 내 남동생이야. 우린 생물학 수업 같이 들어요.

O: 만나서 반갑습니다. 전 한국에서 온 Olivia라고 해요.

T's mom: Olivia, 만나서 반갑구나. 너에 대해 들은 게 많아. Cheryl 이라고 부르고 편하게 있으렴.

O: 감사합니다, 아주머니.

T's dad: 환영한다. 난 Michael 이고 만나서 반갑구나.

T: 아빠는 중고등학교의 수학 선생님이셔.

T's brother: 안녕, 난 Liam 이야. Tom한테 너에 대해서 정말 많이 들었어.

T: 동생은 Portmayer 대학에서 심리학을 전공하고 있어. 기숙사에서 지내다가 휴일에만 집에 와.

O: Liam, 만나서 반가워.

T's mom: 뭐 좀 마실래? 에그녹 좀 줄까?

O: 죄송해요. 제가 유제품에 알레르기가 있어서요. 커피 마셔도 될까요?

T's mom: 그럼.

T's brother: 넌 여기 혼자 온 거야?

O: 응, Portland에 온지 6개월 됐어. 난 여기가 좋고 사람들도 친절해.

T: Olivia 는 진짜 똑똑해. 과목 전부 다 A 받았고 나를 많이 도와주지.

T's brother: 어, 너희 미슬토 아래에 서 있잖아. 미슬토 아래에서 다른 사람이랑 서 있으면 뭐 해야 하는 줄 알아? 서로 키스 해야 돼.

O: 뭐? (얼굴이 붉어짐)

T: 동생이 놀리는 거야. 신경 쓰지 마.

O: 와, 냄새가 근사한데. 뭐야?

T: 엄마가 저녁에 먹을 칠면조 준비하시는 거야.

O: 나 칠면조 고기 먹어 본 적 없는데. 처음 먹어보는 게 되겠다. 이런 전통에 관해서 많이 읽었는데 책에는 항상 미국 전통에서는 칠면조가 나오더라고. 하지만 난 미국 전통은 하나도 경험해 본 적이 없어. 빨리 먹어보고 싶다.

T: 지금은 저녁 식사하기에는 너무 이르니까 기다리면서 모노폴리 게임이나 하자.

O: 좋아!

Section 4. Find a place to move

상황: 첫 번째는 아파트 관리인과 고객이 전화로 하는 대화입니다. 다음은 아파트 상태를 점검하기 위해 아파트에서 일어나는 대화이고 세 번째 대화는 계약서에 사인하기 위해 아파트 관리실에서 일어나는 대화입니다. [A=아파트 관리 직원, S=학생]

A: 안녕하세요. Forrent Management입니다. 전화 받은 사람은 Cindy입니다. 어떻게 도와드릴까요?

S: 안녕하세요. 신문 광고에서 본 방 1개짜리 아파트 보고 관심이 있어서요. 아직 방 있나요?

A: 어떤 걸 보신 거죠? 저희가 여러 군 데의 아파트를 관리해서요. 주소를 알려주시겠어요?

S: 광고에서 나온 주소는 East Lexington에 89 Hills Lane입니다.

A: 아, 네. 그건 가구가 다 포함된 방이 하나인 아파트에요. 오늘 보러 오시겠어요?

S: 네, 몇 시에 볼 수 있나요?

A: 오후 3시 정도 어떠세요?

S: 좋습니다. 아파트 건물 앞에서 뵈면 될까요?

A: 좋습니다.

S: 그럼 3시경에 뵙겠습니다. 제 이름은 Emma Lee입니다.

A: 좋아요, Emma. 3시에 보죠.

[아파트에서]

A: 보시다시피, 이 아파트는 풀 옵션이에요.

S: 좋아 보이네요. 그런데 세탁기는 어디 있어요?

A: 각 층마다 다용도실에 하나씩 있어요. 이 건물 근처에서 운영되는 세탁실도 있고요.

S: 아, 그거 편리하네요. 근처에 편의 시설은 어떤가요?

A: Seven-Twelve 편의점이 이 건물 바로 앞에 있고요. 가장 가까운 버스 정류장과 전철 정거장은 5분 정도 밖에 안 걸려요.

S: 잘됐네요! Lexington University까지 가는 데는 얼마나 걸릴까요?

A: 버스로는 7분 정도 걸리고 걸어서는 20분 정도 걸리죠.

S: 알겠습니다. (아파트를 다시 둘러보며) 이 카펫은 갈아야 될 거 같은데요. 얼룩이 졌고 정말 낡았네요.

A: 문제없습니다. 렌트비가 모든 관리비 다 포함해서 850달러면 정말 좋은 가격이죠.

S: 음… 가격은 괜찮은 거 알고요. 이 아파트 좋네요. 계약할게요.

A: 좋아요. 서류 작업하러 사무실로 가시죠.

[아파트 관리실에서]

A: 이 서류를 작성해 주세요. 사진이 있는 신분증을 복사해야 합니다.

S: 여기 있습니다.

A: 감사합니다. 아시다시피 1년 계약이고요. 이사하시는 날, 보증금과 한달 렌트비는 선금으로, 모두 해서 1,700달러를 내셔야 합니다. 자, 오늘 선금은 얼마 내시겠어요?

S: 200달러요. 그럼, 언제 이사할 수 있나요?

A: 비어있으니까 언제든 괜찮습니다.

S: 좋습니다. 이번 주 토요일에 이사하고 싶습니다. 그때까지 새 카펫 깔아주실 수 있으세요?

A: 그럼요. 토요일에 나머지 비용 내시고 열쇠 받으러 사무실로 오세요. 이사하는 날 1,500달러를 가져오셔야 합니다. 여기다 사인해주세요.

S: 알겠습니다.

Section 5. Install TV, Internet, and cell phone

상황: 이 대화는 Brian과 Jamie의 대화입니다. Brian은 대학교 3학년이고 그의 가족의 친구인 Jamie는 대만에서 2년 간 교환학생으로 미국에 막 도착한 학생입니다. Jamie는 인터넷, TV, 그리고 핸드폰을 연결하고 싶어합니다. Brian이 자신의 집에서 Jamie가 이런 문제들을 해결하는 것을 도와줍니다. [B=Brian, J=Jamie]

J: 안녕, 여기가 너희 집이구나. 전망이 좋은데, 그리고 학교에서도 꽤 가깝고.

B: 응, 나쁘지 않지. 캠퍼스 밖의 아파트에서 살면 개인적인 생활하기에는 더 좋은 것같아.

J: 그런 거 같다. 좋은데.

B: 인터넷 연결은 했어?

J: 아직 못했어. 내가 SSN이 없으니까 네가 나 좀 도와줬음 해.

B: 문제 없어. 난 X-Speed Company에서 제공하는 트리플 플레이 서비스 사용하고 있거든. 인터넷, 케이블 TV 그리고 전화 서비스를 묶은 상품이야.

J: 흠…… 핸드폰은 어때?

B: 핸드폰 서비스는 계약 기간 따라 두 가지 종류가 있어. 너 여기에 1년 이상 살 거야?

J: 응. 내가 알아보니까 계약은 최소 1년은 해야 되더라. 그리고 내가 SSN이 없기 때문에 스마트폰을 하려면 전화 회사에 비싼 보증금을 내야 돼. 내가 스마트폰을 안 쓰고 신용카드가 이미 있으면 보증금을 낼 필요가 없지. 대신에, 선금 서비스를 그냥 사용할 수도 있어.

B: 맞아. 그래도 보증금은 반환되는 거 알지. 인터넷이랑 TV 연결은?

J: 응, 그것도 필요해. 추천할 만한 거 있어?

B: 웹사이트 같이 확인해보자. 이 회사는 이 지역의 대학생들 사이에서 가장 많이 사용되는 회사야. 네가 만약 인터넷이랑 TV를 이 옵션으로 사용하면 한 달에 69달러를 내.

J: 흠. 그렇다면 사는 지역에 따라 비용이 달라진다는 얘기네.

B: 맞아. 이것도 처음에는 굉장히 괜찮아 보였거든. 네가 더블 플레이로 사용한다면 겨우 49달러만 내는 거야. 하지만 이건 홍보 가격이고 처음 6개월만 그 가격이지. 그 이후에는 가격이 119달러로 올라갈 수도 있고, 어찌될 진 모르지. 이 웹사이트 작은 글씨로 쓰여 있어. 계약하기 전에 이런 작은 글씨들도 잘 읽어야 돼.

J: 그런데 XEN Network가 내일 학교에 와서 쿠폰 주는 거 알았어?

B: 아니, 몰랐는데. 그럼 가서 이 옵션이랑 가격을 비교해 봐야지. 가끔은 지정된 가게에서 계약하면 비싼 보증금을 좀 덜 내게 해줄 수도 있거든.

J: 가봐야겠다.

B: 그 박스에 대한 비용 더 내야 되는 거 잊지마.

J: 무슨 말이야?

B: 이건 컨버터라는 건데 네 컴퓨터와 랜 선을 연결시켜주는 거야. 돈을 다시 낼 필요 없이 재사용할 수 있어.

J: 알았어. 고마워! 내일 홍보 부스에 가서 어떤 거 할지 결정해야겠다. 오늘 도와줘서 진짜 고마워.

Section 6. Prepare for a garage sale

상황: 다음은 Sumin과 친구들의 대화로 Sumin의 집에서 일어난 대화입니다. 주말에 중고 물건을 팔려고 계획 중입니다.
[S=Sumin, T=Tim, Sumin의 친구, Z=Zoe, Tim의 여동생]

S: 다음 토요일에 새 아파트로 이사 가서 그 전에 치워버려야 될 물건이 몇 개 있는데.

T: 이번 주말에 옆집들이 중고 물건 세일하더라. 싼 가격에 더 이상 필요 없는 물건들을 치워버릴 수 있지.

S: 그거 좋은 생각인데! 난 책이랑 오래된 DVD도 있고 뜯지도 않은 플라스틱 자동차들도 있어. 또 오래된 야구 카드도 없애 버릴 게 좀 있지.

T: 팔아봐.

S: 그래야겠다…… 돈이 좀 생기면 좋지. 새 아파트로 이사 가는 게 돈이 너무 많이 들어. 아, 중고 물건 판매에 대해선 나는 하나도 모르는데. 좀 도와줄래?

T: 그래, 나도 2번 밖에 안 쓴 MP3 팔까 생각 중이야. 사실 새 거지만 더 이상 사용하진 않을 거거든.

Z: 나도 도와주고 싶다.

S: 고마워, Zoe. 내가 제일 먼저 뭘 해야 되지?

T: 모든 물건을 일단 모은 다음, 용도나 손님들의 눈을 사로잡을 방법이면 어떻게든지 분류할 수 있지. 그런 다음 각각의 상자에 넣으면 돼.

Z: 물건들을 깨끗이 닦고 조심스럽게 포장도 해야 돼.

S: 물건들 가격은 어떻게 하지?

T: 상태가 좋은 물건은 대게 소매 가격의 30 혹은 40% 정도인 걸로 알고 있어.

S: 정말!

Z: 모든 물건에 가격을 다 표시해야지.

T: 우리 이웃인 Mr. Hampton이 메인 거리에 사인을 벌써 걸어놨더라고. 그런 이벤트 같은 거 잘 관리하고 운영하시잖아. 이런 일도 자원해서 하는 걸 좋아하시지.

Z: 그래도 우리 손님들을 끌 만한 사인은 만들어 놓자. 2-3 개 물건은 특별가로 내놓거나 아니면 정말 싼 가격으로 내놓거나 해서 손님들의 시선을 끌면 어때?

S: 좋아. 나는 내 자동차 모델을 2달러에 팔겠어. 하나에 15달러씩 주고 샀거든.

T: 그럼 나는 내가 99달러에 산 MP3 플레이어를 15달러에 팔래. 내가 사고싶은 새로운 모델은 109달러지만 15달러가 모자라서 말이야.

Z: 난 사인을 만들게.

S: 중고 물건 세일은 몇 시에 시작해?

Z: 선전 문구에는 9시로 되어 있고 우리도 그쯤에 준비를 하고 있어야지. 음료수를 제공하는 건 어때?

T: 레모네이드를 준비하자.

S: 내가 레모네이드 믹스 한 봉지 사올게. Zoe는 내가 음료수 만드는 거 도와줄 수 있겠다. Tim, 종이컵 좀 가져오지 않을래?

T: 걱정 마. 그런 건 쉽지. 그런데 내가 우리는 잔돈도 준비해야 된다고 말하려는 걸 깜박할 뻔 했다.

Z: 맞아. 금요일에 은행에 가서 지폐랑 동전 좀 바꿔야겠다.

Unit 3

Section 1. Understand public transportation schedule

상황: Mike는 Main Liabrary로 가는 버스를 타려고 하고, 버스 정류장에서 그 곳에 가는 버스를 찾고 있습니다. 그 다음은 Mike가 버스 기사에게 목적지로 가는 방법을 묻는 대화문이고, 마지막은 신문 가판대의 점원과 Mike의 대화입니다. [M=Mike, D1=운전사 1, D2=운전사 2, P=승객, C=점원]

[버스정류장에서]

M: 실례합니다. 이 버스는 Main Library로 가나요?

D1: 아니요. 347번 버스를 타고 다섯 정거장 뒤에 Kream Street에서 200번 버스로 환승하세요.

M: 347번 버스는 얼마나 자주 오나요?

D1: 15분마다 한 대씩 있어요.

M: 고맙습니다.

[347번 버스에서]

M: 죄송합니다. 저에게 5달러 지폐 말고는 없네요.

D2: 죄송합니다만, 잔돈으로 바꿔 줄 수 없습니다. (버스의 다른 승객 들에게 묻는다) 5달러 지폐를 잔돈으로 바꿔 주실 분 계신가요?

P: 제가 바꿔 드리죠.

M: 감사합니다.

D2: 슬롯에서 잔돈 가져가면 되요.

M: 저는 환승해야 하는데요.

D2: 그런 경우에는25센트를 더 내야 해요.

M: 여기 있습니다. Kream Street로 가려면 어떻게 가야 하나요?

D2: 방송으로 나올 거예요. 그런데 목적지가 어디예요?

M: City University에 있는 Main Library에 가려고 해요.

D2: 이 버스는Civic Park를 지나서Kream street로 가요. 다음 정류장에서 내려서 200번 버스를 타야 해요. 도서관은 Main Square Station에 있습니다. Kream Street에서 세 정거장 뒤에 내리세요.

M: 그 버스는 얼마나 자주 있나요?

D2: 주로 10분에 한 대씩 있죠. 그래도 배차 시간표를 확인해 보세요. 버스 정거장에 있는 가판대나 웹사이트에서 얻을 수 있습니다.

M: 고맙습니다, 기사님.

D2: 다 왔네요. 여기가 Kream Street예요.

M: 감사합니다. 좋은 하루 되세요.

[신문 가판대에서]

M: 안녕하세요, Northwest

방향 버스 시간표 하나 얻을 수 있나요?

C: 몇 장이나 필요하세요?

M: 하나면 충분해요.

C: 버스가 대개 시간표대로 운행하지만 가끔 시간표보다 1-2분씩 빠르거나 늦기도 해요.

M: 알겠습니다. 주말 시간표는 다른가요?

C: 맞아요. 주중과 주말 시간표는 색으로 구분되어 있습니다. 파란색은 Northwest 방향이고 종이 뒷면에 빨간색은 공휴일과 일요일의 시간표예요.

M: 이 시간표 얼마예요?

C: 무료예요. 필요한 만큼 가져가세요.

M: 정말이요! 고맙습니다.

Section 2. Take a taxi

상황: 다음은 택시 배치원과 공항으로 가기 위해 택시를 부르려고 전화를 건 고객 간의 대화입니다. [T=택시 배치원, J=James, 고객, D=운전자]

T: 좋은 아침입니다. Red Cabs입니다.

J: 안녕하세요. 오늘 제 사무실에서 JFK공항으로 갈 택시가 필요해요.

T: 사무실 주소가 어떻게 되시나요?

J: 1020 2nd Avenue입니다. 오후 1시까지 공항에 도착해야 하니, 오전 11시 30분쯤 사무실로 와주세요.

T: 물론이죠. 11시30분 경 사무실 앞에 도착해서 기다리면서 손님께 전화하라고 하겠습니다. 성함과 전화번호가 어떻게 되시나요?

J: James Parker이고 전화번호는 633-1500입니다. 고정 요금인가요 아니면 미터당 요금인가요?

T: 고정 요금입니다. 20%의 팁을 포함하여 80달러입니다.

J: 네, 공항까지는 주로 시간이 얼마나 소요되나요?

T: 1번 터미널에서 출발하십니까, 2번 터미널에서 출발하십니까?

J: 2번 터미널에서 내려야 합니다.

T: 2번 터미널은 교통량이 더 많아서 약 40-50분 정도 걸릴 거예요.

J: 그러면 90분 정도면 국내선을 타기에 충분할거 같나요?

T: 네, 그럴 것 같습니다.

[택시에서]

J: 안녕하세요.

D: 안녕하세요, 손님. JFK 국제 공항에서 출발하시는 거 맞지요?

J: 맞아요. 2번 터미널에서 내려주세요.

D: 네, 몇 시 비행이세요?

J: 오후 1시예요.

D: 걱정 마세요. 안전하게 시간 내에 모셔드릴게요. 혹시 모르니 안전벨트 착용해주세요. Cannale Tunnel 쪽으로 80번 도로를 이용하겠습니다. 40분 정도 걸릴 거예요.

J: 고맙습니다.

[2번 터미널에서]

D: 선생님, 2번 터미널입니다. 90달러입니다.

J: 90달러라니요? 고정요금으로 80달러라고 들었어요.

D: 고정 요금이 90달러예요.

J: 택시 회사에 전화해서 문제를 해결해야겠어요.

D: 물론이죠, 그렇게 하세요.

J: 안녕하세요, James Parker예요. 오늘 아침에 JFK 국제공항으로 가는 택시를 예약했어요. 저는 교환원에게 80달러라고 들었는데 기사 분께서 90달러라고 하시네요.

T: 불편을 드려서 죄송합니다. 예약을 확인할 수 있는 전화 번호를 말씀해주시겠어요?

J: 633-1500예요.

T: 아, 그 교환원이 착오가 있었나 봅니다. 1번 터미널까지 금액이 80달러입니다. 죄송하지만 2번 터미널까지의 요금은 90달러입니다.

J: 세상에! 무슨 이런 일이. 알겠습니다. 신경 쓰지 마세요.

D: 오해하시게 해서 죄송합니다. 안전한 여행되시길 바랍니다.

Section 3. Buy a car

상황: 첫 번째 대화는 두 명의 친구가 약속을 잡는 상황이고 두 번째는 중고차 매장에서 일어난 판매원과 고객과의 대화입니다. [O=Orga, T=Tim, S=판매원]

O: 괜찮은 가격으로 차를 살 수 있는 중고차 가게를 추천해 줄 수 있니?

T: 어떤 차를 찾는 거야? 두 군데가 떠오르는데, 위치나 서비스는 별로지만 좋은 가격에 살 수 있는 곳이 있고, 좋은 위치에 훌륭한 서비스를 갖춘 곳이 있어. 승용차를 사려면 두 번째 장소가 괜찮아.

O: 내 원래 차보다 조금 더 크면 좋겠어. 두 번째 매장부터 가봐야겠다.

T: 좋은 중고차 고르는 방법은 알고 있어?

O: 아니, 사실은 중고차에 대해서 전혀 몰라. 차 사는 것 좀 도와줄래?

T: 물론이지. 언제 갈 거야?

O: 이번 주 금요일 오후는 어때?

T: 금요일 마지막 수업 끝나고는 어때? 오후 1시면 끝날 거야.

O: 좋아. 그러면 1시쯤 학생 회관 로비에서 만나자.

[중고차 매장에서]

S: 안녕하세요, 어떻게 도와드릴까요?

O: SUV나 중형차를 알아보고 있어요.

S: 봐 두신 모델이 있으십니까?

O: 글쎄요. GA 나 Hunda차는 어때요?

S: 저희가 Hunda와 GA 차는 많이 보유하고 있습니다. 이 차는 어떻습니까? 이 차가 Hunda 차 중에 제일 인기가 많은 모델입니다.

O: 네, Sorenson 좋다는 얘기 많이 들었어요. SUV 있나요? 캠핑 가기에는 SUV가 제격이거든요.

S: 정말 그래요. 이 모델은 어떤지요? 내부가 넓어서 성인 6명까지 들어갑니다. 5,000마일밖에 안탔고 GA에서 작년 겨울에 출시되었어요.

T: 연비가 어떻게 되나요?

S: 갤런 당 15마일입니다.

T: 보통이네요. 보증 기간은 어떻게 되지요?

S: 4년 또는 2만 마일까지 됩니다.

T: 사고 경력이 있나요?

S: 아니요. 여기 차량이력카드입니다. 이 차는 가격이 정말 좋죠.

O: 글쎄요, 차는 관심이 있는데 중고차에 대해서 확신이 없어서요.

S: 걱정하실 것 없습니다. 시승해 보실 수도 있습니다.

O: 한번 운전 해 보고 싶어요. 그런데 이 차는 얼마인가요?

S: 이 차는 전매가격이 아직도 높아서 좀 비싼 편이예요. 12,500달러입니다.

O: 와우. 제 예상보다 너무 비싸네요. Tim, 어떻게 생각해?

T: 엔진 소리도 좋고 외관상 흠집이 없긴 하네. 그런데 네가 몰기에는 차가 너무 크지 않아?

O: 안전상 나는 큰 차가 좋아.

T: 11,000달러 정도면 괜찮은 가격일 것 같아요.

S: 그건 너무 낮습니다. 12,000달러는 어떠세요? 제가 드릴 수 있는 최저 가격입니다.

O: 11,500달러로 해주시지요?

S: 음…… 제 상관에게 물어보겠습니다…… 11,800달러 이하로는 안 된다고 하십니다.

O: 그럼, 사도록 하지요.

Section 4. Maintain a car

상황: 다음은 자동차 수리공과 Shanti의 대화입니다. Shanti는 연간 차량 검사를 받고자 합니다.
[M=자동차 수리공, S=Shanti]

M: 좋은 아침입니다. 오늘 어떻게 도와드릴까요?

S: 차량 검사를 받아야 할 것 같아서 왔어요.

M: 오늘 예약을 하셨나요?

S: 아니지만 오늘 받을 수 있을까요?

M: 음, 한 번 볼게요. 예약 중간에 넣어 드릴 수 있지만 차를 두고 가시고 나중에 찾으러 오셔야 해요.

S: 정말 고맙습니다. 사무실이 멀지 않으니 버스를 타고 갈게요.

M: 자동차 등록증을 곧 갱신하셔야 하겠네요.

S: 네, 스티커를 4월까지 바꿔야 하니까 몇 일 남지 않았어요.

M: 알겠습니다. 저기 저 빨간 차인가요?

S: 맞아요. 저기Bluick Laselle이예요.

M: 네, 오늘 오후 5시 정도 까지는 되겠어요. 혹시 더 고칠 부분이 있을 수 있으니 가지러 오시기 전 오후 1시쯤 전화주세요.

S: 그렇게 오래 걸려요?

M: NJ 는 차량 전체 검사를 받도록 하고 있어서 두 시간 반쯤 걸립니다.

S: 알겠어요. 나중에 뵐게요.

[수리공에게 전화]

S: 안녕하세요. George's Garage죠?

M: 네, 그렇습니다.

S: 오늘 아침에 차량 검사로 제 차를 두고 왔는데 1시쯤 전화하라고 하셔서요.

M: 어떤 차죠?

S: 빨간 색 Bluick Laselle입니다.

M: 네, 몇 가지 손 봐야 할 곳이 있어요. 에어 필터와 엔진 오일을 교체해야 하고 한 쪽 헤드라이트도 고장 났어요.

S: 한 번에 다 수리해야 하나요?

M: 모두 수리하지 않으시면 차량 점검을 통과할 수 없습니다

S: 비용이 얼마나 드나요?

M: 다해서 380달러입니다.

S: 별 도리가 없어 보이네요. 모두 수리 해주세요. 오늘 오후에 차를 가지러 가도 되나요?

M: 5시쯤 오세요.

[그 날 오후]

M: 자동차 키 받으세요.

S: 신속하게 해주셔서 감사해요.

M: 이제 다 좋아 보입니다. 전화로 말씀 드린 것처럼, 에어 필터와 엔진 오일 그리고 헤드라이트를 교체 했어요. 엔진 오일이 검은색이었습니다. 차 구입 이후에 엔진 오일을 간 적이 있습니까?

S: 아마 없을 거예요. 제가 차량을 잘 유지하는 방법을 몰라서요.

M: 엔진 오일, 부동액, 그리고 타이어압은 정기적으로 확인해야 합니다. 엔진 오일은 3,000마일에 한 번씩 갈아 주셔야 해요.

S: 좋은 정보 주셔서 고맙습니다.

M: 네.

Section 5. Get or renew a driver's license

상황: 첫 번째 상황은 운전 면허 시험에 관하여 이야기하는 두 친구의 대화이며 두 번째는 차량관리국 사무원과 운전 면허 시험 수험자 간의 대화입니다. [A=Anna, J=John, O1=사무원 1, O2=사무원 2]

J: Anna, 네가 운전 면허증이 곧 만료된다고 도와 달라고 했잖아. 내가 운전면허 센터에 전화해 보니 운행 시험은 안 쳐도 되더라. 필기 시험만 치면 돼.

A: 그러면 시험을 어떻게 준비해야 하지?

J: 시험 안내서를 꼼꼼히 읽어 보지 그래? 내 방 어딘가에 한 권 있을 것 같아. 내 동생이 지난 달에 시험을 봤거든.

A: 필기 시험은 어려워?

J: 그리 어렵지 않아. 만약 합격 못한다 해도 당일만 아니면 언제든 다시 시험을 볼 수 있어. 여권 챙겨서 가야 해.

A: 정말 고마워. 한국어로 시험을 볼 수 있나?

J: New York 에서는 아마 가능할거야. 그럼 넌 언제 가고 싶어?

A: 이번 주 월요일 어떨까?

J: 차량관리국은 월요일에는 문을 닫는 걸로 알고 있어. 수요일 아침에 가자.

A: 좋아.

[차량관리국에서]

A: 안녕하세요. 운전면허 시험을 신청하려고 왔습니다.

O1: 우선, 이 양식을 다 채우시고 시력 검사를 받으신 후 필기 시험을 보시면 됩니다. 시력 검사를 위해 호명될 때까지 기다리세요.

[필기 시험장에서]

O2: 4번 컴퓨터 앞에 앉으세요.

A: 시험 시간이 얼마나 있나요?

O2: 시간은 필요하신 만큼 쓰실 수 있습니다. 문의 사항 있으면 또 말씀해 주세요.

A: 고맙습니다.

O2: 자, 이제 시작하면 됩니다.

[한 시간 후]

J: 합격 했어?

A: 응, 두 문제 틀렸어.

J: 잘했네. 이제 가족 주치의의 사인을 받아야 해. 주치의의 사인과 소인이 찍힌 이 서류를 보내면 교통국에서 새 운전면허증을 보내줄 거야.

A: 나는 가족 주치의가 없는데.

J: 걱정 하지마. 우리 가족 주치의를 소개해 줄게. 의사 선생님이 몇 가지 질문을 할거야. 그런 다음 우편으로 새 운전면허증을 받을 수 있어. 그 이후에는 운전할 자격이 생기는 거지. 그게 다야.

A: 다시 한 번 고맙다.

Section 6. Drive a car

상황: 첫 번째 상황은 손님과 주유소 직원과의 대화이고 두 번째는 경찰관과 그 경찰관에게 정지당한 운전자 간의 대화입니다. [A=Akiko, G=주유소 직원, P=경찰관]

[주유소에서]

A: 실례합니다만, 어떻게 주유하는지 알려주시겠어요?

G: 물론입니다. 주유비는 선불입니다.

A: 현금만 받으시나요?

G: 아니요. 신용카드로도 지불하실 수 있습니다.

A: 신용카드로 어떻게 지불하는 건가요?

G: 신용카드를 삽입한 후 비밀 번호를 입력하세요.

A: 제 비자 카드로 하고 싶어요. (순서대로 한 후) 그 후에는 어떻게 하지요?

G: 먼저 무연, 휘발유, 고급 휘발유 중 원하는 등급을 선택하세요.

A: 어떤 것으로 주유해야 할까요?

G: 주로 자동차 설명서나 주유구에서 확인할 수 있어요. 손님 차에는 무연이 좋겠네요

A: 알겠습니다. (버튼을 누른다)

G: 자, 주유 펌프를 당겨서 노즐을 들어올리세요. 주유 펌프를 차 주유구에 넣은 후 레버를 꽉 쥐세요. 기름을 계속 넣고 싶으면 레버를 잡고 있거나 잠금 장치를 하면 됩니다. 그게 다에요.

A: 고맙습니다. 하나만 더 여쭤볼게요. Irvin으로 가는 가장 가까운 고속도로가 뭔가요?

G: 10번이나 40번 고속도로를 타시면 될 거예요. 40번이 여기서 더 가까울 것 같습니다.

A: 여기서 40번 고속도로로 어떻게 가나요? 고속도로로 가는 길을 못 찾겠어요.

G: 자, 반 마일 정도 직진하면 그 길로 가는 교차로 이정표가 보일 거예요. 찾기 쉬워요. 5 방향 교차로에서 좌회전하세요. 그러면 40번 도로를 타게 됩니다. 그 도로로 가는 연결 부분이 찾기가 좀 어렵죠.

A: 알겠습니다. 제가 교차로에서 길을 잘못 탔었군요.

[집으로 가는 길]

P: 면허증과 자동차 등록증을 보여주십시오.

A: 여기 있습니다. 제가 차에서 내려야 하나요?

P: 아니요, 차에 있으세요. 제가 왜 차를 세우라고 하는지 아십니까?

A: 아니요, 제가 뭘 잘못 했나요?

P: 정지 신호를 무시하고 그냥 지나갔습니다. 완전히 멈춰야 했는데 그렇지 않고 대신 속도를 줄였다가 다시 달리셨습니다.

A: 제가 그랬나요? 저는 완전히 멈춘 줄 알았어요.

P: 기록을 보니 같은 건으로 지난 달에도 경고를 받았었군요. 또 그러셨네요.

A: 티켓을 받게 되나요?

P: 이번에는 어쩔 수 없습니다. 이제부터 정지 신호에는 완전히 멈춰야 합니다.

A: 알겠습니다, 경찰관님. 벌점도 받게 되는 건가요?

P: 이미 벌점 9점이 부과된 상태입니다. 이번에는 티켓만 발급하겠습니다. 한 번 더 위반하면 일정 기간 동안 면허가 정지됩니다.

A: 정말이요!

P: 여기 티켓 있습니다. 하나 더, 브레이크 등 하나가 나갔습니다. 가능한 빨리 교체하세요. 이번에는 경고입니다. 고장 난 브레이크 등 때문에 티켓을 또 받을 수도 있습니다.

A: 교체 하겠습니다. 알려 주셔서 고맙습니다.

Unit 4

Section 1. Go to the library

상황: 첫 번째 대화문은 Sera와 Amy가 대학 도서관에서 나누는 대화입니다. 두 명은 모두 대학교 1학년생입니다. 나머지 대화문은 Sera와 도서관 사서 간의 대화입니다. [S=Sera, A=Amy, L=사서]

[도서관 투어 신청]

S: 얘, 지금 뭐 쓰는 거야?

A: 도서관 투어 지원서 쓰고 있어.

S: 좋은 생각인데. 나도 같이 해도 될까?

A: 물론이지, 투어는 4시에 시작해서 한 25분 정도 걸린대. 이 양식 작성해.

S: 음, 이거 정말 유익하겠다. 도서관 사서가 도서관 각 층을 데리고 다니면서 자료랑 서비스들을 설명해 주기 전에 학교 데이터베이스를 통해서 검색하는 방법에 대해 간단히 설명해준대.

A: 맞아. 내가 이 도서관에서 제일 좋아하는 건 매달 몇 몇의 세션이 있는데 시설을 효과적이고 효율적으로 사용하는 방법에 대한 특별한 세미나도 열어준다는 거야.

S: 정말? 어떤 세미나를 제공하는데?

A: 통계를 사용하는 방법, 예를 들면, SPSS, NVivo 같은 프로그램 사용법 말이야.

S: 끝내주는데! 작문 실력 향상에 관한 세미나도 제공해주니?

A: 아니, 그건 Baker Hall 에 있는 대학 작문 센터에 가면 도움을 받을 수 있어.

S: 우와, 그게 바로 내가 필요한거거든. 필요한 건 그거거든.

A: 예약을 먼저 하고 가면 네 작문 실력을 향상하는 데 도움을 받을 수 있을 거야. 지금 투어가 시작하나 봐. 이거 끝나고 작문 센터에 데려다 줄게.

S: 잘됐다. 고마워.

[책 대출]

S: 실례합니다. 이 저널도 대여되나요?

L: 죄송합니다만, 간행물은 대여가 안됩니다. 도서관 내에서만 보실 수 있어요.

S: 알겠습니다. 이 자료를 복사하려면 복사 카드 있어야 하나요?

L: 있으면 더 편하죠. 복사 카드가 없으시면 동전으로 하셔도 됩니다. 그렇지 않으면, 10달러, 20달러, 30달러 카드 중에서 사실 수 있고 반환금은 1달러 50센트입니다. 필요하실 때마다 카드에 추가로 충전하실 수 있고요.

S: 그럼 20달러짜리 카드 살게요. 그리고 책을 3권 빌리고 싶은데요. 책 대여 기간이 얼마나 되죠?

L: 4주입니다.

S: 꽤 기네요. 이 책들을 대출할게요.

L: 네. 학생증 주세요.

[도서관 상호 대출 신청]

S: 실례합니다. 이 논문이 필요한데요, 이 도서관에서는 찾을 수가 없어서요.

L: 데이터베이스를 다시 볼게요. 아, 다른 대학에 있습니다. 도서관 상호 대출을 신청하셔야겠는데요.

S: 그게 뭔가요?

L: 이 도서관을 통해 다른 곳에서 자료를 빌려올 수 있는 거예요. 여기서 찾아가실 수 있고요.

S: 우와, 그렇게 할 수 있는지 몰랐네요.

L: 신청하시려면 이 양식을 작성하세요. 일주일 정도 걸릴 겁니다. 자료가 도착하면 제가 이메일로 알려 드릴께요.

S: 정말 고맙습니다.

Section 2. Get to know about the course

상황: Hannah 는 첫 스페인어 수업에 막 도착했고 같이 수업을 듣는 친구와 교수님을 만나게 됩니다. Hannah와 친구는 나란히 앉아 프로젝트 파트너가 됩니다. [H= Hannah, J= Jane]

[교실에서]

H: 안녕!

J: 안녕, 너 1학년이구나.

H: 어떻게 알았어? 모든 게 너무 낯설어. 너무 흥분되기도 하고 긴장도 돼.

J: 걱정할 거 없어. 그나저나 난 Jane 이고 3학년이야.

H: 난 Hannah야. 만나서 반가워, Jane. 이 스페인 수업에 사야 할 교재나 리딩 패킷있니?

J: 아니. 없어. 가끔 교재는 중고 서점에 가면 구할 수 있지. 교수님이 지난 학기랑 똑같은 교재를 사용하신다면 말이야.

H: 중고책은 어디서 구해?

J: 서점에서 찾을 수 있어. 서점에서는 모든 과목의 새 책이랑 중고 책을 같은 선반에 두고 판매하고 있어. 또는 어떤 서점이든 온라인에서도 구할 수 있지.

H: 이건 중고책이야?

J: 응, 난 25달러 줬어. 거의 새 거 같지만 말이야.

H: 정말 좋은 아이디어다! 난 왜 생각을 못했지? 다음 학기부터는 좀더 일찍 사러 가야겠다. 저, Jane, 점심 먹었니? 뭐 좀 먹으러 갈래?

J: 좋아. 그럼 나가서 프로젝트도 얘기하자.

H: 그래. 카페테리아 괜찮아?

J: 좋지.

[카페테리아에서]

H: 자, 이 프로젝트에서 우리가 뭘 해야 되지?

J: 멕시코와 관련된 어떤 주제든 조사 해서 파워포인트로 발표해야 돼.

H: 아이구, 어떡하지? 난 스페인어 잘 못하는데.

J: Sarabia 교수님이 좀 점수를 짜게 주시긴 하지만 열심히 하면 살아남을 수 있어. 잘 버텨봐. 내가 가능한 도울게. 몇 학점 신청했어?

H: 15학점 신청했어.

J: 이중언어와 원어민을 위한 일본어 수업 듣니? 그 수업은 일본어 작문이랑 말하기가 엄청 많은데. Hayaku 교수님은 학생들에게 기대치가 높아.

H: 좋은 정보인데. 그 교수님에 대해서 내가 더 알아야 할 게 있을까?

J: 아니, 하지만 내가 아는 한 수업 시간이나 약속한 시간에 정확히 가야만 할꺼야. 굉장히 시간 약속에 엄격하신 분이거든. 그리고 작문 숙제 할 때 절대로 표절하지 않도록 조심해야 해.

H: 응? 못 알아들었어.

J: 인터넷 사이트나 다른 자료에서 다른 사람 것을 네 과제에 베끼거나 복사하고 붙이기 하면 안 된다고. 한 문장에 7단어 또는 그 이상 연속으로 똑같으면, 이러한 경우는 표절이라고 간주해. 그러면 넌 F학점을 받게 되.

H: 조심해야겠다.

J: 그러는 게 좋을 거야. 너도 알겠지만 모든 수업이 다 마찬가지지. 미국인 교수들은 다른 나라와는 달리 학생들의 이러한 태도를 참지 않거든.

H: 정보 고마워. 미안한데, 나 다음 수업 가야겠다.

J: 그래. 나중에 보자.

Section 3. Get a student credit card

상황: Eunji는 한국에서 온 대학교 1학년생이고 학생용 신용카드를 발급받길 원합니다. 첫 번째는 Eunji와 신용카드 회사의 영업사원이 나눈 대화문입니다. 두 번째는 Eunji와 은행 직원이 나눈 대화입니다. [E= Eunji, S=영업사원, B=은행 직원]

[신용카드 가판대에서]

S: 안녕하세요. 어떻게 도와드릴까요?

E: 신용카드 만들고 싶은데요. 어떤 카드가 있는지 알 수 있을까요?

S: 물론이죠 21살 넘으셨어요?

E: 아니요. 19살 인데요.

S: 그런 경우에는 지원서에 부모님이 공동 서명하셔야 되요.

E: 그건 불가능 한데요. 부모님은 한국에 계세요.

S: 그럼 이 서류에 공동 서명해 줄 보호자나 어른 있으세요?

E: 아니오.

S: 죄송합니다. 미성년자 학생 신용카드 관한 법이 작년부터 더 엄격하게 바뀌어서요.

E: 알겠습니다. 감사합니다.

[은행에서]

E: 제가 미성년자여도 신용카드 신청할 수 있나요?

B: 그럼요. 이 양식만 기입하시면 됩니다.

E: 정말이요! 너무 좋네요. 제가 받을 수 있는 카드를 설명해 주실래요?

B: 미성년자인 학생의 경우에는 종류가 한 가지에요. 신용 한도는 300달러 밖에 안되지만 회원비는 없어요. 6개월간 신용이 좋은 상태를 유지하면 회사가 한도를 올려줄 거에요.

E: 이자가 어떻게 되요?

B: 연 22%입니다.

E: 아, 너무 높은데요.

B: 그렇지는 않아요. 한 달 내에 총액을 지불하시면 이자는 없으니까요. 카드 청구서에 표시된 최소액만 지불하셔도 벌금은 없습니다.

E: 뭐라고요? 벌금이 얼만데요?

B: 이자와는 별도로 25달러에요. 제시간에 지불하시면 문제는 없죠. 카드는 위급 상황에는 특히 편리하니까요. 현금이 없을 때 카드를 사용할 수 있잖아요. 지불하는 데는 한 달이라는 기간이 있습니다.

E: 좋아요. 하나 필요한 거 같네요. 위급 시에만 사용 하게요.

B: 사진이 있는 신분증 복사해야 하고요. 신청서와 보통 예금 통장이 필요합니다.

E: 은행 통장이 없는데요. 내일도 근무 하시나요?

B: 그럼요. 질문이 있으시면 여기로 와서 물어보세요.

E: 질문이 하나 더 있는데요. 누가 신용 카드를 발급하나요?

B: 은행이 하는 거죠. 우리 카드는 American Transitional Bank가 발급하고요. 다른 은행도 비자카드를 발급합니다.

E: 정보 감사합니다. 저는 Bank of Citizens에서 은행 거래를 하니까 여기서도 신용카드를 제공하는 지 알아봐야겠어요.

B: 그럼요. 알아보십시오. 저희 은행에서 카드 만들기로 결정하시면 그때 다시 오셔도 됩니다.

E: 그럼 또 뵐게요.

Section 4. Look for a part-time job

상황: 이 대화문은 학생인 Sarah 와 대학교 마케팅 사무실의 직원과의 대화입니다. Sarah는 일자리에 대한 정보를 찾으려고 전화를 걸었고 나중에 면접을 봅니다. [S=Sarah, C=직원, I=면접관]

[전화]

C: 안녕하세요. 대학교 마케팅 사무실입니다. 어떻게 도와드릴까요?

S: 제가 학교 신문에서 광고하는 어시스턴트 매니저 자리를 알아보려고 전화 드렸는데요. 아직 자리 있나요?

C: 예, 있습니다.

S: 그 자리에 대해 좀더 정보를 얻고 싶은데요. 어떤 일을 하게 되는 건가요? 월급은 어떻게 되나요?

C: 음, 어시스턴트 매니저는 기본적인 사무일을 하게 됩니다. 데이터를 구성하고 모으고 분석하는 일을 하죠. 이 자리를 위해서는 통계학에 어느 정도 기본 지식을 갖고 계셔야 되고요. 다른 회사 근무 경험은 없어도 됩니다. 기본 급여는 한 달에 1,850달러입니다. 이 자리에 관심이 있으시면 커버 레터와 함께 이력서를 보내주셔야 합니다. 그러면 자격 요건과 세부 사항을 알아보기 위한 면접을 위해 전화를 드릴 겁니다.

S: 좋습니다. 며칠 안으로 보내드리겠습니다. 감사합니다.

[사무실에서]

C: 안녕하세요. Sarah. 나는 Christine이에요. 전에 통화 했었죠.

S: 네, Christine. 만나서 반갑습니다.

C: 저도 만나서 반가워요. 면접 장소로 안내해드릴게요. 저를 따라오세요.

[면접]

I: 면접하게 되어서 기쁩니다. 앉으시고 편하게 하세요.

S: 감사합니다.

I: 이 자리에 관심을 갖는 이유를 묻는 것부터 시작할게요.

S: 제가 이 분야에서 일한 경력은 많지 않지만 교수님을 도와 데이터 수집과 분석에 관련된 일을 많이 해왔습니다. 교수님을 통해 마케팅 리서치 영역에 관심을 가지게 되었고요. 이 분야에서 더 배우고 저의 실력을 발전시키고 싶습니다.

I: 좋아요. 아직 학생인가요?

S: 네, 4학년입니다 그리고 이번 학기가 마지막 학기입니다.

I: 이력서에 보면 Kaufmann 백화점 고객 서비스에서 어시스턴트 매니저로 일한 경험이 있더군요. 거기서 무슨 일을 했고 왜 그만 뒀죠?

S: 저는 백화점에서 일어나는 일들을 감독하고 한 달에 한 번씩 매니저에게 요약 보고서를 썼었습니다.

I: 큰 책임이 있는 일이었겠군요.

S: 그랬습니다. 그리고 시간이 많이 걸리는 일이었습니다. 그게 제가 일을 그만 둔 가장 큰 이유입니다. 시간도 많이 걸리고 일과 학업을 동시에 잘 해내기가 어려웠습니다.

I: 알겠습니다. 저희가 왜 당신을 고용해야 한다고 생각하나요?

S: 저는 교수님을 도와 마케팅 리서치를 하는 것이 정말 즐거웠습니다. 무엇보다도 저는 사람들과 일하는 걸 즐기고 이 직업이 주는 도전들이 좋습니다.

I: 음, 아주 성실하고 열정적인 사람으로 보이는 군요. 제가 며칠 안으로 결정해서 결과를 알려드리도록 하죠. 마지막으로 질문이 있나요?

S: 아니요. 지금은 없습니다.

I: 만나서 반가웠습니다. 면접을 보러 와줘서 고맙습니다.

S: 감사합니다.

Section 5. Register classes and pay tuition

상황: 다음은 어드바이저와 학생 Minho의 대화입니다. 대화는 어드바이저의 사무실과 재정 사무실에서 일어납니다. [A=어드바이저, M=Minho, FC=재정 사무실 직원]

[상담기간]

A: 안녕하세요 Minho, 어떻게 도와드릴까요?

M: 네, 전 이번에 3학년이 되는데요. 제 전공으로 어떤 수업을 들어야 하는지 알고 싶습니다.

A: 알겠습니다. 기록을 한 번 볼까요…… 교양과목은 다 들었네요. 그렇죠?

M: 네. 그리고 경영을 전공하기로 결정했습니다.

A: 그렇군요. 그렇다면 전공을 정했다는 걸 알리고 전공 커리큘럼에 제시된 과목을 들어야 합니다. 시간표를 훑어보고 원하는 과목을 선택하세요. 학과의 몇 몇 필수 과목과 의무 선택 과목을 들어야 합니다.

M: 무슨 말인가요?

A: 전공에서 필요한 필수 과목을 듣는 것 외에 몇 개의 선택 과목도 레벨별로 들어야 해요. 레벨 100에서 두 과목, 레벨 200에서 세 과목을 들어야 하죠.

M: 수강신청 기간이 지난 다음에 과목을 취소해도 되나요?

A: 네. 하지만 추가/취소 기간에만 되죠. 날짜를 꼭 확인하세요.

M: 수업을 몇 개 청강해도 되나요?

A: pass/fail 학점을 받기를 원하나요 아니면 그냥 수업만 듣고 싶나요?

M: 그냥 수업 듣는 것만 하고 싶은데요. 거시경제학은 패스하기 어려운 과목이라고 들었거든요.

A: 네, 하셔도 됩니다. 하지만 과목을 가르치는 교수님에게 허가를 먼저 받아야 하죠.

M: 네. 알겠습니다. 아, 질문이 하나 더 있는데요. 새로 생긴 재정 사무실은 어디에 있나요?

A: 사무실은 Baker Hall로 옮겼어요. 등록 사무실 바로 오른쪽에 있습니다.

M: 감사합니다. 안녕히 계세요!

[재정 사무실에서]

FC: 안녕하세요. 무엇을 도와드릴까요?

M: 안녕하세요. 등록금 납입이 늦었다는 안내와 학자금 신청에 관한 통지문을 받았습니다.

FC: 잠시만 기다려주세요. 기록을 보니까 국제 학생 자격으로 이전 학교에서 우리 학교로 옮겨왔을 때 왔을 때 I-20 비자와 재정 지원을 받았네요. 하지만 그래도 지원을 신청해야 합니다.

M: 국제 학생이 학자금 대출 지원을 받는 게 가능한가요?

FC: 학생이 교육을 받기 위한 재정적 상황이 안 좋다는 증거를 발견한 경우에만 가능해요. 그리고 학점도 기준에 맞아야 하고요.

M: 그렇다면 저는 지원하겠습니다. 어떤 서류를 제출해야 하나요?

FC: 서류를 가져올게요. 잠시만 기다리세요.

M: 감사합니다.

FC: (서류를 가지고 돌아와서) 이 서류들을 작성하고 나면 내게로 가져오세요. 학과 사무실에 가서 연구 조교 자리가 있나 알아보고요.

M: 그 생각을 미처 못했네요! 정보 주셔서 감사합니다.

Section 6. Get involved in extracurricular activities

상황: Hannah는 아일랜드 출신으로 새로 채용된 기숙사 조교이고 그녀는 파티에서 새로 뽑힌 기숙사 조교 모임에 초대받았습니다. 첫 번째 대화는 기숙사 조교 사무실에서 일어났고 다음은 여성 동아리에서 나눈 대화입니다. [H= Hannah, S= Shelly]

[기숙사 조교 사무실에서]

S: 안녕, 기숙사 조교된 거 축하해

H: 고마워.

S: 난 Shelly야. 넌 1학년이니?

H: 안녕, 난 Hannah야. 티가 나니? 1학년 맞아. 도움을 청하러 네 방에 자주 갈 것 같아.

S: 그래, 도움이 되면 좋지.

H: 그럼 먼저 내가 어떤 일을 하게 되니?

S: 학생들이 기숙사 규칙을 제대로 지키고 있는지 확인해야 하지. 여기 가이드라인이 있어. 12 쪽을 읽고 규칙 10 개는 꼭 외워둬야 해. 학생들이 3번 이상 규칙을 어기면 기숙사에서 나가야 하거든.

H: 알았어.

S: 앞으로 물어볼 거 있으면, 뭘 해야 할 지 알지. 그런데 너 가입한 동아리 있어?

H: 아니, 그런데 여성 동아리에 가입되길 기다리고 있어. Phi Delta Sigma 멤버가 되려고 오리엔테이션 하는 날 사인했었거든.

S: 우와, 내가 그 클럽의 회원인데.

H: 정말 잘됐다. 하지만 내가 회원으로 뽑힐지는 모르지 뭐.

S: 걱정 마. 내가 우리 회원들한테 너를 강력 추천해줄게. 말이 나온 김에 내가 친구한테 전화해서 새로운 회원명단 목록을 다 마쳤는지 알아볼게.

[여성 전용 동아리에서]

H: 안녕, Shelly.

S: 축하해. 네가 이 동아리의 회원이 돼서 아주 기쁘다.

H: 고마워. 나 너무 신나. 내가 이 순간을 얼마나 기다려 왔는지 아니?

S: 상상도 못하겠는걸! 네가 입회식에서 해야 될 일들에 대해 말해줄게. 행사에서 가장 큰 부분은 토요일에 고아원에 갈 지원자와 일요일에 양로원에 갈 지원자를 뽑는 거야.

H: 정말? 그게 입회식이야? 정말 좋은데. 난 아이들하고 노는 거 정말 좋아하거든.

S: 우린 자원 봉사를 한 경험을 기준으로 거의 뽑고 학점도 최소 3.2는 넘어야 돼.

H: 그렇구나. 이 동아리의 회원이 돼서 정말 기쁘다. 자원 봉사 일은 얼마나 자주 가는데?

S: 한 달에 한 번. 모든 회원은 5 - 6 명의 그룹으로 나눠져서 정해진 센터로 가는 거야. 매 달 대 여섯 개의 다른 센터로 돌아가면서 가.

H: 특별히 정해진 일을 하게 될까?

S: 캡틴이 지원서에 쓰여진 걸 보고 네가 좋아하는 걸 기준으로 정해줄 거야.

H: 내가 고아원에 가게 되면 아이들한테 수학을 가르쳐 주고 싶어. 내가 전에 자원 봉사 갔을 때 그게 정말 재미있었거든.

S: 그것도 괜찮은데. 우린 너 같은 사람이 필요했어. 우리가 하는 일은 이런 게 다가 아니니까 오해하진 말고. 거의 매주 토요일 저녁에는 파티도 있어. 회원들이 정말 재미있게 보내. 하지만 학점을 유지해야 되는 거 항상 기억해야해. 2학기 연속해서 학점이 안되면 멤버십이 끝나버리게 되거든. 동아리 소개가 너무 길었네. 자, 친구들한테 돌아가자.

H: 그래. 나중에 더 얘기하자.

Unit 5

Section 1. Open or close a bank account

상황: 다음은 은행에서 은행 직원과 고객인 Heanny와 나눈 대화입니다. Heanny는 은행계좌를 만들고 은행 직원에게 궁금한 점을 질문하고 있습니다. [H=Heanny Lee, B=은행 직원]

[은행에서]

B: 무엇을 도와드릴까요?

H: 은행계좌를 만들고 싶습니다.

B: 일반예금과 당좌예금 중 어떤 계좌를 원하십니까?

H: 둘 다 필요합니다.

B: 사진이 부착된 신분증을 주시겠습니까?

H: 여권을 가져왔는데, 괜찮죠?

B: 물론입니다. 그 사이에 이 신청서를 작성해주시겠어요?

H: 음...... 집 전화번호가 없는데요.

B: 연락 가능한 전화번호가 있나요? 연결될 수 있는 아무 연락처라도 없으신지요?

H: 여기 Seattle에 온 지 일주일이 안됐거든요. 일주일 안으로 집전화를 설치할 예정인데, 그 때 번호를 가져와도 될까요?

B: 알겠습니다. 신청서를 다 작성하셨습니까?

H: 네, 여기 있습니다.

B: 오늘 예금할 예정이신가요?

H: 일반예금에 2,500달러, 당좌예금에 1,750달러를 입금하고 싶습니다.

B: 알겠습니다. 입금 진행하도록 하겠습니다.

H: 당좌예금에 대해서 몇 가지 궁금한 점이 있는데요.

B: 네, 말씀하세요.

H: 수표는 어떻게 작성하나요?

B: 우선 날짜와 금액, 그리고 수표를 받는 사람을 기재하셔야 합니다. 마지막으로 하셔야 할 일은 수표에 서명을 하시는 거고요. 금액을 기재하실 때 0의 개수에 유의하셔야 합니다. 또 한가지 중요한 것은 수표에 메모를 적고 수표책에 수표의 용도를 메모하고 가지고 계셔야 합니다.

H: 알겠습니다. 만약 제 계좌에 잔금이 충분치 않고 예금을 늦게 하면 어떻게 되나요? 예금부족에 대하여 벌금을 물게 되나요?

B: 상황에 따라 다릅니다. 수표를 받은 분이 고객님의 예금부족 계좌에서 현금으로 출금하려고 시도한 경우 부도수표로 처리되어 25달러의 벌금을 물게 됩니다. 고객님께서 수입과 지출을 잘 맞추시고 정기적으로 확인하신다면 크게 문제될 일은 없습니다. 혹은 고객님께서 은행에 오실 때마다 창구에서 계좌의 잔고를 늘 확인하실 수도 있습니다.

H: 알겠습니다.

B: 궁금한 점이 있으시면 전화 주시거나 은행으로 오시면 됩니다. 자, 이제 은행에서 고객님께 몇 장의 수표를 드릴 텐데요, 그래도 수표책을 주문하셔야 합니다. 여기에 카탈로그가 있으니 보시고 원하는 스타일과 디자인을 고르시면 됩니다.

H: 음…… 파란 배경으로 된 이 IS290으로 주문하고 싶습니다. 얼마나 걸릴까요?

B: 일주일 정도 걸립니다.

H: 한 가지 더 궁금한 게 있습니다. 매달 정기적으로 받는 고지서가 있는데요. 다른 계좌로 자동이체 되도록 설정할 수 있나요?

B: 죄송하지만 그건 저희 은행에서 제공하지 않는 시스템입니다.

H: 정말이요? 번거롭겠네요. 매달 수표를 써야겠군요.

B: 죄송하지만 그렇게 하셔야 할 듯 합니다. 또 필요한 게 있으신지요?

H: 직불카드로 ATM에서 현금 인출을 할 수 있나요?

B: 네, 물론입니다.

H: 이제 다 되었네요.

B: 자, 여기 고객님의 일반예금과 당좌예금 계좌입니다. 감사합니다, 좋은 하루 되세요! 다음 고객님.

Section 2. Deposit or withdraw money

상황: 첫 번째 대화는 은행 직원과 고객인 Sumin의 대화입니다. Sumin은 수표를 현금으로 바꾸는 방법과 현금인출하는 방법을 은행 직원에게 질문하고 있습니다. 두 번째는 Sumin과 친구인 Holly가 은행의 입출금 내역서 읽는 방법을 이야기하고 있습니다. [B=은행 직원, H=Holly, S=Sumin]

[은행에서]

B: 다음 고객님. 안녕하세요! 무엇을 도와드릴까요?

S: 네, 여행자 수표와 개인수표를 현금으로 바꾸고 싶은데요.

B: 죄송하지만 오늘은 개인수표를 현금으로 바꾸실 수 없습니다. 먼저 고객님의 계좌에 수표를 예치하셔야 하고, 그 수표가 승인될 때까지 기다리셔야 합니다. 최대한 빠르게 인출하실 수 있는 시간은 내일 오후 12시 이후입니다.

S: 알겠습니다. 당좌예금에 입금할게요.

B: 수표들에 이서해주시기 바랍니다.

S: 네?

B: 수표 뒷면에 서명 부탁 드립니다. (서명을 마친 후) 여기 영수증 있습니다. 또 필요하신 건 없으세요?

S: 제 당좌예금에서 돈을 인출해야 하는데, 어떻게 하나요?

B: 지불란에 "현금"이라고 쓰시고 오늘 날짜와 인출하실 금액을 써주세요. 그리고 뒷면에 서명해주시면 됩니다. 사진이 부착된 신분증을 제시해주시기 바랍니다.

S: 여기 학생증이요.

B: 죄송하지만 학생증은 안됩니다. 운전면허증이나 여권과 같이 정부에서 발행된 신분증이어야 합니다.

S: 아, 알겠습니다. 여기 여권 있습니다.

B: 감사합니다. 뒷면에 이서해주시겠어요?

S: 네. (수표에 서명한다.)

B: 현금은 어떻게 드릴까요?

S: 20달러짜리 다섯 장, 5달러짜리 일곱 장, 그리고 1달러짜리 열 장이요.

B: 네. 여기 다섯, 넷, 셋, 둘…... (고객에게 돈을 세어준다.)

S: 한 가지 더 필요한 게 있습니다. 일반예금 계좌에서 당좌예금 계좌로 175달러를 송금해야 해요.

B: 여기 고객님의 일반예금 계좌의 출금 신청서와 당좌예금 계좌의 예금전표를 작성해주시기 바랍니다. 일반예금 계좌 통장을 가지고 계신가요?

S: 여기 있습니다.

B: (모든 거래 과정을 마치고) 자, 다 되었습니다. 좋은 하루 보내세요!

[친구 Holly에게 은행의 입출금 내역서를 읽는 방법에 대하여 질문]

S: Holly, 이 은행 내역서 보는 것 좀 도와줄래?

H: 그래, 문제가 뭔데?

S: 이 당좌예금 입출금 내역서에서 NSF가 무슨 뜻이야?

H: 그건 누군가 네가 쓴 수표를 현금으로 인출하려고 했을 때 네 계좌에 돈이 충분하지 않았다는 소리야. 다행히 은행이 너한테 이것에 대한 수수료를 부과하진 않았네. 네가 매달 내역서를 받을 때에는 모든 수표들이 현금으로 인출되었는지 아닌지를 잘 보고, 또 월초와 월말의 잔고가 맞는지를 확인해서 너의 당좌 예금 계좌 통장의 잔고와 맞는지를 비교해 봐야 해.

S: 만약에 잔고가 안 맞으면 어떻게 해야 해?

H: 그러면 부과된 수수료나 현금으로 인출되지 않은 수표들이 있는지 전표를 살펴보고 하나하나 확인해야지. 그것들을 내역서의 최종 잔고에서 빼보면, 이 금액이 네 수표책의 최종 잔고랑 맞을 거야.

S: 알겠다. 이제 훨씬 더 이해하기 쉬워졌어. 고마워.

Section 3. Solve problems related to banks

상황: 다음은 은행 직원과 고객의 대화입니다. 이들은 은행 입출금 내역서와 신용카드의 재발급에 관련된 문제들에 대하여 이야기하고 있습니다. [C=고객, B=은행 직원]

[은행에서]

B: 다음 고객님. 안녕하세요! 무엇을 도와드릴까요?

C: 네, 지난달 입출금 내역서 사본이 필요합니다.

B: 공인 사본이 필요하신가요 아니면 일반 사본이 필요하신가요?

C: 공인 사본으로 부탁합니다. 대출회사에서 제 신용도 확인과 보관용으로 사본이 필요하다고 하더군요.

B: 일주일 전쯤에 내역서를 보내드렸기 때문에 재발급에는 수수료가 부과됩니다.

C: 얼마인가요?

B: 2.5달러입니다.

C: 알겠습니다. 여기 있습니다. (돈을 주며)

B: 네, 여기 사본 있습니다. 또 필요하신 일은 없으세요?

C: 제 당좌예금 내역서에 대해서 궁금한 점이 한 가지 있는데요. 부도수표에는 보통 얼마의 요금이 부과되나요?

B: 은행에서는 부도 처리되는 수표마다 25달러의 요금을 부과하고, 또한 고객님이 수표를 써주신 대상에게도 초과인출 수수료 25달러가 부가되게 됩니다.

C: 진짜요? 수표에 관련된 잔액을 더 정기적으로 확인하고 잔고 확인을 더 자주해야겠군요.

B: 고객님의 계좌 잔고는 온라인으로 모든 ATM 또는 어느 지점에 가셔도 확인 가능하십니다. 또한 입출금 내역서 역시 매달 댁으로 발송됩니다.

C: 알겠습니다. 눈 여겨 봐야겠네요. 이 내역서에 대해서 궁금한 게 한 가지 더 있습니다. 제 급료지불수표 바우처에는 급료 총액이 185달러라고 되어있는데, 이 내역서에는 제가 105달러를 예치했다고 나와있습니다. 한 번 확인해주시겠어요? 여기 바우처 사본이 있습니다.

B: 확인해드리겠습니다, 잠시만 기다려주세요. (몇 분 뒤 돌아와서) 죄송합니다, 이 예금전표에 실수가 있었네요. 고객님께서 이 전표에 보시는 대로 105달러라고 쓰셨어요.

C: 둘 다 실수한 것 같은데요. 숫자 "8"이 "0"처럼 보여서 구별하기가 어려웠겠군요.

B: 차액은 고객님 당좌예금으로 입금될 예정입니다.

C: 감사합니다.

[전화]

C: 실례합니다만, 제가 신용카드를 잃어버렸습니다.

B: 카드 번호를 알고 계신가요?

C: 아니요. 어딘가에 적어 뒀는데 기억이 나질 않네요.

B: 알겠습니다. 고객님 성함과 사회보장번호(SNN)를 알려주시겠습니까?

C: 제 이름은 Abdul Ahad이고 아직 SSN은 없지만 다음주에 받을 예정입니다. 비자카드는 이 은행에서 발급받았고요.

B: 그거면 됩니다. 아직 고객님의 카드를 아무도 사용하지 않은 것 같네요. 지금 카드를 정지시켰으니 더 이상 아무도 이 카드는 사용할 수 없게 됩니다. 새 카드를 발급해서 우편으로 발송해 드리겠습니다.

C: 새 카드를 받는 데 얼마나 걸리나요?

B: 평일 기준으로 5일에서 7일 정도 소요됩니다. 등기우편으로 발송될 예정이니 카드를 받을 수 있도록 댁에 누군가가 계셔야 합니다.

C: 알겠습니다. 감사합니다.

Section 4. Transfer or wire Money

상황: 다음은 은행에서 일어나는 거래에 관련된 내용으로, 고객, 은행 직원, 매니저, 보안 요원이 대화를 나누고 있습니다. [C=고객, B=은행 직원, M=은행 매니저, S=은행보안요원]

[은행으로 전화]

B: 안녕하세요, Trans America Union 은행입니다. 무엇을 도와드릴까요?

C: 국제송금을 하고 싶습니다. 어떤 서류들을 준비해야 하나요?

B: 이런 경우에는…… 송금인과 수령인에 대한 정보가 필요합니다. 송금인의 경우 성함과 고객님의 은행 주소, 계좌번호와 고객님이 송금하시는 일반예금의 통장이 필요합니다. 또한 수령인의 성함, 전화번호나 연락 가능한 정보, 은행명과 주소, 계좌번호 그리고 은행식별코드나 은행인식코드(BIC)가 필요합니다. 위의 사항이 모두 준비되면 은행으로 방문하셔서 송금하시면 됩니다.

C: 은행식별코드나 은행인식코드(BIC)가 무엇인가요?

B: 해당 은행을 확인하는 코드입니다. 모든 은행은 부여된 코드가 있거든요. 일종의 SSN이라고 보시면 됩니다. 고객님의 수령인께서 거래하시는 은행도 별 문제없이 정보를 제공할 겁니다.

C: 감사합니다.

B: 아, 송금인과 수령인의 성함을 성과 이름을 모두 써주시기 바랍니다. 모두 여권상의 이름과 동일해야 합니다.

C: 알겠습니다.

[은행에서]

C: 실례합니다, 국제송금을 하려면 이 줄에 서면 되나요?

S: 아니요. 줄을 설 필요는 없습니다. 이 줄은 일반 은행거래업무를 하시는 고객님들의 줄입니다. 여기 은행 매니저가 도와드릴 겁니다.

M: 안녕하세요! 무엇을 도와드릴까요?

C: 한국으로 송금하려고 합니다. 요청하신 모든 서류는 제가 여기 모두 가지고 있습니다.

M: 그럼 이 신청서를 작성해주시는 걸로 송금을 시작하도록 하죠. 신청서에 표시된 곳에 금액을 포함하여 모든 정보를 적어주시기 바랍니다. 들으신 대로 송금액이 10,000달러 미만인 경우 18달러의 송금수수료가 부과됩니다. 금액이 그 이상이면 수수료는 더 올라갑니다.

C: 알겠습니다. 요즘 환율은 어떤가요?

M: 음, 나쁘지 않아요. 오늘 환율은 조금 내려갔네요. 어제는 달러당 1,155원이었는데 오늘은 1,140원입니다.

C: 잘 됐네요. 오늘 3,500달러를 송금하고 싶습니다.

M: 그럴 경우 총 3,518달러가 필요합니다. 한 번 확인해보겠습니다…… 잠시만요…… 고객님 계좌에서 돈을 송금하실 건가요?

C: 네. 일반계좌에서 인출할 예정이고 여기 제 계좌 통장이 있습니다. 신청서는 다 작성했습니다.

M: 출금 청구서도 작성하셔야 합니다.

C: (작성을 마치고) 여기 있습니다.

M: (몇 분 뒤에 돌아와서) 이 서류를 읽어보시고 여기에 서명 부탁 드립니다…… (고객이 서명한다) 다 되었습니다. 여기 사본 받으시고요. 모두 완료되었습니다. 감사합니다.

Unit 6

Section 1. Find a good doctor and make an appointment

상황: 다음은 Kelly와 몸이 아픈 친구 Helen과의 대화문입니다. Helen은 한국에서 온 교환 학생입니다. Kelly는 그녀가 병원 예약하는 것을 도와줍니다. [K=Kelly, H=Helen, N=간호사]

[집에서]

K: 얘, 너 지금 뭐 먹는 중이야?

H: 음…… 한국 스타일의 죽이야. 내가 아팠을 때 엄마가 만들어주셨던 거야.

K: 지금은 괜찮아?

H: 아니, 요즘 몸이 계속 좋지 않고 배가 자주 아파.

K: 다가오는 시험 때문에 그래?

H: 잘 모르겠어. 전에는 복통이 극심했거든, 있잖아, 월경 전 증후군. 그런데 이번에는 좀 달라. 증상이 훨씬 심해. 편두통과 요통까지 있어. 이런지 일주일이 더 됐어.

K: 아이구…… 엄청 아프겠다. 병원에 가보지 그래?

H: 글쎄, 내가 듣기로는 병원에 가는데 비용이 많이 든다던데. 내 보험으로 이게 커버될 지 모르겠어.

K: 그래도 병원에 가서 검사 받는 게 좋을 거야. 그렇지 않으면 아픈 게 더 오래가고 심각해 질 수 있어.

H: 전적으로 동감이야!

K: 내 여동생도 비슷한 문제가 있어서 엄마가 병원에 데리고 갔어. 그런데 한 달만 늦었으면 수술해야 했을 거야. 내 동생이 갔던 같은 병원에 한 번 가볼래?

H: 그러지 뭐. 전화번호 알아?

K: 엄마한테 물어볼게. 옐로우 페이지에서도 의사를 찾아볼 수 있어. 모든 산부인과 의사의 목록이 거기 있거든.

H: 이름이 너무 많으면 누구를 선택해야 할 지 모를 것 같아.

K: 맞아, 나도 그렇더라. 번호를 알아 볼게. 잠깐만, 여기 이름과 전화번호, 그리고 주소가 있다. 내 생각에는 네 보험사를 통해서 다시 한번 보장 내역을 알아 보는 게 좋을 것 같아.

H: 그래, 방금 네가 너희 엄마와 통화하는 동안 알아봤어. 학생 정보처에 전화해보니 내 보험으로 보장이 된다고 하네.

K: 잘됐다! 가능한 한 빨리 예약을 잡아.

H: 고마워.

K: 별 말씀을. 의사 선생님 이름은 Dr. Peterson이야.

H: 고마워.

[병원에 전화]

N: 좋은 아침입니다. Dr. Peterson의 무슨 일이신가요?

H: 안녕하세요, 예약을 하고 싶은데요.

N: 네. 저희 병원에 처음 방문하시는 건가요?

H: 네.

N: 금요일 10시와 오후 3시가 가능해요. 주중 다른 날은 예약이 다 찼습니다.

H: 10시가 더 낫겠어요.

N: 좋아요. 이름이 어떻게 되시죠?

H: Helen Park이예요. 성은 P-A-R-K 로 철자를 쓰고요.

N: Helen 씨, Peterson 선생님과 금요일 10시로 예약해 드렸어요.

H: 고맙습니다. 안녕히 계세요.

Section 2. Have a health interview

상황: Dr. Sims의 진료실에서 환자, 간호사 그리고 의사가 나눈 대화입니다. 일주일 뒤에 환자는 병원에 다시 방문합니다. [P=환자, N=간호사, D=Dr. Sims]

P: Sims 선생님과 10시에 예약했고, 여기에 처음 방문했습니다.

N: 그러시면, 이 양식을 작성해주시겠어요?

P: 이건 왜 쓰는 거예요?

N: 환자 분이나 가족 분 중 암이나 중대 질환을 앓은 사람이 있는지 등의 병력에 대한 정보가 필요합니다. 환자분의 건강 보험 정보도 필요해요. Blue Cross and Blue Shield 또는 Medicare 같은 보험에 가입되어 있나요?

P: 학교에서 제공하는 학생 보험이 있어요.

N: 그거면 될 거예요.

P: 죄송하지만, 여기 있는 몇 개의 병명은 잘 모르겠고 전에 들어본 적도 없어요.

N: 들어 본 적이 없는 것들이라면, 해당 사항이 아닌 병일 거예요. 페니실린에 알레르기 반응이 있나요?

P: 없는 것 같아요.

N: 할 수 있는 만큼만 양식을 작성하세요.

P: 알겠습니다.

N: (잠시 후) Sims 선생님은 준비 되셨으니 들어가시면 됩니다.

P: 고맙습니다.

D: 좋은 아침입니다. 한번 봅시다. 무슨 문제가 있나요?

P: 이게 문제인지 잘 모르겠지만, 월경 전 증후군이 너무 심각해서요

D: 어떤 증상이 있나요?

P: 편두통과 요통이 있어요. 어떤 때는 약하게 오는데 어떤 때는 극심해져요. 지금 일주일이 넘었어요.

D: 흠. 여기 누워보세요. 제가 가볍게 배를 눌러볼 테니 아프면 말하세요. 아시겠죠? 여기 아픈가요?

P: 아, 거기요! 아파요! 거기도요.

D: 초음파를 해봐야겠어요, 소변검사와 혈액 검사도 받고요.

P: 문제가 심각한가요?

D: 아직 확실하지 않지만 정보가 조금 더 필요해요. 이 간호사를 따라 가세요. 모든 검사가 끝나야 확실한 답변을 드릴 수 있습니다. 검사 결과는 일주일 이내에 나올 거예요. 그 동안 통증을 완화할 수 있는 약을 처방해 드릴게요. 하루에 두 번, 아침 저녁 식사 후에 드세요.

[일주일 후]

D: 검사 결과가 음성으로 나왔습니다.

P: 휴. 그렇다니 다행이에요.

D: 다 좋아 보입니다. 환경이나 식단이 바뀌었나요? 아니면 스트레스가 심해요?

P: 음……저는 대학원생인데, 최근에 서울에서 Austin으로 왔어요. 서양식 식사에 적응하는 것이 쉽지 않네요. 무엇보다도 중간고사가 코 앞이라 하루에 고작 몇 시간 밖에 못 자고 있어요.

D: 그렇군요. 지금도 여전히 아파요?

P: 처방해주신 약을 먹은 이후로는 아프지 않아요.

D: 스트레스를 덜 수 있는 것을 좀 해보고 잠도 충분히 자야 해요.

P: 네, 선생님. 고맙습니다.

D: 오늘은 여기서 마칠게요.

Section 3. Perform CPR and give a simple first aid

상황: Sally의 집에서 Sally와 Mike가 나눈 대화입니다. 둘은 심폐 소생술에 대해 이야기를 나누고 있으며 응급 처치에 대한 문제를 다루고 있습니다. [S=Sally, M=Mike]

S: 너 심폐 소생술 하는 법 배웠다고 들었는데, 맞아?

M: 응, 그게…… 10학년인가, 11학년쯤에 배웠지. 왜 묻는 거야?

S: 내일 심폐소생술 시험이 있는데 복습도 하고 누군가와 연습해 봐야 해.

M: 글쎄, 잘 모르겠지만 일단 해 보지 뭐.

S: 좋아! 도와줘서 정말 고마워.

M: 연습하는데 이 인형을 쓰자. 첫 순서가 뭔지 기억나?

S: 흠…… 환자의 입을 벌리기?

M: 그거 전에! 처음으로 해야 할 일은 환자의 목 옆을 두 개의 손가락으로 지긋이 눌러서 맥박을 확인하는 거야.

S: 이렇게?

M: 그렇지. 그 다음에는 흉골을 부드럽게 문지르며 환자를 깨워 보는 거야.

S: 알겠어. 다음은?

M: 흉부 압박을 5회 실시해. 이제 환자 입을 열고 숨소리를 들어보거나 움직임이 있는지 또는 의식이 깨어날 어떤 징후라도 있는지 체크해.

S: 환자 입에서 마늘 냄새가 안 났으면 좋겠는데.

M: Sally, 진지해져 봐!

S: 미안해, 계속해. 그래서 아무 징후가 없으면 어떻게 해?

M: 환자가 숨을 쉬지 않으면 머리를 뒤로 젖히고 숨을 한 번 불어 넣으며 구강대구강 인공호흡을 하는 거야. 흉부가 오르내리는지 확인하며 해야 해. 아무 변화가 없으면 한 번 더 숨을 불어 넣고 이 과정을 반복해.

S: 아주 어렵지는 않구나.

M: 이 인형에 몇 차례 연습해봐. 아는 거 하고 해보는 거 하고는 다르니까. 아니면 나한테 연습해도 괜찮아.

S: 뭐라고?

M: 장난이야. (몇 분 후) 아야!

S: 무슨 일이야?

M: 손가락을 베였어.

S: 피가 많아 나잖아. 이리 와서 이 수건으로 상처를 눌러. 내가 구급 상자를 가지고 올게.

M: 피가 멈춘 것 같아.

S: 좋아. 이제 가서 수돗물에 상처를 씻어. 어서!

M: 아파! 비누를 써야 할까?

S: 아냐, 그럴 필요 없어. 어차피 비누는 세균에 별 도움이 안돼. 오, 아직도 피가 조금 나네. 구급 상자에서 소독약과 밴드를 찾았어. 여기, 이 소독 거즈로 상처를 덮어.

M: 고마워. 상처가 좀 나아진 것 같아.

S: 내가 도와 줄게. 손가락 움직이지 말고 가만히 있어 봐.

Section 4. Identify an appropriate department

상황: 첫 번째 대화는 Shaun과 Molly의 대화입니다. Shaun은 허리 통증을 겪고있으며 어떤 진료과로 가야 할지 알아보고있는 중입니다. 두 번째는 병원 입원실에서 나눈 대화입니다. [S=Shaun, M=Molly, N=간호사]

[Shaun의 집에서]

S: 내 허리 통증은 어떤 진료과에 가야 하는 걸까?

M: 글쎄, 내 생각에는 정형외과, 스포츠 의학과나 척추 지압과에 가야 할 것 같아. 그런 과들이 엉덩이, 허리, 무릎, 목, 다리나 발목에 오는 통증과 관련 있잖아. 일어서거나 쭈그려 앉을 때 아프니?

S: 아파서 내 일상 생활에 방해가 될 정도야.

M: 어떤 종류의 운동이든지 시도해보기 전에 의사와 상담을 먼저 해야 할 것 같아.

S: 그렇게 해야겠다.

M: 똑바로 서거나 앉고, 앞뒤로 걷기는 가능해? 어쩌면 나쁜 자세로 인한 통증일지도 몰라.

S: 아마 네 말이 맞을 거야. 네 조언을 잘 생각해보고 도움이 되는지 볼게.

[병원에서]

S: 실례합니다. 소화기내과를 찾아 왔는데요.

N: 3층에 있습니다.

S: 감사합니다.

[301호 병실에서]

M: Shaun, 무슨 일이 있었던 거야?

S: 지난 주에 며칠 동안 계속 두통이 심하고 메스껍고 구토하기도 했어. 그래서 의사 선생님이 몇 가지 검사를 받으라고 했어.

M: 컨디션은 어때?

S: 글쎄, 여기에 이틀 동안 있으면서 검사를 많이 받았어. 이제 MRI와 위내시경 검사를 기다리는 중이야. MRI는 한 번도 받아 본 적이 없어서 조금 떨려.

M: 그럼 어제 저녁은 안 먹었어?

S: 오늘 아침도 안 먹었어! 너무 배고프고 힘도 없어.

M: 검사만 끝나면 거창하게 밥 한 번 살게.

S: 고마워. 의사 선생님이 당분간 스테이크를 먹지 말라고 했는데 나는 거대한 립 아이 스테이크에 Merlot 한 잔 먹고 싶은 생각이 간절해.

M: 너 퇴원하면 내가 정말 건강하고 맛도 있는 음식을 만들어 줄게. 아침 내내 인터넷으로 조리법을 찾았어. 다음에 올 때 가지고 올게.

S: 넌 정말 친절해. 고마워, 그런데 나는 의사 선생님 분부대로 특별한 다이어트를 시작해야 할 것 같아. 그런데 간호사에게 MRI하고 위내시경이 얼마나 걸리는지 물어봐 줄 수 있어?

M: 이미 물어봤어. 간호사가 보통 40분 정도 걸린대. 어떤 물약을 먹고 기계 위에 누워있어야 해. 일단 기계 위에 올라가면 많이 움직여서는 안돼. 아픈 건 전혀 없어. 온갖 종류의 이상한 소리가 들리겠지만 걱정하지마, 검사는 금방 끝나니까. 최소한 주사는 안 맞잖아.

S: 그건 잘됐네. 나는 주사 바늘이 정말 싫거든.

M: 결과는 언제 받는 거야?

S: 아직 모르겠어.

Section 5. Go to the drugstore

상황: 첫 번째는 병원 진료실에서 Hannah와 Dr. Lashivia가 나눈 대화입니다. 두 번째는 약국에서 Hannah와 약사가 나눈 대화입니다. [H=Hannah, L=Dr. Lashiva, P=약사]

[의사 진료실에서]

H: Lashivia 선생님, 제가 왜 MRI와 혈액검사를 받아야 하나요?

L: 환자분의 의사가 갑상선 정밀 검사를 받으라고 이 곳에 보낸 거예요. 갑상선 부위에서 작은 혹이 느껴졌고 종양이나 암의 가능성이 있다고 판단한 거죠. 이런 경우에는 생체 검사 같은 추가 검사를 받을 필요가 있어요.

H: 정말이요? 심각한 건가요?

L: 검사 결과부터 받아야 더 나은 답변을 드릴 수 있어요. 그 사이에는 너무 염려하지 마세요. 만약에 그런 게 있다고 해도, 종양은 덜 심각한 종류고 제거하는 과정도 훨씬 간단해요.

H: 확실한가요?

L: 말기로 발견된다고 해도, 생존율이 95% 정도 됩니다.

H: 그래요? MRI 검사한 다음에 결과를 받기까지 얼마나 기다려야 하나요?

L: 일주일 정도입니다. 너무 걱정하지 마세요. 잠시만요. 목을 한 번 봅시다. 그냥 작은 혹 같아요. 여기 느껴지네요. 이쪽을 스캔해 봅시다.

[일주일 후]

H: Lashiva 선생님, 결과는 받으셨나요? 저 암인가요?

L: 아니에요. Hannah. 어떤 종류의 악성 종양도 찾지 못했습니다. 건강해요. 그냥 조직 수축으로 인한 거였어요.

H: 정말이요? 검사 결과에 대해 정말 걱정했어요. 이제 좀 낫네요. 그런데 여전히 두통과 메스꺼움은 있어요.

L: 스트레스 때문일 거예요. 약을 좀 처방해 줄게요. 페니실린 같은 약에 알레르기 증상이 있어요?

H: 아니요, 선생님. 제가 알기로는 없어요.

L: 이 약을 먹으면 조금 졸릴 거예요. 며칠 동안 운전하면 안 됩니다.

H: 하지만 직장과 학교에 운전해서 가야 해요.

L: 그런 경우라면, 표시 되어진 약들은 밤에만 복용하세요.

[약국에서]

P: 안녕하세요. 다음 분?

H: 안녕하세요. 처방전대로 약을 지어 주세요.

P: 물론이죠. 복제약과 일반약 중 어떤 것을 원하세요?

H: 복제약도 괜찮아요.

P: 15분 정도 걸릴 거예요. 쇼핑을 마치고 다시 와도 됩니다.

H: 이 처방전의 약도 다시 주시겠어요?

P: 이 약은 다시 받을 수 없어요.

H: 그러면 어떻게 해야 하지요?

P: 의사에게 전화해서 저나 다른 약국에 유선으로 처방전을 다시 주라고 할 수 있어요.

H: 괜찮아요. 의사 선생님이 약을 다시 못받게 처방하신 데는 이유가 있으시겠죠. 제가 의사 선생님을 다시 만나서 처방전을 받아야겠어요.

Section 6. Discuss how to work out

상황: 다음은 카페테리아에서 Helen과 Jessica가 운동과 운동을 잘 하는 방법에 대해 나눈 대화입니다. Helen은 운동을 시작하려고 하고 Jessica는 조언을 주고 있습니다. 둘은 대학 친구입니다. [H=Helen, J=Jessica]

H: 안녕, Jessie. 요즘 너 운동하니?

J: 그럼. 이 학교에 오고 나서 규칙적으로 조깅하기 시작했어. 이틀에 한 번씩 캠퍼스 주변을 달려. 비가 오는 날은 실내 체육관에 있는 트랙에 가지. 기숙사 바로 옆에 있잖아.

H: 흠……

J: 왜? 운동을 시작해 보려고 생각 중이야?

H: 응, 진지하게. 솔직히 말하자면 나는 운동이 정말 싫은데 요즘은 해야 할 거 같아. 몸무게가 지난 3개월동안 5파운드나 늘었어!

J: 그렇게 많이 찌지는 않았네.

H: 나한테는 엄청난 거야. 정말 불편하게 느껴져. 왜 그렇게 살이 많이 쪘는지 알 것도 같아. 이번 몇 달 동안 하루 종일 컴퓨터 앞에 앉아 있었어. 수업 들으러 이동할 때를 제외하면 움직일 시간도 별로 없었어.

J: 하하하. 학기 중에는 모두가 다 그렇지. 늘 도서관 책상에만 붙어 있잖아.

H: Jessie, 주로 하루에 언제 그리고 얼마 동안이나 조깅해?

J: 주로 아침 6시쯤 거의 50분 정도 조깅해. 움직이기 전 10분 정도는 스트레칭을 먼저 하고 10분 간 빠르게 걷기 그 다음 30분은 달리지. 의사들이 심장을 위해서 최소한 20분은 달리라고 권하더라.

H: 얼마나 빠르게 달려?

J: 빠르게 달릴 필요는 없어. 너만의 속도를 정해야지. 마치기 전에 스트레칭을 한 번 더 하는 것도 잊지마. 나에게는 조깅이 체중 감소에 많은 도움이 돼. Helen, 너도 운동 하는 게 좋아. 기분도 정말 좋고 몸 전체가 변하는걸 느낄 거야.

H: 너를 보니 알 것 같아. 건강해 보이고 날씬하잖아. 어떻게 그렇게 유지하는 거야? 뭐 다른 것도 하는 거야?

J: 고마워, 체육관에서 아령 들기도 해. 무거운 것으로 들면 안돼. 남자처럼 큰 근육이 생길 수 있으니. 이런 운동은 지방을 연소하고 신진대사를 활발하게 하지.

H: 어떻게 꾸준하게 운동을 할 수 있는 거야? 너는 정말 열심인 것 같아.

J: 나도 가끔씩 달리고 싶지 않을 때가 있지만 운동을 마치고 나면 얼마나 기분이 좋을지를 생각하면서 스스로를 밀어 붙이는 거야. 고등학생 때 입었다가 옷장 한 구석에 걸려있는 4사이즈 청바지를 입게 될 순간을 생각하기도 하고 말이야.

H: 맞아, 나도 그래! 나도 늘 그런 사이즈의 청바지를 입을 수 있길 원했어. 그건 그렇고 너 피부가 참 맑다.

J: 응, 규칙적으로 조깅하고 아령 들고, 운동으로 땀을 빼는 것 말고는 특별한 것을 하지는 않아. 아마도 운동 때문에 내 피부가 맑고 깨끗해 지나봐. 막힌 모공은 이제 안녕. 그나저나 체육관에 무료 요가 강습 있는 것 알았어?

H: 농담이지? 학생들에게 무료라고?

J: 그래, 학교 신문에 났어. 그런데 금요일에만 수업이 있대. 한 번 확인해 볼래?

H: 당연하지. 요가가 건강을 증진하는 운동이라고 들었어. 너도 등록할거야?

J: 꼭 해야지. 늘 요가 강습을 받아보고 싶었어.

H: 잘됐다. 우리 같이 하자.

이미지 출처

Unit 1 At the Airport

[Ken Fielding] https://commons.wikimedia.org/wiki/File:N118UA_B747-222_United_FRA_29JUN13_(9188696501).jpg (19p)

[Cassiopeia_sweet] https://commons.wikimedia.org/wiki/File:NWA_Airline_Ticket_JL2703.jpg (19p)

[User:Mattes] https://commons.wikimedia.org/wiki/File:VTBS-Thai_Check-In-Counters.JPG (19p)

[Austrian Airlines] https://commons.wikimedia.org/wiki/File:Austrian_Airlines_flight_attendant_and_passenger.jpg (19p)

[Robert Couse-Baker] https://commons.wikimedia.org/wiki/File:Traveling_in_airport_terminal.jpg (19p)

[M.O. Stevens] https://commons.wikimedia.org/wiki/File:Portland_International_Airport_security_check.jpg?uselang=ko (19p)

[The original uploader was Airodyssey at English Wikipedia]
https://commons.wikimedia.org/wiki/File:ETicketAirline.png (27p)

[A MAGIC] https://commons.wikimedia.org/wiki/File:100_2902.JPG (35p)

[Nutjaru] https://commons.wikimedia.org/wiki/File:CSDC.jpg (45p)

[Sebastian White from New York, United States] https://commons.wikimedia.org/wiki/File:Turkish_Airlines_Business_Class_meal,_Istanbul%E2%80%94Cairo.jpg (45p)

[Iduke] https://commons.wikimedia.org/wiki/File:Vancouver-yvr-terminal.id.jpg (55p)

[ukhomeoffice] https://en.wikipedia.org/wiki/File:Manufacturing_passports_of_the_United_Kingdom.jpg (55p)

[Minnaert] https://commons.wikimedia.org/wiki/File:SeaTacTerminalSecurity.jpg (65p)

[User:Mattes] https://commons.wikimedia.org/wiki/File:Kofferanh%C3%A4nger.pbair.JPG (65p)

Unit 2 At Home

[Kurman Communications, Inc.] https://www.flickr.com/photos/kurmanphotos/15108076463 (67p)

[Adam Caudill] https://commons.wikimedia.org/wiki/File:Party_foods.jpg (67p)

[The original uploader was Mruk20 at English Wikipedia. Image rotated, cropped, and enhanced by Dwaterson]
https://commons.wikimedia.org/wiki/File:Sittingroom-edit1.jpg (67p)

[User:Zink Dawg] https://commons.wikimedia.org/wiki/File:User_Zink_Dawg_2009_Christmas_Tree.jpg (67p)

[Catalarem] https://commons.wikimedia.org/wiki/File:Imac17pouces.png (67p)

[Maysooneille] https://commons.wikimedia.org/wiki/File:Citymovers.nl_Amsterdam.jpg?uselang=ko (67p)

[Jim Chute] https://commons.wikimedia.org/wiki/File:Tag_Sale_Sign.jpg (67p)

[Jinho Jung] https://commons.wikimedia.org/wiki/File:Korean_food-Bibim_ssambap_ingredient-01.jpg(75p)

https://en.wikipedia.org/wiki/Motion_Picture_Association_of_America_film_rating_system(85p)

[Dinner Series] https://commons.wikimedia.org/wiki/File:Eggnog2.jpg?uselang=ko (95p)

[AlbertHerring] https://en.wikipedia.org/wiki/File:Colonial_Williamsburg_(December,_2011)_-_Christmas_decorations_73.jpg (95p)

[Ildar Sagdejev] https://commons.wikimedia.org/wiki/File:2011-02-12_Yard_sale_on_Green_St_1.jpg?uselang=ko (123p)

[Jim Chute] https://commons.wikimedia.org/wiki/File:Tag_Sale_Sign.jpg (123p)

[Wolffystyle] https://commons.wikimedia.org/wiki/File:Rosemont_Flea_Market.jpg (123p)

[Linaduliban] https://en.wikipedia.org/wiki/File:The_Market_NYC.jpg (123p)

Unit 3 Transportation

[Robert McConnell] https://commons.wikimedia.org/wiki/File:NYCT_R142A.jpg (127p)

[Mariordo Mario Roberto Duran Ortiz] https://commons.wikimedia.org/wiki/File:Articulated_Metrobus_DC_2010_10_546.jpg (127p)

[Joseph Plotz] https://commons.wikimedia.org/wiki/File:NYC_taxis.JPG (127p)

[CZmarlin] https://commons.wikimedia.org/wiki/File:Car_dealership_in_Rockville_Maryland_Jeep.jpg (127p)

[Jeff dean] https://commons.wikimedia.org/wiki/File:Motorofficer.jpg?uselang=ko (127p)

[Michigan Department of State] https://en.wikipedia.org/wiki/File:Pure_Michigan_base_plate.jpg (127p)

[Melsta Logistics(Pvt)Ltd] https://commons.wikimedia.org/wiki/File:Using_of_Correct_Tools.jpg?uselang=ko (127p)

[Ad Meskens] https://commons.wikimedia.org/wiki/File:Yellow_cabs_2.jpg?uselang=ko (145p)

[Kelley Blue Book] https://commons.wikimedia.org/wiki/File:Kelley_Blue_Book_horizontal.JPG (153p)

[Jgera5] https://commons.wikimedia.org/wiki/File:PennDOTinspection.jpg (163p)

[J187B] https://commons.wikimedia.org/wiki/File:DMV_logo,_De_Meijerij_Veghel.jpg (171p)

[John Stephen Dwyer] https://commons.wikimedia.org/wiki/File:Registry_of_Motor_Vehicles.jpg (171p)

Unit 4 Campus Life

[Patrickneil] https://commons.wikimedia.org/wiki/File:Georgetown_Jesuit_Residence.jpg?uselang=ko (183p)

[AndrewHorne] https://commons.wikimedia.org/wiki/File:UniversityofMichiganLawLibrary.jpg (183p)

[PHPEric] https://commons.wikimedia.org/wiki/File:Harkness-method.jpg?uselang=ko (183p)

[Petr Kratochvil] http://www.freestockphotos.biz/stockphoto/6134 (183p)

[bpsusf] https://commons.wikimedia.org/wiki/File:Job_interview_0001.jpg (183p)

[Mosborne01] https://commons.wikimedia.org/wiki/File:Ashs-teacher-and-students.jpg (183p)

[carmichaellibrary] https://commons.wikimedia.org/wiki/File:Student_Government_Booth_(1260128581).jpg (183p)

[KF at English Wikipedia] https://commons.wikimedia.org/wiki/File:London_books.JPG (201p)

[Petr Kratochvil] http://www.freestockphotos.biz/stockphoto/11701 (211p)

[Pike Place Market] https://commons.wikimedia.org/wiki/File:Pike_Place_Market_-_Starbucks_circa_1977A.jpg (219p)

[revolution cycle] https://commons.wikimedia.org/wiki/File:Dog_walker_-_Buenos_Aires.jpg (219p)

[Huw Williams] https://commons.wikimedia.org/wiki/File:Alpha_Xi_Delta_sorority_rush.png (239p)

[Brewski919] https://commons.wikimedia.org/wiki/File:Gamma_Phi_Beta_trike_race.jpg (239p)

Unit 5 At the Bank

[Coolcaesar] https://commons.wikimedia.org/wiki/File:Porter_Ranch_Bank_of_America.jpg (241p)

[Airodyssey] https://commons.wikimedia.org/wiki/File:ClientCardSample.png (241p)

[Stahlkocher] https://commons.wikimedia.org/wiki/File:Fr%C3%BCher_Bankautomat_von_Nixdorf.jpg (241p)

[www.tOrange.us] http://www.torange.us/Objects/money/dollars-on-your-desktop-1506.html (241p)

[Evan Bench] https://commons.wikimedia.org/wiki/File:Receptionists.jpg (241p)

[Sergio Ortega] https://commons.wikimedia.org/wiki/File:SampleBankbook.png (249p)

[Sergio Ortega] https://en.wikipedia.org/wiki/File:BankStatementChequing.png (259p)

[Andyhi18] https://en.wikipedia.org/wiki/File:USDnotes.png (279p)

Unit 6 At the Hospital

[User:Nephron] https://en.wikipedia.org/wiki/File:Toronto_Western_Hospital_(Krembil_Neuroscience_Centre).jpg (283p)

[U.S. Navy photo by Mass Communication Specialist 1st Class Brian Finney] https://commons.wikimedia.org/wiki/File:US_Navy_090427-N-9318F-054_Lt._Cdr_Gayle_Kostyack,_a_U.S._Public_Health_Service_dentist,_performs_an_oral_examination_on_a_patient_aboard_the_Military_Sealift_Command_hospital_ship_USNS_Comfort_(T-AH_20)_in_support_of_Continuin.jpg (283p)

[Ilmicrofono Oggiono] https://www.flickr.com/photos/115089924@N02/16256199615 (283p)

[Rama] https://commons.wikimedia.org/wiki/File:CPR_training-04.jpg (283p)

[Elliot Grieveson] https://en.wikipedia.org/wiki/File:Lister_Hospital,_STEVENAGE.jpg (283p)

[Rhoda Baer] https://en.wikipedia.org/wiki/File:Man_consults_with_pharmacist.jpg (283p)

[Ed Yourdon] https://en.wikipedia.org/wiki/File:Jogging_couple.jpg (283p)

[Tomasz Sienicki] https://commons.wikimedia.org/wiki/File:Telefonbog_ubt-1.JPG (291p)

[Andrew Sullivan] https://commons.wikimedia.org/wiki/File:Auckland_Yellow_pages.jpg (291p)

[ProfDEH] https://commons.wikimedia.org/wiki/File:Fluorescent_flower_display.jpg (321p)

[Neutrality] https://commons.wikimedia.org/wiki/File:Newsstand.jpg (321p)

[Ragesoss] https://commons.wikimedia.org/wiki/File:Regular_strength_enteric_coated_aspirin_tablets.jpg (331p)

[User:Vberger] https://commons.wikimedia.org/wiki/File:Xi%27an_traditionnal_medecine_market_(18).JPG (331p)

[gildemax] https://commons.wikimedia.org/wiki/File:Marrakech_103.JPG (331p)
https://commons.wikimedia.org/wiki/File:Natacio.jpg (341p)

[Greenstrat] https://commons.wikimedia.org/wiki/File:AlumniGymB.jpg (341p)

[www.localfitness.com.au] https://commons.wikimedia.org/wiki/File:Gym_Free-weights_Area.jpg?uselang=ko (341p)

ANSWER SHEET

UNIT1 At the Airport		
Sec	EXERCISE FOR USEFUL EXPRESSION	DIALOGUE PRACTICE PART3
1-1	booked, discounted, put on, itinerary, penalty	1-d, 2-a, 3-b, 4-e, 5-f, 6-c
1-2	1-b, 2-a, 3-d, 4-e, 5-c	1-a, 2-c, 3-b, 4-d
1-3	1-b, 2-c, 3-b, 4-c, 5-d	1-b, 2-d, 3-a, 4-c
1-4	1-d, 2-c, 3-d, 4-b, 5-a	1-d, 2-c, 3-b, 4-e, 5-a
1-5	1-d, 2-b, 3-e, 4-a, 5-c	1-b, 2-a, 3-d, 4-c

UNIT2 At Home		
Sec	EXERCISE FOR USEFUL EXPRESSION	DIALOGUE PRACTICE PART3
2-1	1-d, 2-a, 3-b, 4-c, 5-e	1-d, 2-e, 3-b, 4-a, 5-c
2-2	catch up, episodes, reruns, rated	1-c, 2-b, 3-a, 4- d
2-3	1-c, 2-a, 3-b, 4-d, 5-e	1-b, 2-a, 3-d, 4- c
2-4	1-c, 2-d, 3-a, 4-b, 5-a	1-a, 2-c, 3-b, 4-d
2-5	1-c, 2-d, 3-b, 4-b, 5-a	1-b, 2-a, 3-d, 4-c
2-6	1	1-c, 2-b, 3-a, 4-d

UNIT3 Transportation		
Sec	EXERCISE FOR USEFUL EXPRESSION	DIALOGUE PRACTICE PART3
3-1	3	1-c, 2-a, 3-b, 4-d
3-2	1-False,2-True, 3-False, 4-True,5- True	1-b, 2-c, 3-a, 4-e, 5-d
3-3	1-a, 2-c, 3-b, 4-d, 5-e	1-c, 2-d, 3-a, 4-b
3-4	1-d, 2-e, 3-b, 4-c, 5-a	1-b, 2-a, 3-d, 4-c
3-5	expired, examinees, vision test, terminal, permit	1-d, 2-c, 3-b, 4-a
3-6	1-d, 2-c, 3-a, 4-c, 5-b	1-c, 2-d, 3-a, 4-b

UNIT4 Campus Life		
Sec	EXERCISE FOR USEFUL EXPRESSION	DIALOGUE PRACTICE PART3
4-1	1-e, 2-d, 3-a, 4-c, 5-b	1-d, 2-a, 3-b, 4-c
4-2	1-c, 2-b, 3-d, 4-a, 5-c	1-c, 2-a, 3-b, 4-d
4-3	1-c, 2-d, 3-e, 4-a, 5-b	1-c, 2-a, 3-b, 4-d
4-4	statistics, cover letter, position, qualifications, indicates	1-e, 2-b, 3-c, 4-a, 5-d
4-5	4	1-b, 2-c, 3-a, 4-d
4-6	1-True, 2-False, 3-False, 4-True, 5-True	1-c, 2-b, 3-a, 4-d

UNIT5 At the Bank		
Sec	EXERCISE FOR USEFUL EXPRESSION	DIALOGUE PRACTICE PART3
5-1	1-d, 2-c, 3-e, 4-a, 5-b	1-b, 2-d, 3-a, 4-c
5-2	1-c, 2-a, 3-b, 4-e, 5-d	1-c, 2-a, 3-b, 4-d
5-3	overdrawn, loan agency, bank statement, registered mail, issue	1-b, 2-a, 3-d, 4-c
5-4	1-b, 2-c, 3-d, 4-b, 5-c	1-b, 2-c, 3-a, 4-d

UNIT6 At the Hospital		
Sec	EXERCISE FOR USEFUL EXPRESSION	DIALOGUE PRACTICE PART3
6-1	1	1-c, 2-b, 3-a, 4-d
6-2	1-c, 2-b, 3-a, 4-d, 5-a	1-a, 2-d, 3-b, 4-c
6-3	1-False, 2-True, 3-False, 4-True, 5-True	1-c, 2-a, 3-b, 4-d
6-4	posture, crouching, chiropractic, consult	1-d, 2-c, 3-b, 4-a
6-5	1-b, 2-e, 3-d, 4-c, 5-a	1-c, 2-a, 3-b, 4-d
6-6	1-c, 2-b, 3-a, 4-a, 5-d	1-d, 2-b, 3-c, 4-a

유학영어 길라잡이

초판 인쇄	2016년 2월 1일
초판 발행	2016년 2월 5일

지은이	Jennifer M.Yi · 김미연 · 김영하 · 박혜원 · 이원희
발행인	김인철
기 획	장지호 Director, University Press
편집장	신선호 Executive Knowledge Contents Creator
도서편집	김민정 Contents Creator
도서·전자책편집	최인우 e-Contents Creator
마케팅	곽용창 Chief Marketing Creator
재무관리	권미경 Chief Managing Creator
발행처	한국외국어대학교 지식출판원
	02450 서울특별시 동대문구 이문로 107
	전화 02)2173-2493~7
	팩스 02)2173-3363
	홈페이지 http://press.hufs.ac.kr
	전자우편 press@hufs.ac.kr
	출판등록 제6-6호(1969. 4. 30)
디자인 · 편집	디자인퍼브 02)2254-4308
인쇄 · 제본	네오프린텍 02)718-3111

ISBN 979-11-5901-043-9 13740 정가 24,000원

*잘못된 책은 교환하여 드립니다.

HUINE은 한국외국어대학교 지식출판원의 어학도서, 사회과학도서, 지역학 도서 Sub Brand이다. 한국외대의 영문명인 HUFS, 현명한 국제전문가 양성(International+Intelligent)의 의미를 담고 있으며, 휴인(携引)의 뜻인 '이끌다, 끌고 나가다'라는 의미처럼 출판계를 이끄는 리더로서, 혁신의 이미지를 담고 있다.